2006 WORLD CHAMPIONS
2007 AFC SOUTH CHAMPIONS
INDIANAPOLIS
COLTS

INDIANAPOLIS COLTS

The Complete Illustrated History

BY LEW FREEDMAN

First published in 2013 by MVP Books, an imprint of MBI Publishing Company, 400 First Avenue North, Suite 400, Minneapolis, MN 55401 USA

MVP Books titles are also available at discounts in bulk quantity for industrial or sales-promotional use. For details write to Special Sales Manager at MBI Publishing Company, 400 First Avenue North, Suite 400, Minneapolis, MN 55401 USA
To find out more about our books visit us online at www.mvpbooks.com

978-0-7603-4330-2

Library of Congress Cataloging-in-Publication Data

Freedman, Lew.
Indianapolis Colts : the complete illustrated history / by Lew Freedman.
p. cm.
Summary: "A complete illustrated history of the National Football League's Indianapolis Colts, including the team's early era in Baltimore"--Provided by publisher"-- Provided by publisher.
ISBN 978-0-7603-4330-2 (hardback)
1. Indianapolis Colts (Football team)--History. I. Title.
GV956.I53F73 2012
796.332'640977252--dc23
2012012638

Edited by Josh Leventhal
Design manager: James Kegley
Designed by Sandra Salamony
Layout by Kim Winscher

Printed in China

On the front cover: (top left) Johnny Unitas, circa 1968, photo by Focus on Sport/Getty Images; (center) Colts flag, 2009, photo by Scott Boehm/AP Photos, and Colts fans, 2007, photo by Joe Robbins/Getty Images; (top right) Bert Jones, 1980, photo by Al Messerschmidt/Getty Images; (lower right) Andrew Luck, 2012, photo by Joe Robbins/Getty Images; (lower left) Peyton Manning, 2008, photo by Jeff Gross/Getty Images.
On the frontispiece: AP Photo/Tom Strickland
On the title page: AP Photo/Paul Spinelli

Contents

Colts fans have been fortunate enough to enjoy two of the greatest field generals the game has ever seen—Johnny Unitas and Peyton Manning (page 9). FOCUS ON SPORT/ GETTY IMAGES

Introduction

The horseshoe has made the entire journey. The Baltimore Colts and the Indianapolis Colts are family, one the linear descendent of the former, both wearers of white helmets with blue horseshoes imprinted on the sides. That horseshoe is the common connector between the players who have represented the team in two cities. Both versions of the club have had their heroes and their successes, both winning Super Bowls and competing in others.

This team is not as old as the founding father Chicago Bears. Storied franchises such as the Green Bay Packers and Pittsburgh Steelers have been around longer as well, but the Colts do predate most National Football League expansion clubs, playing their first downs in the 1950s (not accounting for their old affiliation under another name in the defunct All-America Football Conference).

Baltimore and Indianapolis have both been proud homes to the Colts, with fanatic fans in different eras of NFL play. The Baltimore Colts had Johnny Unitas to rally around. The Indianapolis Colts had Peyton Manning. Unitas handed the ball off to Lenny Moore and Alan Ameche. Manning stuck the ball in the belly of Edgerrin James and Joseph Addai. And, oh yes, thoroughbreds such as Eric Dickerson and Marshall Faulk also took turns toting the pigskin for Indy. Raymond Berry, John Mackey, and Jimmy Orr possessed the skills to run free so Unitas could find them with passes. Marvin Harrison, Reggie Wayne, and Dallas Clark were guys Manning could count on.

Originally, it was Carroll Rosenbloom with the cash. For the last 30 years it has been the Irsay family, but the Colts have always known the stability and continuity of ownership with single chiefs, as opposed to being run by corporate entities and complex boards of directors.

In both cities, although there were other sports allegiances, the Colts were the kings of the castle, the most prominent rooting interest and unifying entity in the community.

These days in Indianapolis a person can't walk along a downtown street without coming to the conclusion that half the population must belong to the same fraternity because of all the blue Colts gear on display. And in recent years, judging by the nameplates displayed by the many people wearing No. 18 football jerseys, it seemed as if half the residents of Indianapolis were named Manning.

Surely the same sartorial passion would have been evidenced in the 1950s if the NFL had been in the business of selling individual players' jerseys back then—there would have been a slew of Unitases.

From the start, though, there was identification with the horseshoe. The Colts were the most popular horses around, even with the Preakness Stakes—a Baltimore institution—contested each May.

The Colts got their nickname when a man named Charles Evans of Middle River, Maryland, submitted the suggestion in a contest during the waning days of 1946. The football team formerly known as the Miami Seahawks relocated to Baltimore for play in the long-defunct All-America Football Conference.

The league died, but the team persevered the hard way. After the Seahawks (no relation to the Seattle franchise) went bankrupt, the Colts represented Baltimore in the AAFC between 1947 and 1949 and in the National Football League beginning in 1950. Those Colts folded but were revived when the Dallas Texans shifted to Maryland.

In 1953, under the ownership of Rosenbloom, the Colts began their modern era in Baltimore. For the next 31 years they earned the love of the community with the superior play of Hall of Fame athletes such as Art Donovan, Raymond Berry, Gino Marchetti, Lenny Moore, Jim Parker, John Mackey, and of course Johnny Unitas. All the while, the melodious voice of Chuck Thompson wooed fans on broadcasts.

In many quarters, Unitas is viewed as the greatest quarterback of all time. He was the living embodiment of the flat-top haircut that made him appear freshly discharged from the Marines— a true Joe Everyman with his white socks and conservative style. Yet even within the Colts organization there is competition for that title of greatest-ever, because quarterback Peyton Manning, the best Colt since Unitas, certainly achieved enough on the field to gain standing in any rankings argument.

The Colts of their very earliest days gained little distinction. Indeed, John Steadman, who in a half-century as a Baltimore newspaper columnist and someone who also worked for the club as public relations official, once wrote a story insisting that the Colts of 1950 were the worst team in NFL history. The Colts finished 1–11 that year, for the second season in a row. Steadman cited lowlights that included losing to the Los Angeles Rams by a score of 70–28 and surrendering 2,857 yards rushing in a 12-game season as proof to buttress his bleak argument.

Apparently, the only way opposing ball carriers were tackled that season was by accident. That squad did feature future Hall of Famers Y. A. Tittle (better known for his signal-calling work with the San Francisco 49ers and New York Giants) and Donovan, who once looked at muscled-up linemen who had a close familiarity with barbells and said the only weight he ever lifted was a beer can.

Depending on the eyesight of observers, those old Colts wore either green and silver or green and white uniforms. In either case it was widely acknowledged that the fashion pattern would provoke a stroke in any Parisian designer who gained a glimpse of them. In 1953, the Colts adopted the more familiar blue-and-white uniforms that have lasted, traveling to Indianapolis along with the famed horseshoe insignia in 1984. The horseshoe remains one of the iconic symbols of the NFL.

Even older fans might not realize that, for a short period of time as the Colts were being absorbed into the NFL, consideration was given to dumping the nickname in favor of something fresh. Rosenbloom and general manager Don Kellett huddled but decided not to call an audible.

"We thought of changing the name of the Colts when we first came to Baltimore," Kellett said years later. "After all, it was a fresh start, and the name Colts having been associated with a loser may not have been a good carryover. Neither Carroll nor I could come up with a better name."

So the Colts they remained, and the Colts they remain. After the Colts took root in Baltimore in 1953, they were regarded as a civic treasure. The players were viewed more as adopted sons, partially because many lived in the community year-round and partially because pro football players were not yet seen as celebrities whose paychecks greatly exceeded those of the average working stiff.

In those days, you may have run into Johnny U at the grocery store or bumped into Gino Marchetti at the movie theater. They were just guys—admired men for certain, but not on pedestals. Heck, they even worked at some of the same types of jobs as their fans, to supplement their meager football salaries. Parker sold cemetery plots. Unitas worked for a time at Bethlehem Steel wielding an acetylene torch. Marchetti worked in a bowling alley. Duckpin bowling and watching Blaze Starr strip off her clothing on "The Block" were the main contenders for Baltimore's disposable income dollars, with the baseball Orioles running far behind.

The 1950s were a time of innocence in America after World War II, and the Korean War had supposedly made the world safe for democracy. Cheap housing attracted young couples, who drove their new cars on the open road when they weren't riveted by the likes of Milton Berle, Sid Caesar, and the other performers barging into the new medium of TV.

No one foresaw that the Colts would become as popular as the fine local delicacy of crab cakes; that Unitas would become as popular as Lord Baltimore, the city's namesake; or that Memorial Stadium would become as favored an entertainment venue as Chesapeake Bay. You couldn't beat the value at the box office, paying $6 for a 50-yard-line seat.

The Colts became a team of characters such as Gene "Big Daddy" Lipscomb, the NFL's first great gargantuan player, and Johnny Sample, who wrote a book titled ***Confessions of a Dirty Ballplayer***. They displayed artistry, too, as halfback Lenny Moore wiggled, squirmed, and dashed to innumerable touchdowns, while Unitas, the rock in the pocket, rallied his team from hopeless situations to victory.

In 1958, the Colts defeated the New York Giants in the NFL championship game that has forevermore been judged as the first great milestone of the league's success. Immediately dubbed "The Greatest Game Ever Played," with no serious challenges mounted for that title, the game introduced the words "sudden-death overtime" to the American sporting public. The first overtime playoff game in league history provided the Colts with a compelling forum to showcase their talents and for the NFL to display its best. The nationally televised triumph created a level of buzz that had never before crossed over to the casual sports fan. From then on the graph chart of NFL growth in attendance and TV ratings only pointed upward.

After the Colts silenced all of New York by notching the victory at Yankee Stadium, about 30,000 fans greeted the team at Friendship International Airport in Baltimore. A year later, with less drama but equal satisfaction, the Colts repeated, winning a second straight NFL crown. The same two teams met, but the Colts won handily this time.

After the NFL merged with the American Football League and the Super Bowl era began, the 1969 Colts were embroiled in a tussle regarded as one of the league's true milestone contests. Heavily favored and representing the established NFL in Super Bowl III, the Colts were upended by the New York Jets and their brash quarterback Joe Namath, who guaranteed a victory for his upstart team and delivered. From then on it was generally agreed that parity had been reached between the old-line NFL and the less-than-a-decade-old AFL.

That core group of Colts, however, did not go unrewarded. Two years later, in 1971, Baltimore captured the Super Bowl by edging the Dallas Cowboys 16–13.

The championships were appreciated, but the Colts were always loved by their fans, fans who fielded a Baltimore Colts Marching Band and sang along with a team theme song even when the club faltered in the win-loss column.

However, despite devotion and passion, dark days were ahead for Baltimore. Owner Robert Irsay first flirted with moving

ANDY LYONS/GETTY IMAGES

MVP BOOKS COLLECTION

The horseshoe on a Colts helmet is an image that has resonated across generations, from Baltimore to Indianapolis and beyond.

the team to other cities as he tried unsuccessfully to convince Maryland officials to build him a new stadium in the early 1980s. In a day that lives in Baltimore infamy, moving vans arrived and hauled the entire Colts operation to Indianapolis under cover of darkness. Edgar Allen Poe, buried in Baltimore, never wrote such a horrifying story or poem. Nevermore, Colts fans despaired.

That transition in 1984 broke the hearts of many Baltimore fans but created a ripple effect that eventually led to the Cleveland Browns moving to Maryland in 1996 to fill the void. They changed their name to the Baltimore Ravens, while Indianapolis ushered in a new era of prosperity for the Colts.

The Colts were rejuvenated in Indianapolis. Initially playing in the Hoosier Dome, which was later renamed the RCA Dome, they now play in the spectacular Lucas Oil Stadium, which was chosen as the site for Super Bowl XLVI even though Indianapolis is not a warm-weather winter city.

The Indianapolis Colts first built a playoff dynasty around quarterback Jim Harbaugh and Hall of Fame running back Eric Dickerson. Later, the squad was led by quarterback Jeff George, and the team eventually introduced a new generation of even bigger stars—from Hall of Fame back Marshall Faulk to receivers Marvin Harrison and Reggie Wayne, defensive stalwarts Robert Mathis and Dwight Freeney, and then to the biggest star of all, Peyton Manning.

The Colts' No. 1 draft choice in 1998 stepped into the starting lineup as a rookie and never missed a regular-season or playoff game until 2011 when an injury sidelined Manning at the start of the season. By then Manning had emerged as one of the greatest quarterbacks in history and led the Colts to annual double-digit victory totals and playoff appearances. In February 2007 the Colts won their first Super Bowl for Indianapolis by besting the Chicago Bears. In February 2010 the Colts worked their way back to the Super Bowl but fell to the New Orleans Saints.

The ongoing success of the Colts has uplifted football's profile around the entire state. Long considered the No. 1 basketball mecca in the country, some dare to suggest that the resulting brilliance of the Colts in Indianapolis now outshines any of the myriad high school and college basketball teams in Indiana, despite their longtime traditions.

During 14 years of Manning's guidance, the Colts were perennial winners—the dominating team in the AFC South Division. But the series of neck surgeries Manning underwent wiped out his 2011 campaign and led to his departure from the Colts. In 2012, Manning and the Colts headed in separate directions, and a new savior was brought in to carry the team to a new era.

Using the top overall pick in the NFL draft, Indianapolis selected All-American Andrew Luck of Stanford as its quarterback of the future. In his first season, Luck played like a veteran, much as Manning had done during his own rookie year. Stunning the football establishment, the Colts finished 11-5 and reached the playoffs. Indianapolis was back.

In the two main epochs of franchise history, both the Colts of Baltimore and the Colts of Indianapolis have shined. Both versions of the team have made their fans proud of the horseshoe. And both versions of the team were fortunate to have accomplished and famous leaders who are among the game's all-time greats. Johnny Unitas and Peyton Manning represented the best of the Colts over decades of football history. Hopes are high in Indianapolis for another return to glory.

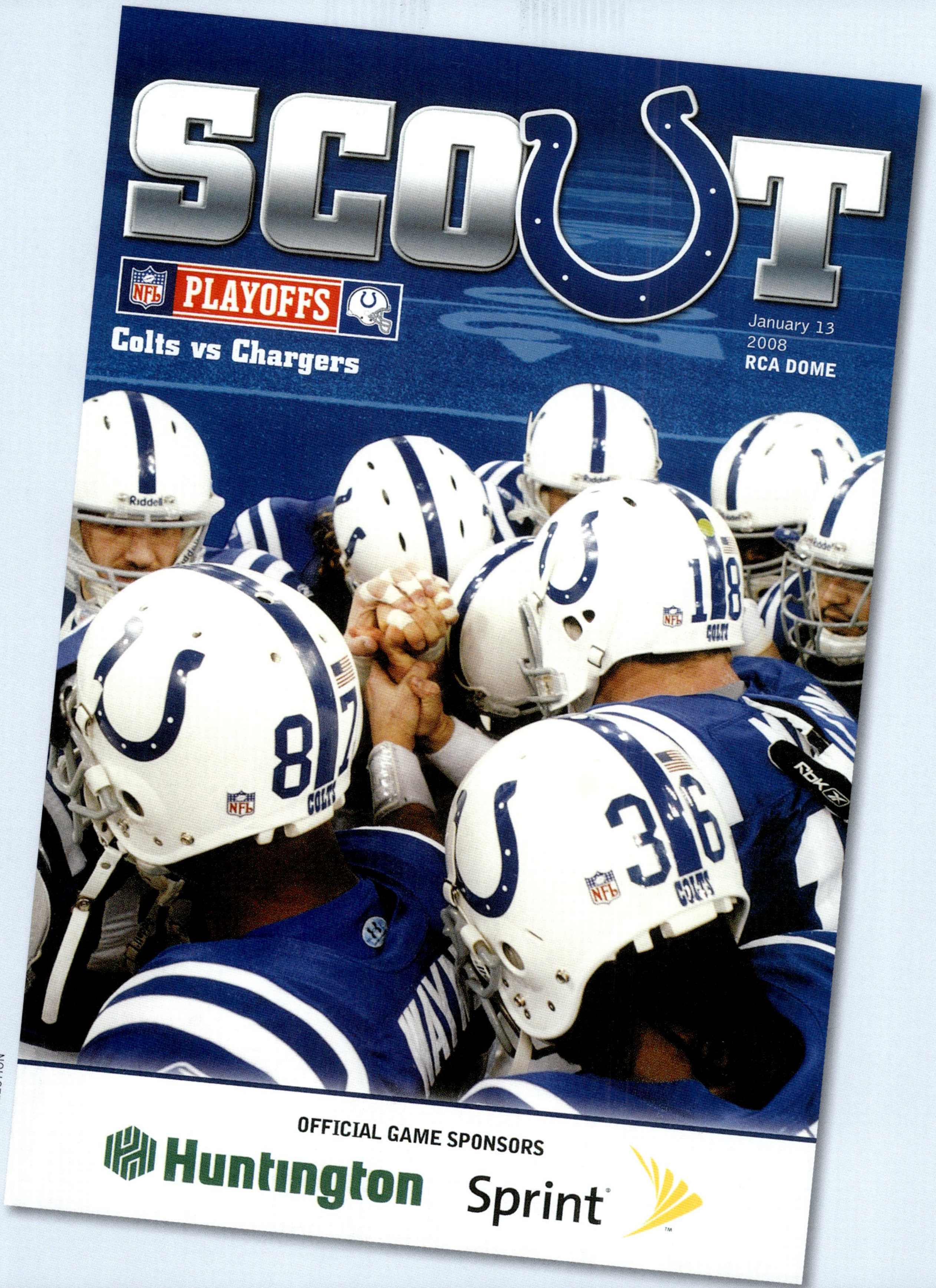

MVP BOOKS COLLECTION

SCOUT

NFL PLAYOFFS

Colts vs Chargers

January 13
2008
RCA DOME

OFFICIAL GAME SPONSORS

Huntington

Sprint

Hall of Famer Y. A. Tittle, started his career with the Colts—his tenure predated even the team's iconic blue and white uniforms.
NFL PHOTOS/ AP PHOTO

Part I

BIRTH—1984

The Baltimore Colts as we knew them sprang into existence for the 1953 season with optimistic expectations and the passionate support of a populace that already loved the game. By the end of the decade, they were the best football team on the planet, winners of two championships and the helpmates that ushered in a television era of football that expanded and grew the game beyond any of their imaginations.

Baltimore was the winner of the 1958 NFL title game over the New York Giants that was quickly pronounced "The Greatest Game Ever Played," an event that has yet to be downgraded. It was the first sudden-death overtime playoff game, a game of such drama and suspense that it created fresh fans and became only more appreciated in lore.

The Colts of the 1950s were composed of colorful and talented players, many of them among the greatest ever at their positions, from the incomparable Johnny Unitas at quarterback to the studious Raymond Berry at wide receiver and from the always joking Art Donovan at defensive tackle to the ferocious Gino Marchetti at defensive end.

It was an era of innocence in professional sport, where the players did not make enough money from their games alone to support their families and had to work in the community they represented in the offseason. Perhaps no city fell as deeply in love with its football players as Baltimore.

The team was good, the fans were rabid, and it seemed as if the special relationship between team and town would last forever. But it didn't. To disbelieving observers, the Colts era in Baltimore expired after the 1983 season.

BALTIMORE

MVP BOOKS COLLECTION

THE NFL COLTS ARE BORN

Carroll Rosenbloom had the money and the passion for football, and National Football League Commissioner Bert Bell made sure he channeled them into the Baltimore Colts. The man in charge of the league put a full-court press on his potential investor to become the financial backbone of a team for Baltimore.

The Colts began their existence in the old All-America Football Conference in 1947 and competed through 1949. Both the team and the league folded. The awful 1–11 Colts represented Baltimore in the NFL in 1950 but disintegrated, too. However, when the original, pre–American Football League Dallas Texans conceded that the dismal life as they knew it in Texas had run its course, they transferred to Baltimore for the 1953 season and became the born-again Colts, the team we know now.

Rosenbloom, who had played halfback for the University of Pennsylvania where Bell was an assistant coach, made his fortune in clothing manufacturing. The Colts were essentially orphans living a hardscrabble existence, and Bell did not want to see the team disband and be left with an 11-team NFL.

Bell was a good salesman. He convinced Rosenbloom that ownership of an NFL team was a prestigious thing and was like being accepted into an exclusive club. That is true today but was a difficult argument to support in the early 1950s. Rosenbloom put up enough money to become a 52 percent owner, and the Colts began their love affair with Baltimore.

The Colts won four championships under owner Caroll Rosenbloom, who eventually left for the sunny skies of California. AP PHOTO

"It's a good thing he's in the shirt business, because he's going to lose his." —Bert Bell on Rosenbloom's investment in the Colts

Bell was seeking a quick fix to his problem. He did not imagine the Colts would become successful at the box office, and he told friends of Rosenbloom's investment, "It's a good thing he's in the shirt business, because he's going to lose his."

That did not occur. The price of an NFL franchise in those days was not wallet-busting for millionaires. Rosenbloom originally needed to pledge just $13,000 to take control. A key element in returning football to Baltimore was a prerequisite that the city guarantee the sale of 15,000 season tickets. With that accomplished, the Colts were given a $300,000 kitty to work with.

Although the Colts were not very good on the field, Baltimore embraced the team. The community enjoyed its newfound big-league status. The St. Louis Browns relocated and became the Baltimore Orioles in 1954, the nickname stemming from Maryland's appreciation of its state bird. So suddenly, Baltimore had teams in both the NFL and Major League Baseball.

MVP BOOKS COLLECTION

Colts president and general manager, Don Kellett, meets with NFL commissioner Bert Bell and representatives from each of the league's teams on January 22, 1953, in Philadelphia. AP PHOTO/SAM MYERS

MVP BOOKS COLLECTION

That first Colts season under coach Keith Molesworth—his only year as boss—the team went a mediocre 3–9. Molesworth, who had been a halfback with the Chicago Bears in the 1930s, moved into the Baltimore front office and stayed there for the rest of his life, until he died of a heart attack in 1966.

One highlight of that otherwise pedestrian 1953 season was an NFL-record 56-yard field goal kicked by Bert Rechichar against the Chicago Bears. The old record had been a 55-yard drop kick by Paddy Driscoll in 1924, and the Rechichar boot held up as the league record until 1970 when Tom Dempsey stroked a field goal 63 yards.

Rechichar was a piece of work, often gruff to his teammates, always outspoken to opponents. When playing safety he announced to the ends he covered in advance what he was going to do to them. That meant hitting them so hard their teeth would rattle. One of 10 children from Belle Vernon, Pennsylvania, whose father was murdered for his payday profits, Rechichar had never before kicked a field goal before lining up that day with four seconds left in the first half. He said later he didn't know how far the kick was going to be but that he looked down at holder Tom Keane and ordered him to place the ball quickly "because I've got to go to the bathroom."

In 1957, Rechichar, by then a veteran of such attempts, kicked field goals of 52, 44, 42, and 41 yards and was voted Most Valuable Player in the Pro Bowl.

Molesworth was replaced by Weeb Ewbank, a diminutive man whose size left him forever looking up at the football players he commanded. Ewbank had prepped under Cleveland Browns coach Paul Brown, regarded as one of the sport's great innovators. Ewbank was never acclaimed as a great game coach, but he was an excellent judge of talent and a good motivator. None of that did him much good his first season when the Colts again finished 3–9. The only difference was that they looked better losing in 1954 than they had the year before.

Even in 1953 the Colts had the core of a good defense in the making. Among the starters on that side of the ball were Gino Marchetti, on his way to the Hall of Fame; Don Shula, on his way to the Hall of Fame as a coach; snarling Bill Pellington at middle linebacker; Bert Rechichar; Carl Taseff; and a character named Art Donovan at defensive tackle.

GINO MARCHETTI

Old School Tackler

The ferocity that Gino Marchetti brought to the sport and his relentless drive are what most impressed his teammates during his Hall of Fame career. He was a ruthless defensive end who ate quarterbacks for lunch and halfbacks for snacks.

An 11-time Pro Bowl selection with the Colts between 1953 and 1966, the 6-foot-4, 245-pound Marchetti was not especially large by modern-day standards. But he was the most feared pass rusher around, especially when a team faced a third-down–and-long situation. The quarterback knew that Marchetti was going to be in his face trying to rip his head off.

Marchetti is on the short list of greatest pass rushers and thrived on employing his quickness to run around blockers. It is ironic that when Marchetti was just starting out in the game his parents warned him to stay out of the way of the other boys so they wouldn't hurt him. It turned out that Marchetti delivered most of the pain.

Marchetti hardened up with World War II service and played for the University of San Francisco at a time when the school was a West Coast power. He broke into pro ball with the old Dallas Texans and was one of the leftover players who joined the Colts when the team shifted to Baltimore. "I was signed for a $500 bonus, and it thrilled me to death," Marchetti said. "Imagine getting all that dough for doing something I loved to do. My first pro contract was for $6,500."

Gino Marchetti was an imposing presence on Baltimore's defensive line for 13 seasons. He was an 11-time Pro Bowler and 7-time First-Team All-Pro. KIDWILER COLLECTION/DIAMOND IMAGES/GETTY IMAGES

MVP BOOKS COLLECTION

Marchetti stands on the sideline next to a fellow future Hall of Famer, coach Don Shula, during a 1964 game at Memorial Stadium in Baltimore. KIDWILER COLLECTION/DIAMOND IMAGES/GETTY IMAGES

Marchetti became rich later—not as a direct result of his playing skills but through those he got to know as a player. Colts owner Carroll Rosenbloom helped finance Marchetti's foray into the fast-food restaurant business, and teammate Alan Ameche became a partner. At its peak, before the chain was sold to Marriott in 1982, Gino's restaurants totaled 359 outlets and employed thousands.

As a player, Marchetti let crashing through offensive linemen do much of his talking. His teammates respected him mightily, and they listened closely when he did speak. It was Marchetti who predicted that Johnny Unitas would be a permanent fixture when he replaced an injured George Shaw. "He's never going to be the quarterback again," Marchetti said of Shaw. "Unitas is the quarterback." That was one accurate crystal ball reading.

When Rosenbloom weighed the dismissal of coach Weeb Ewbank in 1963, he asked Marchetti for advice. "He asked me to recommend a coach," Marchetti said years after the meeting. "I told him [Don] Shula." Shula was only 33 and had been a teammate in the defensive backfield with some longer-serving Colts players. But the hire worked out, and Shula became the winningest coach in NFL history.

ART DONOVAN, BUDDY YOUNG HELP MAKE COLTS FAMOUS

Arthur Donovan Jr. was an original personality, if not the original Baltimore Colt. Donovan, whose father, Arthur Donovan Sr., was a world-famous boxing referee, played college football for Boston College, and his pro days went back to the All-America Football Conference. With 300 lumpy pounds distributed over his 6-foot-2 frame, Donovan earned the nickname "Fatso." It was not an insult but a term of endearment from teammates. At least they said so.

Donovan did not look the part of sculpted athlete, but he was such a fine defensive tackle that he was voted into the Hall of Fame. He was a guy who liked to talk, drink beer, talk some more, eat, and talk some more. Donovan was a gourmand, not a gourmet. He subsisted on pizza, hot dogs, baloney sandwiches, and cheeseburgers washed down preferably by Schlitz beer. Once, at a Baltimore Lions Club party, Donovan said he ate 37 hot dogs before anyone complained about his intake.

"I was a light eater," Donovan wrote in his autobiography. "When it got light, I started eating."

Eating big, as if every meal was a buffet, was one of Donovan's notable traits, but although it might seem that the two habits were related, his penchant for throwing up before each game was about nerves, not food. When his teammates heard him barfing in the locker-room bathroom, they knew he was ready to play.

When Weeb Ewbank took over the team, he took note of Donovan's training habits and wrote a clause into his contract that his tackle had to weigh no more than 270 pounds in order to play. Some weeks at his weigh-ins Donovan stripped off not only all of his clothes to make weight but also removed his false teeth. Hitting that weight also meant Donovan earned a $2,000 bonus.

Donovan hadn't even received All–New England recognition with BC, so he didn't expect to make it as a pro when he tried out for the Colts in 1950. Shocked when he saw 150 players at the preseason camp, he felt he was doomed. But Donovan made the team, earning a meager $4,500 in 1950, and he played until 1961.

The NFL of the early 1950s was rough around the edges. Only 33 players were kept on rosters, and many played on both offense and defense. Kicking specialists were unheard of, with the guy booting field goals also playing elsewhere on the field. Donovan said the NFL of his day was about "as sophisticated as a tong war."

Donovan was well-equipped to compete in such an environment. His grandfather, Mike Donovan, had been the middleweight boxing champion in the 1870s. Father Arthur was

"I was a light eater. When it got light, I started eating." —Art Donovan

(BOTH) MVP BOOKS COLLECTION

the third man in the ring for the two Joe Louis–Max Schmeling heavyweight duels. Once, when he blew his cool, Art Jr. shouted at an official, "My old man's a ref, a better ref than you'll ever be, and I know a bad call when I see one."

The discrimination against blacks in the United States in the 1950s was a widespread disgrace. Most black athletes who wished to make a mark professionally preferred to play in the North or California. Baltimore was a segregated city, and that was the world Claude "Buddy" Young—who, like Donovan, was one of the earliest Colts to make a long-term impact—walked into. After bouncing around with soon-to-be-defunct teams such as the New York Yankees and Dallas Texans, Young played the final years of his pro career with the Colts between 1953 and 1955. He was one of the first black players in Baltimore and at 5-foot-4 is one of the shortest players in NFL history.

Young first played a football game in Baltimore with a visiting team in 1947, and nasty fans ridiculed him by painting their faces with lampblack and yelling profanities at him. "I didn't know if I was here to play in a football game or a minstrel show," Young said later. Young did have allies in coping with segregated Baltimore. Cecil Isbell, the old Green Bay quarterback who coached the Colts in the AAFC said, "If you don't like Buddy Young, then you don't like people."

Young was a world-class sprinter for the University of Illinois track team and was called the "Bronze Bullet." His best 100-yard dash time was 9.4 seconds. Young won both NCAA and AAU championships, and his blinding speed was an asset on the gridiron that helped offset his small stature. He made the Pro Bowl for the Colts in 1954. As a publicity gimmick the Colts cajoled the reluctant Young to race against a horse. Young had a better start and beat the horse easily over 100 yards.

Young averaged 4.6 yards per carry for his career, more than 28 yards per kickoff return, and about 15 yards per pass reception. He was a trailblazer for blacks on the team, and when he was cut in 1955 to make room for rookie Lenny Moore, he stayed on with the Colts in the front office.

Moore said he was sorry that his advancement came at the cost of the termination of Young's playing career and that he felt he had much to learn from him. Moore felt the NFL quota was seven black players per team at the time, and that was the main reason Young was shunted aside. But the two men never got along well after that.

Hall of Fame defensive tackle Art Donovan at training camp, 1960s.
AP PHOTO

Buddy Young was a world-class sprinter for the University of Illinois track team and was called the "Bronze Bullet."

RAYMOND BERRY

Self-Made Hall of Famer

Raymond Berry breaks free to get open for a pass during a game at Memorial Stadium in the mid-1960s. FOCUS ON SPORT/GETTY IMAGES

Raymond Berry couldn't run very fast, partly because one of his legs was shorter than the other. He couldn't see very well, so he wore contact lenses. He had no record of being a superior end at Southern Methodist University. All he did was work harder than anyone on the planet and use the one natural gift he possessed—good hands—to make himself into the best professional pass catcher of his era.

Almost daily, Berry drilled and drilled a package of 88 moves that he felt could help him beat defensive backs on his routes. He worked overtime to develop timing with Colts quarterback Johnny Unitas, and the twosome developed the rhythm of a duet on the dance floor. He practiced potential game situations the way no one ever had before and few have since. "In all my time in coaching . . . in high school, college, and the pros, I have never seen a more serious athlete," said Colts coach Weeb Ewbank in 1958.

One of the least likely success stories in Colts history, Berry didn't start on his high school team until his senior year—and his father was the coach. He caught just 33 passes during his entire college career. Berry was surprised to be drafted by an NFL team, but when the Colts took him in the 20th round of the 1954 draft, he seized the opportunity. When he showed up for training camp, he emphasized to always call him the formal Raymond, never Ray, in accordance with family tradition. Berry's teammates weren't impressed with him at first. "He had very limited ability," said fullback Alan Ameche, "but he was the hardest working guy anybody ever saw."

Known for his perfectionism and consistency, Berry fumbled just once in 13 seasons—and claimed the official blew the call on that one. It was an upset that Berry ever became a pro, but he blossomed in a Colts uniform. He spent his entire playing career in Baltimore, catching 631 passes for 68 touchdowns and 9,275 yards between 1955 and 1967. At the time the 631 catches was a league mark. Now he is barely in the top 50. Teams just didn't throw as often back then.

Berry was named all-pro six times and was voted into the Hall of Fame in 1973. Then he became a coach, taking the New England Patriots to the Super Bowl in 1985 after becoming the first NFL team to win three playoff games on the road.

In a career full of highlights, Berry shined in the 1958 championship against the New York Giants, in what was termed "The Greatest Game Ever Played." Berry caught 12 passes for 178 yards and a touchdown in that milestone game. Ewbank estimated that Berry spent 40 hours watching game film of the Giants to get ready. "One play may make the difference in winning or losing a game," Berry said. "I must be prepared to make my own luck." He always did.

MVP BOOKS COLLECTION

Raymond Berry grabs a 13-yard touchdown pass thrown by Johnny Unitas during a 20–0 rout of the Redskins in 1960. AP PHOTO

BUILDING A RAPPORT WITH THE CITY

Several early Colts players were active in the Baltimore community. Running backs Alan Ameche and Buddy Young pose here with some members of the Police Boys Club in 1955. AP PHOTO/NFL PHOTOS

Carroll Rosenbloom, Don Kellett, and Weeb Ewbank would turn the Colts into the best team in the world by 1958. Kellett was Rosenbloom's choice for general manager, and they hired Ewbank to make the personnel judgments that changed the team's fortunes.

Ewbank promised a championship in five years, and the key event that enabled him to make good was the 1955 draft. Baltimore had two first-round picks, selecting quarterback George Shaw and running back Alan Ameche, and then the team selected Dick Szymanski, L.G. Dupre, and Jack Patera in later rounds.

Ameche was the Heisman Trophy winner from Wisconsin, and his selection energized the fan base. The first time he carried the ball from scrimmage in a regular-season game, Ameche scampered 79 yards for a touchdown. The item was reported nationally in a ***Ripley's Believe It Or Not*** syndicated newspaper column. Ameche rushed for 194 yards in his debut, making the draft choice look very wise. In his second game Ameche ran 57 yards for a score, and the back-to-back long runs surprised even him. "I thought I suddenly turned into something I wasn't," he said. "I had always been a grind-it-out fullback, certainly not a breakaway runner. What happened was a fluke."

It couldn't have been much of a fluke because Ameche led the NFL in rushing that season with 961 yards.

Shaw became the starting quarterback until he got hurt and was uprooted by Johnny Unitas. Szymanski became the starting center and later the team's general manager. Dupre and Patera made useful contributions as well. The Colts also hit big with their No. 1 picks in 1956 and 1957, choosing two future Hall of Famers: Lenny Moore out of Penn State and Jim Parker from Ohio State.

Coach Weeb Ewbank goes over the game plan with Colts quarterbacks Johnny Unitas and George Shaw. AP PHOTO

There were growing pains, of course. They needed experience and to mesh as a team, but the 5–6–1 record of 1955 and the 5–7 record of 1956 represented slow but steady improvement. By then, when the Colts were playing at a near-.500 level and rounding up exciting young players, the fans had become disproportionately devoted. Baltimore residents were still grasping the designation of being a big-league pro sports town. It was not as cosmopolitan as New York or Washington.

From the first, back in the All-America Football Conference days, any noise the Colts made on the field was accompanied by the music of the Baltimore Colts Marching

The first time he carried the ball from scrimmage in a regular-season game, Alan Ameche scampered 79 yards for a touchdown.

"It felt like we were attached to this town at our very core. You understand what I'm saying? It felt like we **were attached at our souls.**" —Mike Curtis

The Colts marching band plays in the end zone at Baltimore's Memorial Stadium before a game against the New York Giants on December 27, 1959. AP PHOTO

Art Spinney (63) and Big Jim Parker (77) were cornerstones of the great Colts teams of the 1950s, while Jim Welch (46) joined them as a rookie in 1960 and stayed for eight seasons. ROBERT RIGER/GETTY IMAGES

Band. Founded in 1947, the band quickly became an institution in Baltimore. Major football-playing colleges featured bands staffed with coordinated students, but the Colts' band was staffed by volunteer adults who brought their own tubas to the fight.

Also dating to 1947, the team had "The Baltimore Colts Official Theme Song," and the sheet music indicated it was to be played at "march tempo." The cover of at least one version of the sheet music had a horse (presumably a colt) playing the piano. The words and music were a collaboration of Benjamin Klasmer and Jo Lombardi (no known relation to Vince). Generally speaking, the theme song was outside of Klasmer's wheelhouse. He was a well-respected classical musician, a professional violinist in Baltimore. Lombardi was the musical director of Baltimore's Hippodrome Theatre.

The song in part goes this way: "Let's go you BAL-TI-MORE COLTS/And put that ball a—cross the Line/So/Drive on you BAL-TI-MORE COLTS/Go in and strike like light—ning bolts/FIGHT, FIGHT, FIGHT./Rear up you COLTS and let's fight." With all that fighting being advocated, perhaps Arthur Donovan Sr. should have been there to officiate.

Broadcaster Chuck Thompson built goodwill for the team on the air, too. His signature phrase of encouragement and excitement was "Go to war, Miss Agnes!" which he often exclaimed after a Colts touchdown.

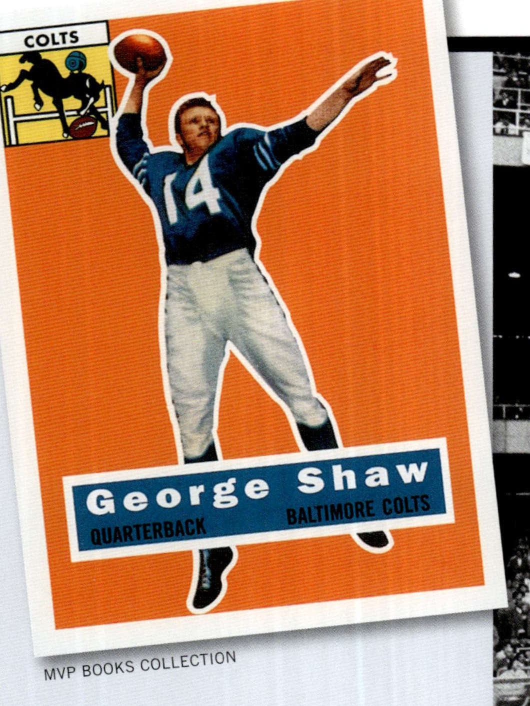

MVP BOOKS COLLECTION

The Colts were also the only team in the NFL that had a live horse for a mascot, predating their acquisition of the human "Horse," Alan Ameche. Starting in 1949, every time the Colts scored a touchdown or field goal, a white horse named Dixie, with a rider decked out in western regalia, galloped around the perimeter of the field.

Sprints around the stadium by the horse were a tradition from 1949 to 1963, when the act was axed. Fans loved the celebratory maneuver, and there was at least one documented occasion of the horse getting on opposing players' nerves—which wasn't all bad, either. "With that horse running around every time the Colts scored, I didn't know if I was at a football game or at Santa Anita," said Rams linebacker Les Richter on a particularly bad day for his team when the Colts ran up 56 points. He might have had a better day betting at the racetrack.

Finally, Colts Corrals, branches of the team fan club, sprang up all over the city and the suburbs starting in 1957. There was even a chapter in a prison. Those clubs remain in existence today, though allegiance has transferred to the Baltimore Ravens. Baltimore showed its love for players in many ways as they began winning games.

Members of the "Colts Corral" fan club impersonate Dixie during halftime of a 1958 game at Memorial Stadium. PAUL SCHUTZER/TIME LIFE PICTURES/GETTY IMAGES

One reason the relationship was so tight was because the Colts were not just mercenaries passing through. They were of the community as well as part of the team. Players and their wives ate in restaurants where other Baltimore residents ate. They drank in bars where workers drank. They worshipped in the same churches. Sure, they were Colts and on a pedestal of sorts, but they were people who didn't make salaries 50 times greater than the ticket buyers. Most of the players stayed in town year-round, and most of them worked offseason—and in some cases, additional in-season—jobs.

Gino Marchetti worked in a bowling alley for a while. Art Donovan sold liquor and made a career out of it after football. Parker sold cemetery plots and later ran a profitable liquor store. Imagine, pro athletes needing the bucks from working at regular-guy jobs.

" . . . We were connected at the hip with these people," said linebacker Mike Curtis. "It felt like we were attached to this town at our very core. You understand what I'm saying? It felt like we were attached at our souls."

Baltimore
Memorial Stadium
★
October 31, 1953
OFFICIAL
PROGRAM
50¢
COLTS
PACKERS

ALAN "THE HORSE" AMECHE

A Major Catch

When the Baltimore Colts made Alan Ameche their No. 1 draft pick in 1955, it was a symbol of a downtrodden team taking the plunge into the big time.

Fans could hardly believe their good fortune. They were used to the bottom-feeding Colts always losing out on the best talent. They rooted for a team that hadn't been able to pluck athletes of Ameche's caliber, who was awarded the Heisman Trophy as the finest player in college football in 1954.

Born Lino Dante Ameche to a strong Italian family, Ameche was an All-American running back at the University of Wisconsin. At the time, his 3,212 yards was the NCAA record for career rushing. He was fast and strong, the type of back a team could build its offense around. He was also very much a gentleman, and as time went on he proved to be a huge community asset through his volunteer work with nonprofit charitable agencies.

First Ameche made his mark on the playing field. Lined up as a fullback on the first carry of his pro career, Ameche burst free behind the line of scrimmage and rumbled for a 79-yard touchdown. The 6-foot, 218-pound Ameche immediately lived up to his college reputation by being named the NFL Rookie of the Year when he led the league in rushing with 961 yards. Four times Ameche was selected to play in the Pro Bowl game in a six-year career that was cut short by injury. Ameche gained more than 4,000 yards from scrimmage for the Colts and also caught 101 passes.

The consistent star was appreciated in Baltimore for his weekly exploits, and Ameche's enduring national fame hinges on the pivotal role he played in the Colts' 1958 NFL championship victory over the New York Giants. Ameche scored the winning touchdown on a one-yard run. Head down, he blasted through a spacious hole created by his offensive linemen, sealing the 23–17 victory in sudden-death overtime.

Alan Ameche tries to break free from a Packers defender during a 1956 contest. VERNON BIEVER/GETTY IMAGES

The circumstances were unique—the first NFL overtime game. But Ameche, a down-to-earth fellow, did not add flowery description to the play. To him, it was an ordinary call from the playbook, embellished in memory because of the high-profile situation. "Ironically, there was nothing to it," said Ameche, who was so self-effacing about his athletic achievements that he kept his Heisman trophy in a box out of sight at home. "It was very routine, very anticlimactic."

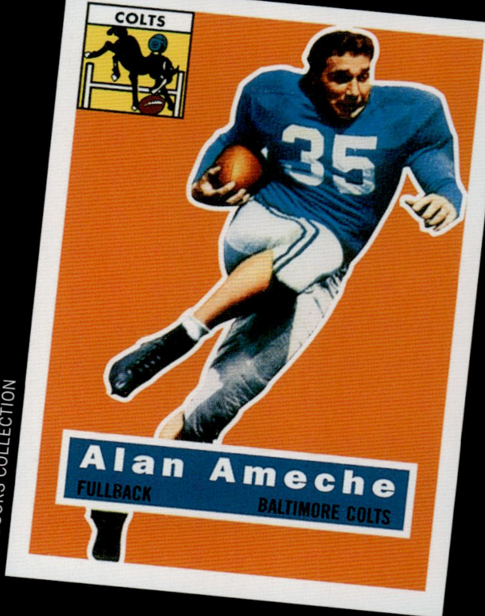

MVP BOOKS COLLECTION

Ameche's comparison to the strength and power of a free-running horse saddled him with a nickname he was indifferent to at first. But when asked to pose for a picture with the famous thoroughbred Native Dancer, he warmed up to it. As soon as the publicity shot made the rounds, it was fair game to note that "The Horse" stampeded through opposing defenses for yardage.

After retirement, Ameche and Colts teammate Gino Marchetti entered the fast-food restaurant business together, selling more hamburgers than they ever gained yards. The investment made him a millionaire, but he joked that business was too good because he gained 15 pounds eating his own product. Whether it was poor eating habits or something else that harmed him, Ameche was only 55 when he died undergoing heart surgery.

AND THE BAND PLAYED ON

For some fan observers, it probably seemed as if the band played on in futility as the *Titanic* sank. But the Baltimore Colts Marching Band had remarkable perseverance on its seemingly foolish errand.

Formed on September 7, 1947, the Baltimore Colts Marching Band goes back to the days when the franchise was founded and played in the All-America Football Conference. It remained viable during the years after the original Colts folded, remained brassy during the golden era of the Colts in Baltimore, and refused to go away when the Colts did. When the team was kidnapped to Indianapolis in 1984, the Marching Band refused to yield. The band even played at empty Memorial Stadium at times.

For many years it appeared that the Baltimore Colts Marching Band was the patron saint of lost causes. Band members gathered to practice weekly and played gigs when asked, at everything from Little League baseball games to parades, all the while hoping against hope that they would once again represent a Baltimore NFL franchise. They endured 12 years of playing to empty houses, a bit like Moses wandering around in the desert for 40 years, awaiting instruction from the Lord.

The Baltimore Colts Marching Band has run longer continuously than *As the World Turns* did. There was even a documentary made about the band by Hollywood director Barry Levinson. Levinson was the creator of the movie *Diner* with a subplot illustrating Baltimore's devotion to the Colts. The documentary was called *The Band That Wouldn't Die.*

The band was created to demonstrate the city's enthusiasm for the Colts. It is an all-volunteer musical group, and only through a combination of luck and conspiracy did the band retain the uniforms, which were being dry-cleaned when the team fled to Indianapolis. Owner Bob Irsay did not give the uniforms to the band, but a plan was hatched to capture them.

The group played on and on until the NFL let Baltimore swipe the Cleveland Browns, who became the Baltimore Ravens in 1996. The Cleveland Browns had been uprooted by owner Art Modell, who was pulling an Irsay. Irsay was vilified in Baltimore, extolled in Indianapolis. Modell was vilified in Cleveland, extolled in Baltimore.

After it was finalized that the Browns were on their way to Baltimore, David Modell, son of the owner, appeared on a local talk show with band president John Ziemann. On the airwaves, Ziemann asked Modell if the Marching Band could become the official Ravens Marching Band. With supreme grasp of understatement, Modell said, "I thought you already were."

So now the same group is the Baltimore Ravens Marching Band.

The tuba section of the Baltimore Colts Marching Band exits the field through the end zone at Memorial Stadium. PAUL SCHUTZER/TIME LIFE PICTURES/GETTY IMAGES

MVP BOOKS COLLECTION

ROUGH, TOUGH COLTS

General manager Don Kellett was the public face of the Colts franchise, the man who helped bridge the distance between the young team and its receptive public. A three-sport athlete at the University of Pennsylvania who played briefly for the Boston Red Sox and coached some college football, Kellett was Carroll Rosenbloom's right-hand man in establishing the Colts in Baltimore. Kellett made promotional speeches in front of just about any organization that would have him. He gave more talks promoting his cause than a politician running for office, and that did the Colts no harm.

On the field, the Colts were definitely putting together a better product. One of the other holdovers from the Colts' earliest days, besides Buddy Young and Art Donovan, was linebacker Bill Pellington.

Pellington came out of Rutgers and served time on the Colts' 1953 team that got clobbered more often than not. But he outlasted most of his teammates with a rough, aggressive style that coaches love. The 6-foot-2, 235-pound Pellington intercepted 21 passes and recovered 14 fumbles during his career that lasted through 1964, all with the Colts. His signature play was a so-called "neck-tie" tackle. During those days, the NFL had no rules against tackling a ball carrier by his head—Pellington's technique would be illegal in today's game and was more akin to a wrestling move than a tackle.

If people thought Pellington was hard on opponents, he also sacrificed his own body in committing mayhem. In the end, Pellington was so worn out from his own broken bones and bruises that teammate Don Shinnick used to help him peel off his uniform following games. After one game, that need for assistance peaked when owner Carroll Rosenbloom cut through the locker room and offered to pull off Pellington's jersey for him.

Football players are known for their toughness, but in private meetings Colts coaches talked about Pellington's grit in hushed voices. Once, they voted him the player they would most like to have on their side in a street fight. Assistant coach Charlie Winner said, "He'll hit anybody or anything, friend or foe, that he can reach. He has the killer instinct, and that's something you can't teach."

Unless the injury was so severe that doctors would tackle him before he could reach the field, Pellington played with whatever pain accrued from his reckless style, and Colts fans ate it up, just as they did the huge platters of food he later offered at The Horse, a popular restaurant he owned that featured gargantuan serving portions.

Years into retirement, Pellington met a sports writer at The Horse. On that occasion he was asked to list his injuries and did so, noting problems he suffered with a knee, hand, arm, and his nose. The arm was a doozy of an injury. He showed off a years-old five-inch scar, incurred when he clubbed Detroit Lions running back Tom Tracy to the turf. Nothing illegal about that at the time, though such a move is grounds for a fine and suspension today.

> **". . . the best players are those with the fewest worries and personal problems. That's my job, to take their worries off their back." —Carroll Rosenbloom**

Pellington carried the souvenir scar from the play, but Tracy got the worst of the collision. "I knocked him out," Pellington said. "They had to call a time out for him." Pellington wrapped tape around his arm and continued to play—but only for a little while. Even he couldn't tolerate the pain from this injury. After visiting a hospital, Pellington learned the arm was broken.

In the early days when he was just learning the ropes of being an NFL owner, Rosenbloom was very popular with his players. He tried to treat them well, even if he didn't go overboard on the salary scale any more than other owners. He tried to reward the longest-serving players with assistant coach jobs and even made loans to set them up in businesses that would nurture them in retirement. Rosenbloom supplied the seed money that helped Gino Marchetti and Alan Ameche start the wildly successful fast-food restaurant chain called Gino's.

"Football games are won by football players, not coaches," Rosenbloom once said. "Coaches are overrated. And the best players are those with the fewest worries and personal problems. That's my job, to take their worries off their back."

Players generally appreciated Rosenbloom's attitude. Lineman Jim Parker was one of those fans. "I played for him for 11 years, and I wouldn't want to play for anyone else," Parker said. "He's always been a fair man. I've never met a man who worked for Carroll Rosenbloom who didn't like him."

Players are one thing, but fans are another. Rosenbloom presided over the Colts becoming winners, and that's one way to keep the masses happy. Of course, one way to become a winner is to find the right personnel.

Bill Pellington was a rough and tough presence on the Colts defense for more than a decade.
WILLIAM GREENE/SPORTS STUDIO PHOTOS/GETTY IMAGES

The 6-foot-2, 235-pound Bill Pellington intercepted 21 passes and recovered 14 fumbles during his career that lasted through 1964.

SOME GUY NAMED JOHNNY U

The greatest bargain in pro football history fell into the Colts' lap when they discovered the availability of Johnny Unitas. Unitas played college ball at Louisville and was drafted by the Pittsburgh Steelers. They never gave him a chance to win the quarterback job and cut him swiftly. Unitas took a job and played semipro ball once per week, hoping he would get another chance at the NFL.

He did. Don Kellett invested 80 cents in a telephone call to invite Unitas to attend the Colts' training camp in 1956. They would try him out along with another player from the semipro Bloomfield Rams. Unitas had to borrow the gas money to make the short trip, but as soon as he got his foot in the door, he kept that door open. Weeb Ewbank was smart enough to see the potential in Unitas, even if he was not yet the polished article.

The as-yet untapped potential was unveiled over time, as Unitas threw at least one touchdown pass in a league-record 47 straight games between 1956 and 1960, a mark that still stands.

George Shaw, out of the University of Oregon, was the No. 1 pick in the 1955 NFL draft, and the Colts installed him as their quarterback of the future. Unitas was retained the next year to be Shaw's backup. In just the fourth game of the 1956 season, against the Chicago Bears, Shaw broke his leg, and Unitas was thrust into action. This was no storybook start to a Hall of Fame career, though, as Unitas looked every bit the timid youngster. The first pass of his career was intercepted and run back for a touchdown.

But Shaw was out, and the Colts needed Unitas. He eased into the role as the starter, even if he didn't light up the stat sheet. He threw for nine touchdowns but also had 10 interceptions. The next season, when the Colts began to show indications of the Ewbank plan coming to fruition, the fans got vintage Unitas, the player they would grow to marvel at. He completed 57.1 percent of his passes for 2,550 yards and 24 touchdowns. Those were great numbers in a running league, and after the 7–5 campaign Unitas was selected as first-team all-pro for the first time.

The Colts might even have finished better. With two weeks left in the season they were 7–3 and in position to claim a division title. But then they traveled to the West Coast, and as was their habit, lost to both the San Francisco 49ers 17–13 and the Los Angeles Rams 37–21. Although the Colts let the title slip away, they recognized that they were on the verge of something big, that they would be ready to take the next step in 1958.

"This was the season we truly came together as a team," said halfback Lenny Moore. "All the major pieces were in place, and it was in this campaign that we learned to compete as a unit."

MVP BOOKS COLLECTION

The Colts had no idea what they were getting when they invited Johnny Unitas to training camp in 1956—but it sure worked out well. HULTON ARCHIVE/GETTY IMAGES

Johnny Unitas threw at least one touchdown pass in a league-record 47 straight games between 1956 and 1960, a mark that still stands.

JOHNNY UNITAS QUARTERBACK KING

Johnny Unitas takes the snap from center during a game against the Chicago Bears on October 6, 1963. ROBERT RIGER/GETTY IMAGES

Johnny U is what many called him, almost as if he was a famed gunslinger—which in a way he was. Johnny Unitas is one of the most famous football players in history, and even those who follow the game only casually know that he was perhaps the greatest quarterback of all time. Even those who never saw him play in person and know little else about him know he was a winner and a leader whose deeds lifted the spirits of an entire city.

As great as the cast surrounding him turned out to be after judicious drafting and trading, without Johnny U there would have been no Baltimore Colt championships in the 1950s. George Shaw was good, but the difference between good and great became apparent when Shaw got hurt and Unitas stepped in as quarterback. Unitas was the man who made everything run smoothly.

The legend of Johnny Unitas lives on, long past his retirement in 1973 and his death from a heart attack in 2002. In Unitas' case, neither he nor anyone else has ever burnished the legend with colorful tales or boastful stories. He took care of business on the field, and there was no need to embellish excellence.

In a career that spanned 1956 to 1973, Unitas threw for 290 touchdown passes. He set a record by throwing at least one touchdown pass in 47 straight games. And he passed for 40,289 yards at a time when the sport's preoccupation with the running game relegated passing to the second option.

If "Broadway Joe" Namath introduced showmanship to the quarterback position, Unitas was more like an astute military officer who planned precision attacks. His flat-top haircut added to the image. And like a captain who had the respect of his troops, Unitas' Colts believed in him completely. When reporters sought interviews about how something was accomplished, Unitas was basically analytical, never likely to pour any hot fudge on his vanilla ice cream.

Unitas was Lithuanian and experienced a hard upbringing after being born in Pittsburgh, Pennsylvania, in

1933. His father died when he was four, and his mother worked two jobs to support the family. Although he was a good athlete, the 6-foot-1 Unitas was skinny. Major college football programs ignored his skills because he didn't look the part of a big-time quarterback. A tryout for the Notre Dame Fighting Irish earned him a letter saying officials there thought he was too small. Indiana University didn't even write a rejection after Unitas tried out for the Hoosiers. He may have wanted attention from Notre Dame, but he matriculated at the University of Louisville.

Unitas showed he could perform in college, passing for more than 3,000 yards and 27 touchdowns, but the pros, with the inexact scouting of the era, did not study him enough to see the magic in his arm. His hometown Pittsburgh Steelers drafted Unitas in the ninth round of the NFL draft, but coach Walt Kieseling, making one of the most infamous blunders in pro sports history, never even allowed Unitas to take a snap in training camp before releasing him. "For a good many years," Unitas said, recalling the bad times, "it looked as if I'd never make it. I was the quarterback nobody wanted."

Married with a baby, Unitas needed work. He returned to Pittsburgh and took a job in construction. Although his prospects seemed bleak, he didn't give up on his football dream, once per week leading the semipro Bloomington Rams into gridiron battle. He was paid $6 per game. When Unitas and a teammate received an invitation to try out with the Colts, he had to borrow money for gas to make the trip. Coach Weeb Ewbank let Unitas show his stuff, and he signed the quarterback to back up Shaw. When Shaw got hurt in the fourth game of the 1956 season, Unitas became Baltimore's starter. The rest is the stuff of legend.

Ewbank deserves points for his judgment of talent. Younger fans probably don't realize how close America came to missing out on Unitas altogether. It wasn't long before Unitas, a 10-time all-star and a three-time Most Valuable Player, became a star. More than a star, really—he was more like the focal point in a constellation. Unitas quickly transitioned from unwanted to indispensable. Unitas was chosen as the quarterback of the NFL's all-time team during the league's 50th anniversary celebration in 1970.

FOCUS ON SPORT/GETTY IMAGES

One Unitas nickname was "Mr. Clutch." He had a knack for bringing his team back when it trailed, instigating rallies in the fourth quarter regularly at a time when no one kept track of such doings. Unitas was probably the most dangerous player in the league in the sense that he was never beaten until the last seconds ticked off the clock. He was always gunning for more yards, more points, no matter how far behind his team was. "I can't relax when Unitas is out there," said Green Bay Packers coach Vince Lombardi. "I'm scared to death when he's on the field."

Unitas possessed that indefinable quality of champions, an ability to ooze leadership so that men listened when he spoke and followed when he carved out a path. Otto Graham, who developed his own credentials as a Hall of Fame quarterback for the Cleveland Browns, put Unitas in a class of his own. "He's simply as good a quarterback as has ever been seen in pro football," Graham said.

Unitas was not a glamour boy. He didn't dress flashy. He was a family man and didn't go out on the town much. He exuded confidence in his actions on the field, even when the Colts were behind, but never talked a big game. Polite off the field, he was a dictator in the huddle. Only his voice was to be heard.

Johnny U–the clean-cut, working-class hero with a golden arm and an uncanny ability to lead a team. SPORTING NEWS ARCHIVE/GETTY IMAGES

His choice of play was the law. Ewbank may have supplied play recommendations, but Unitas managed the game and he was sure he knew best. If he didn't like the coach's call, he substituted his own. Usually, his play worked and no one complained.

Once, a writer for *Sport* magazine categorized Unitas' play-calling in a situation as risky and asked him what if the other team had intercepted the ball and run it back all of the way for a touchdown. Unitas acted as if such a thought had never clouded his mind. "When you know what you're doing, they're not intercepted," he said. Unitas' world was a world of certainty. In the chess game running through his head, he was five moves ahead of the opponent.

Unitas pretty much demonstrated those smarts in the 1958 NFL Championship Game against the New York Giants, billed as "The Greatest Game Ever Played." This was the Colts' first taste of life on the big stage, the first time Ewbank's squad was in position to win it all. The game, the victory, and his own sterling performance put Unitas on the map in much bigger letters than ever before, too. The attention on the sport, but also the Baltimore star, multiplied.

"People who never knew I was alive before now come up and say, 'You're Johnny Unitas of the Baltimore Colts, aren't you? I'd like to shake hands,'" Unitas said. "Kids ask for autographs. I'd be a liar if I said I didn't like it."

Neither Ewbank, nor his successor as Colts coach, Don Shula, interfered with Unitas' ideas on how to run an offense. They had proposals, but they trusted Unitas' instincts and ability to read defenses. They comprehended that he was the smartest guy on the field, that he knew what was going on between the 22 players on the field better than anyone else. Besides, his own record proved Unitas might be daring but was never reckless. Unitas was not some inexperienced rookie who thought he knew it all. Heck, Unitas probably did know it all. "You have to have a reason for every single thing you do out there," Unitas said.

For most of Unitas' career, the NFL schedule consisted of 12-game seasons. Late in his career teams played 14. For the times, Unitas threw a lot, though not nearly as much as teams routinely do now. Unitas' best stats were 3,481 passing yards gained in 1963 and 255 passes completed in 1967. He threw for a career-high 32 touchdowns in 1959—and that was in a 12-game season.

Impressive stuff, but Unitas never made a big deal out of his totals. "Why should I care about records?" he said. "I'm just not concerned with them. I am concerned with only one thing—winning."

One way that Unitas gained admiration around the league was by brushing off hard hits from the game's biggest and strongest defenders, who crushed him for sacks in the pocket and in the split second after he released the ball. Unitas played through pain, wrapping himself into a flak jacket to protect broken ribs instead of sitting one Sunday out. The behemoths of the defensive line try to make quarterbacks cringe and quit. Hall of Fame defensive end Deacon Jones of the Rams said it didn't work that way with Unitas. "You can't intimidate the man," said Jones, who weighed about 80 more pounds than Unitas' 195. "You could hit him hard enough to break him in two, and yet he'll come back on the next play and throw a touchdown pass."

Unitas played football until his arm felt as if it was going to fall off. He struggled through his final season in Baltimore in 1972, was bitter when the Colts didn't want him anymore, and then in what seemed like slow motion, he played out a last, unsatisfying year with the Chargers in 1973 before retiring.

After that, the only thing left was Unitas' election to the Hall of Fame in 1979, as soon as they would have him in Canton.

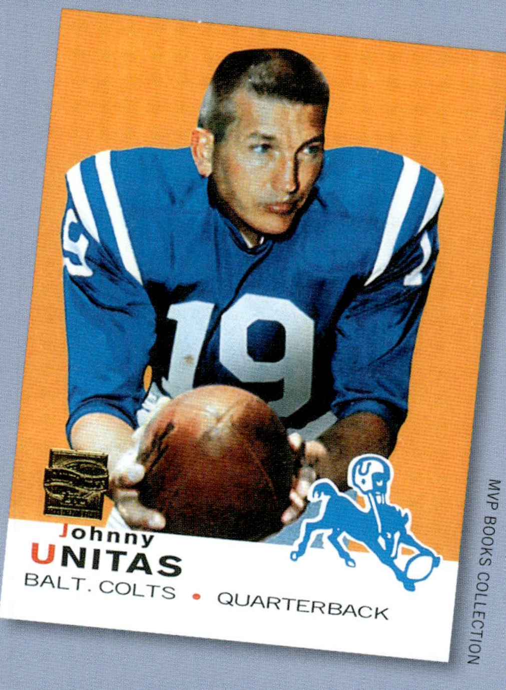

Johnny
UNITAS
BALT. COLTS • QUARTERBACK

MVP BOOKS COLLECTION

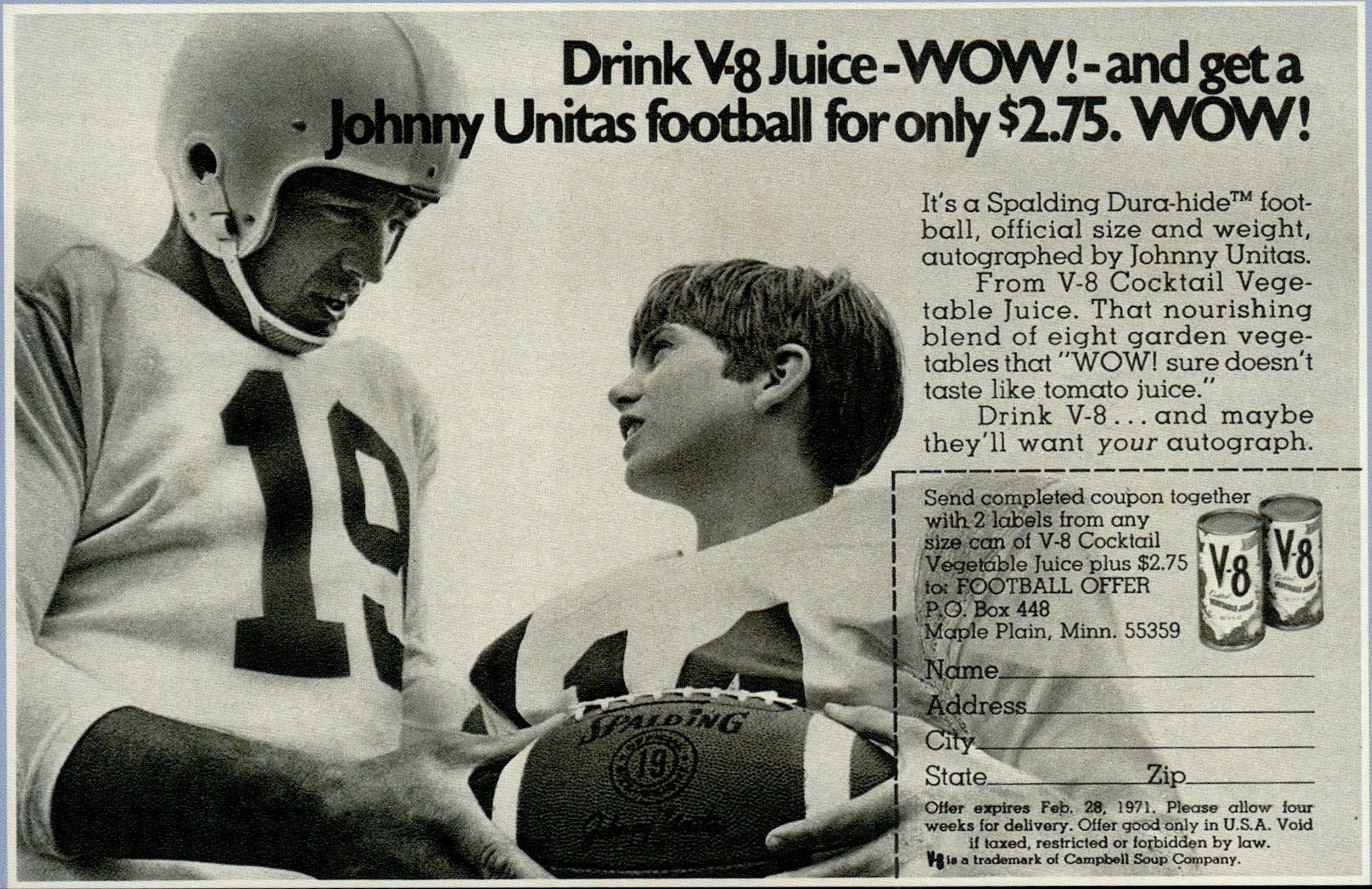
Drink V-8 Juice-WOW!-and get a Johnny Unitas football for only $2.75. WOW!
It's a Spalding Dura-hide™ football, official size and weight, autographed by Johnny Unitas.
From V-8 Cocktail Vegetable Juice. That nourishing blend of eight garden vegetables that "WOW! sure doesn't taste like tomato juice."
Drink V-8 . . . and maybe they'll want your autograph.
Send completed coupon together with 2 labels from any size can of V-8 Cocktail Vegetable Juice plus $2.75 to: FOOTBALL OFFER P.O. Box 448 Maple Plain, Minn. 55359
Name
Address
City
State Zip
Offer expires Feb. 28, 1971. Please allow four weeks for delivery. Offer good only in U.S.A. Void if taxed, restricted or forbidden by law.
V8 is a trademark of Campbell Soup Company.
V-8
SPALDING
19

MVP BOOKS COLLECTION

1958: THE COLTS CAPTURE THEIR FIRST TITLE

The Horse gallops through a massive hole to score the winning touchdown in "The Greatest Game Ever Played." AP PHOTO

The 1958 season, culminating with the first Colts championship, is one of the warmest memories in Baltimore sports history. This was the year the Colts became the ***Colts***. They won their first six games, lost by three points to the New York Giants, and then won three straight. They sat at 9–1 with the Western Division already clinched before making their dreaded end-of-season West Coast trip. Although it didn't matter much, the Colts lost yet again to both the 49ers and Rams, but they had captured the Western Conference crown just the same.

"The man who made it all go, of course, was John Unitas," Weeb Ewbank said. "He quickly blossomed into one of the great quarterbacks in the league. I don't mean it all happened by magic. Nothing happens that way. If you want to excel at something like football, you've got to work for it. John was one who worked for what he wanted."

There was another extraordinary aspect to the 1958 regular season. Rookie running back Lenny Lyles, the Colts' No. 1 draft pick out of Louisville, Unitas' old school, returned two kickoffs of more than 100 yards for touchdowns. One went for 103 yards against the Bears in early October, and the other went for 101 yards against the Redskins three weeks later. In the entire history of the team, in Baltimore and Indianapolis, the Colts have had just five kickoff returns that long.

All of this was merely the opening act for "The Greatest Game Ever Played," the NFL championship game against the New York Giants in Yankee Stadium. If the game were a building, it would have been put on a list of National Historic sites. The Colts' 23–17 victory in sudden-death overtime was the most meaningful ever played. The exposure to 45 million television viewers showed what the game could be like at its best.

"There are certain elements that go into the making of a great game, and this one had them all," Ewbank said.

Commissioner Bert Bell, who would not live to see the coming popularity of the NFL, was in the stands that day and instantly recognized what the drama of the tight game could mean to the league. Everyone there realized it was a special game, and the label stuck when *Sports Illustrated* anointed the contest—and Madison Avenue and TV networks took notice.

The Giants were established. Many of their same top players had been on their 1956 championship team. Frank Gifford, Charlie Conerly, Andy Robustelli, Roosevelt Brown, Rosey Grier, and Sam Huff were all celebrities in New York. The Colts were coming of age, ripening together under the leadership of Ewbank and Unitas. There were a few old-timers left who had lived through the bad times with the team, but to a man they felt they were the best team on December 28, 1958, and that by the end of the afternoon the world would know it, too.

"Just the fact that it was the first overtime in championship play, that was enough to make people feel they had seen something fantastic." —Johnny Unitas

The first quarter did not start spectacularly. On Baltimore's first possession Unitas was hit by Huff and he fumbled. Giant safety Jimmy Patton recovered. The Giants did not capitalize. Don Heinrich was clobbered by Gino Marchetti, and he fumbled it right back to the Colts' defensive end. On Baltimore's second try, Unitas was intercepted throwing to Raymond Berry.

"Both teams were a little tight at first," said Baltimore linebacker Don Shinnick, "which is natural for an important game." Shinnick agreed that this was the finest game he ever played in.

Before the end of the quarter, Pat Summerall nailed a 36-yard field goal for the Giants, and it was 3–0 New York.

The Colts' offense resembled its better self in the second quarter after Gifford fumbled for New York. Baltimore took over on the Giants' 20-yard line and scored five plays later on a two-yard run by Alan Ameche. More impressive was a Colts 86-yard drive closer to halftime. Although the Colts earned their points on a 15-yard toss from Unitas to Berry, they had made a good chunk of their yardage on the ground, with handoffs going to Ameche and Lenny Moore. It was 14–3 Baltimore at halftime.

The Giants fought back. Charlie Conerly, in at quarterback, hit Kyle Rote with a pass, and Rote ran to the Baltimore 25-yard line. Baltimore safety Andy Nelson, the team leader in interceptions that season

Colts fans arrive in New York to cheer on their team in the 1958 NFL Championship Game.
PAUL SCHUTZER/TIME LIFE PICTURES/GETTY IMAGES

Johnny Unitas throws a pass during overtime in the 1958 NFL Championship Game at Yankee Stadium. Unitas hit Raymond Berry on a handful of key plays in the greatest game. ROBERT RIGER/GETTY IMAGES

with eight, hit Rote, and he bobbled the ball. However, fullback Alex Webster, trailing the play, grabbed the loose ball and ran to the 1-yard line, where he was pushed out of bounds by Carl Taseff. Mel Triplett scored on the next play for New York, and the score was 14–10.

Before the end of the third period, the Giants took the lead, with Conerly hitting tight end Bob Schnelker for a touchdown. The later in the day it got, the colder in the stadium it got. Players wore cloaks over their uniforms as they stood on the sidelines.

The Giants couldn't hold Baltimore. Starting at their own 14 for the second time, the Colts marched to the other end of the field. When players think back on the offensive production in this contest, the first thing they recall is the precision passing from Unitas to Berry. On this drive the duo combined for three completions for 62 yards before Steve Myhra kicked the tying 20-yard field goal with seven seconds left in regulation time.

Before that, as the Colts rose up to deny Gifford a crucial first down on a running play, Baltimore defensive tackle Gene "Big Daddy" Lipscomb fell on Marchetti and broke his ankle. Marchetti was carried off the field on a stretcher but insisted on watching the game from the Colts' sideline. Some players sought to use Marchetti's injury for motivation and yelled, "Win it for Gino!"

Although Berry was always credited with having a wider repertoire of moves downfield than Bobby Fischer had on the chess board, he downplayed his creativity. "Actually, six to ten patterns is all you need," Berry said. "If you have a couple of sideliners, a couple of deep and a couple of inside patterns with good timing, you've got all you need."

However, Tom Landry, who became a Hall of Fame head coach with the Dallas Cowboys, thought there was more to it. Landry was the Giants' defensive coordinator during the title game, and when Berry retired a few years later, he hired him as an assistant coach in Dallas.

"Berry developed something new in pro football in his ability to fake," Landry said. "Until he came along, most of us didn't really see a lot of fakes. Never did we see the multiple fake system he brought to the game. Berry started faking with the first step. This was revolutionary. And he had so many variations."

The NFL had adopted a rule making a provision for overtime so no season would end with a tie in the title game. But many of the players were unaware of it because it had never been used. The league was prepared for this scenario, though. The Giants won the new coin toss and got the ball but couldn't make headway.

Rookie Lenny Lyles returned two kickoffs of more than 100 yards for touchdowns in 1958.

A Don Chandler punt to the Colts set Baltimore back on its own 20.

Right from the start, the Colts moved. L. G. Dupre ran for 11 yards and a first down on the first play. Unitas mixed Dupre runs with his passes, and key throws of 21 and 12 yards went to Berry. As Baltimore threatened, Unitas fired a pass to tight end Jim Mutscheller that put the ball on the 1-yard line.

"It was a straight slant pattern," Mutscheller said. "After I caught the ball, I was unable to cut up the field because the ground was frozen near the goal, so I just continued on a straight line out of bounds."

The Colts won the championship on the next play when Ameche toted the ball over the goal line from the 1-yard line.

Berry caught 12 passes for 178 yards. Unitas threw for 349 yards and was voted the Most Valuable Player of the game. Yet Unitas, the "Cool Hand Luke" of the sport, was not particularly caught up in the post-game hype.

"I've always felt that it wasn't a real good football game until the last two minutes and then the overtime," he said. "Just the fact that it was the first overtime in championship play, that was enough to make people feel they had seen something fantastic."

At home, Baltimore erupted into a friendly riot. Some 30,000 people clogged the airport to greet the team.

Art Donovan, whom Ewbank had pressured to lose weight and had been a Colt since the AAFC days, credited his coach for shaping the team into a winner.

"Weeb was a teacher," Donovan said. "He taught Unitas, took a guy from the sandlots and made him into the greatest quarterback of all time. He took a lot of ragtag football players and made us world champions."

Twice, in fact.

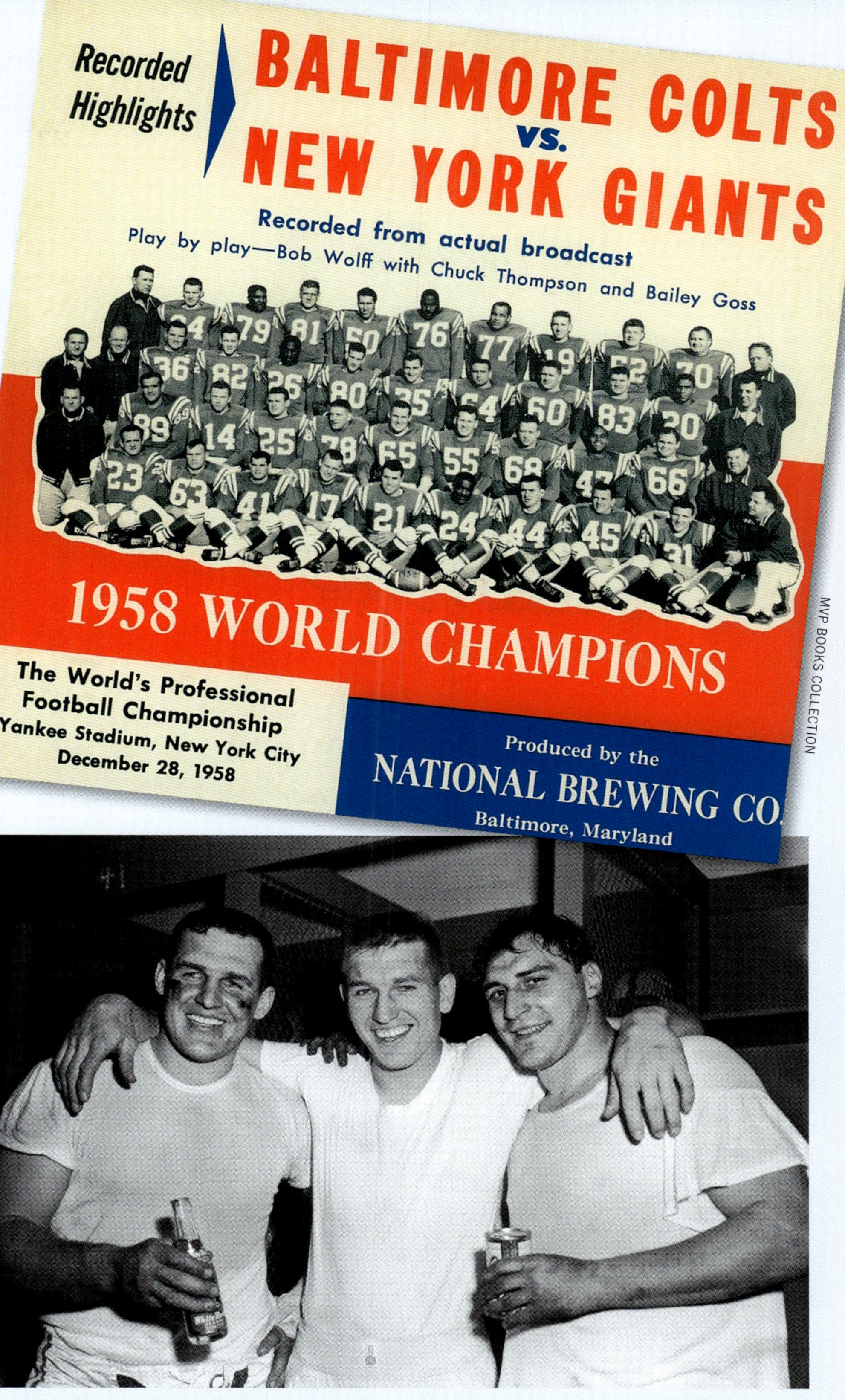

MVP BOOKS COLLECTION

Guard Steve Myhra, Johnny Unitas, and Alan Ameche celebrate in the locker room at Yankee Stadium after their thrilling overtime victory. KIDWILER COLLECTION/DIAMOND IMAGES/GETTY IMAGES

THE GREATEST GAME IN NFL HISTORY

It is impossible to rate the significance of the 1958 NFL Championship Game between the Baltimore Colts and the New York Giants simply by reviewing the play-by-play. There was tremendous drama on that chilly afternoon in Yankee Stadium, but the pure quality of play did not elevate this showdown to its ranking. Still, the label of "The Greatest Game Ever Played" was slapped on the game soon after it was contested, and it has endured ever since.

Some may say it is a misnomer to label the Colts' 23–17 victory as the greatest game, but there is little doubt it is the most important of all pro football games. The sport was never the same after the nation tuned in to the compelling performance showcased on the national stage.

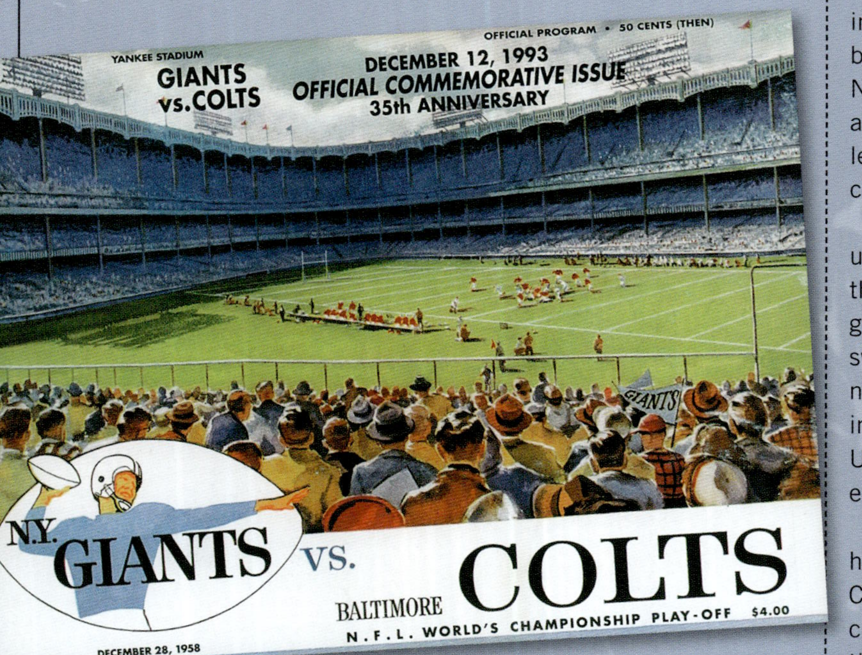

MVP BOOKS COLLECTION

1958 NFL CHAMPIONSHIP GAME

BALTIMORE COLTS 23 **NEW YORK GIANTS** 17

	1	2	3	4	OT	Total
BALTIMORE COLTS	0	14	0	3	6	23
NEW YORK GIANTS	3	0	7	7	0	17

About 45 million people viewed the contest on television, in addition to the 64,185 fans inside a stadium that was better known for hosting Yankees World Series than Giants NFL triumphs. It was the first overtime game in NFL history and introduced the words "sudden death" into the sport's lexicon. The stars of both teams were household names in their communities, beacons of the sport.

It was a game that fans talked about for days and one that ushered in a new era for the NFL—the television era—with all of the exposure and money that followed, to grow and finance the game. The contest propelled football on an upward popularity swing that eventually enabled it to eclipse baseball as America's national sport. "I think that particular game accelerated football into what it's become now," said Colts quarterback Johnny Unitas in 1998, "in everybody's living rooms on just about every Sunday."

The game was not even a sellout—Yankee Stadium could hold 71,000 for football—and an estimated 15,000 hardcore Colts fans made the journey north, many by train. So the crowd was not completely hostile to Baltimore, a first-time title game competitor.

In the Colts' locker room before the game, coach Weeb Ewbank did something he had never done before. Harkening

When the scoreboard read 17–17 at the end of the game, few Americans knew what "sudden death overtime" was. The Colts and the Giants taught them all about it. HY PESKIN/SPORTS ILLUSTRATED/GETTY IMAGES

back to the humble beginnings of his squad, Ewbank reminded each player in personal terms of the rejections they had encountered from other teams. It was a solid pep talk designed to motivate his men.

The game began in sunshine, but as the day wore on the sun faded and the stadium grew colder. By the third period the lights were more than a casual accessory. Baltimore built a 14–3 halftime lead following catastrophic Giants fumbles, and the Colts felt they might cruise to victory and the team's first championship. But nothing came easy in this game.

Baltimore had a chance to send the Giants reeling early in the third quarter, but New York's gallant defense, led by linebacker Sam Huff, defensive end Andy Robustelli, defensive tackle Rosey Grier, and defensive backs Emlen Tunnell and Jimmy Patton, rebuffed the Colts with a goal line stand.

Quarterback Charlie Conerly, New York's old pro whose craggy face landed him a gig as the Marlboro Man, directed a desperate 95-yard charge downfield. Fullback Mel Triplett's one-yard touchdown was set up by a quirky play that began as a Conerly pass to Frank Gifford. Gifford fumbled but was rescued when trailing Alex Webster scooped up the ball for the Giants.

Trailing 14–10, the Giants grabbed their first lead of the day when Conerly hit tight end Bob Schnelker on a 46-yard pass play, followed by a 15-yard touchdown throw to Gifford. That made it 17–14 New York in the fourth quarter. A little later there was a crucial play on a Giants possession that could have altered the outcome and the history-making nature of the game. New York had the ball needing short yardage for a first down, and Gifford lunged forward on a handoff. The Colts' front four met him at the line of scrimmage, but Gifford was certain he made the first down. However, the pileup was slow to unravel. Baltimore defensive end Gino Marchetti couldn't stand up because he had broken his ankle. His 300-pound teammate, Gene "Big Daddy" Lipscomb, had fallen on him.

Art Donovan, the rugged Colts defensive tackle who later proved to be a popular talk-show guest because of his sense of humor, tried to shout down Gifford's protests, yelling, "Aw, shut up and go back to the huddle. What are you hollering about? You didn't make it."

There was confusion as Marchetti was carried off the field on a stretcher. Although game film indicated he was short, Gifford always felt the ball placement was incorrect and he

The Unitas-Berry connection was a huge factor in the Colts' victory over the Giants at Yankee Stadium. KIDWILER COLLECTION/DIAMOND IMAGES/GETTY IMAGES

really got the first down. But instead the Colts took over the ball.

Team captain Marchetti refused to be evacuated to the locker room. He insisted on being wrapped in his team cloak and propped on the sideline to watch. As the clock ran down, Unitas guided Baltimore on an 86-yard drive that culminated with a Steve Myhra field goal to tie the game at 17. The phrase "two-minute drill" had not yet been invented, but that's what Unitas ran, whipping the team swiftly toward the goal line, sometimes without a huddle. The clock ran out, and for the first time ever, the NFL, which was founded in 1920, was faced with a tied championship game.

Not everyone, including players, knew about the rule installed in 1955 that extended play beyond four quarters in the event of a tie. The sudden-death rule—meaning that the first team to score would win the game—had never been used. There were no second chances. Several players thought the Giants and Colts were going to be co-champions. Certainly that would have been an anticlimactic ending that would have defused all future hullabaloo. But there was going to be a winner declared this day.

Unitas was one of the players who wondered what was next. "We never discussed anything about an overtime," Unitas said of Colts game preparation. "When we tied the football game, we were all standing around there scratching our heads waiting for someone to make our decision on what we were going to do."

MVP BOOKS COLLECTION

What they were going to do was have another kickoff following a fresh coin toss. Unitas made the call for the Colts, saying tails. It came up heads, and the Giants got the ball first, a potentially fatal circumstance for Baltimore. But the Colts' defense stiffened, and the Giants had to punt the ball away on their first possession of OT. They would not get another.

The Colts started on their own 20-yard line and Unitas, with the same bloodless aplomb he brought to regular-season

Alan Ameche bursts into the end zone for the winning touchdown in the 1958 NFL Championship Game. ROBERT RIGER/GETTY IMAGES

games, led his team down the field. Play after play his passes hit end Raymond Berry for first downs. The duo was among 12 participating players from that day that were eventually chosen for the Pro Football Hall of Fame.

Huff, who said he was angry when he walked off the field, admitted later the frustration the Giants' defense had in trying to stop the Unitas-Berry combination. "It's Unitas to Berry, Unitas to Berry, Unitas to Berry," Huff said. "After 40 years that still rings in my ear. We couldn't stop it, and we didn't stop it, and that was the difference in the game."

The Colts worked their way to the Giants' 7-yard line, and Ewbank nearly swooned when Unitas threw to tight end Jim Mutscheller rather than running the ball. Mutscheller made a terrific catch, putting the Colts on the 1-yard line. "I'm glad John had that kind of confidence, but it scared me plenty," Ewbank said.

On the 1-yard line, Unitas made the conservative call. He sent fullback Alan Ameche into the teeth of the Giants' defense. But like the Red Sea parting for Moses, the Colts' offensive line cleared out a hole so large a school bus could have been driven into the end zone.

In famous photographs of the play, Ameche is shown head down, plunging forward as if he expects to encounter stiff resistance. But the space he had to run through was gigantic, and he scored the winning touchdown easily. Game over. Ameche's is probably the most famous touchdown in NFL history, one of the league's most memorable plays, and it heralded the beginning of something new.

"That was a great game," Gifford said. "There's no question about it. It had a lot of drama to it. It brought a great focus on pro football that wasn't there before."

1959: BACK TO BACK CHAMPS

Still glowing from their first championship, the Colts ramped up for the 1959 NFL wars with fresh confidence, carrying the firm belief they could repeat as title winners.

Although their record was again 9–3, they were in every game until the end. They never lost by more than a touchdown and, for a change, actually swept the 49ers and Rams out west.

Despite winning the 1958 championship by such a slender margin, the Colts believed in themselves as true champions and felt all along they could repeat. They won four of their first five regular-season games in 1959 and their last five in a row as well. They outscored opponents 374–251.

"The Colts were the kind of team that took themselves and their jobs seriously enough to make another successful run at the title," coach Weeb Ewbank said.

The drama from the 1958 sudden-death overtime game was still fresh in fans' minds. When the New York Giants repeated their emergence from the Eastern Division, the setting for an intense rematch seemed perfect. The Giants were renowned for their defense. In fact, fans at Yankee Stadium invented the cry of "Dee-fense! Dee-fense!" That chant spread and persists in the game today, employed by crowds to encourage the home team's efforts. Given a second chance, the Giants were certain they would be able to contain Johnny Unitas and his receivers. They were hungry for revenge.

"The Giants' personnel was pretty much the same as the team we had beaten a year earlier," Ewbank observed. There was one major change for the Giants' defense: an already strong defensive backfield featuring Jimmy Patton, Dick Nolan, and Linden Crow was joined by Dick Lynch. "This was as good a secondary as you'd want to see anywhere," Ewbank said.

Of course, that's the group who went man-to-man trying to best Baltimore's dangerous receivers with the idea of limiting Unitas' options. That's how the optimistic thinking went in New York, anyway.

Lenny Moore is off to the races for a 60-yard touchdown reception in the first quarter of the 1959 NFL Championship Game against the Giants. No overtime was necessary, as the Colts won 31–16 at Memorial Stadium.
ROBERT RIGER/GETTY IMAGES

After the classic overtime performance of 1958, the rematch figured to be anyone's game. But it did not play out that way. This time the Colts didn't make as many mistakes as they had the first time and dominated the contest in the later going. No overtime was necessary, as the Colts won 31–16 in their home, Memorial Stadium. This was a team that had perfected its act.

"After that talk about the Giants' defense, I'm certainly glad that our defense came through the way it did," said Colts fullback Alan Ameche, hero of the 1958 championship. "Our defense set us up."

Baltimore took the lead in the first quarter on a 60-yard Unitas-to–Lenny Moore touchdown pass. The Giants retaliated with three Pat Summerall field goals of 23, 37, and 22 yards, before the Colts assumed control on a four-yard Unitas TD run.

Before New York could score again, the Colts had added touchdowns on a 12-yard strike from Unitas to Jerry Richardson and a 42-yard interception return by Johnny Sample, as well as a 25-yard Steve Myhra field goal.

The Colts prepare to kick off at Memorial Stadium, circa 1959. GEORGE SILK//TIME LIFE PICTURES/GETTY IMAGES

Richardson conferred with Ewbank on the sideline before being sent into the huddle. The coach did not send a specific play with the receiver, only instructions for Unitas that illustrated his supreme confidence in the quarterback: "Just tell Unitas to score."

So he did, on the throw to Richardson.

Richard Nixon, then vice president under Dwight Eisenhower, visited the Colts' locker room after the game and joked around with Unitas. One of the politician's fans yelled, "Nixon and Unitas for president." Nixon laughed and said, "But if we do it, I'll let Johnny call the signals."

Letting Johnny call the signals was always a bright idea. All season Unitas was phenomenal. He threw for 32 touchdown passes, 14 to Raymond Berry alone, who grabbed 66 passes in all. With a balanced running game and a stingy defense (Baltimore allowed 123 points fewer than it scored), the Colts were an impressive team. Seven players—Unitas, Berry, Moore, guard Art Spinney, Jim Parker, Gino Marchetti, and defensive tackle Big Daddy Lipscomb—were selected for the Pro Bowl.

The 1959 team has forever been overshadowed by the 1958 team, although most of the components were the same. The title gets mentioned almost as an afterthought, even though a title is a title. "I have to laugh," Art Donovan said of the '58 game being designated as "The Greatest Game Ever Played." He acknowledges the importance of that game but doesn't believe the Colts played as well that day. "We weren't even as good in '59 as we were in '58."

Not everyone agreed. Ewbank, for one, thought that the Colts of 1959 were better, and winning back-to-back crowns was special. "That was the peak for the Colts during my nine seasons with them," he said. "And I believe this was as good a team as ever won a world championship. Champions often have trouble repeating."

Johnny Unitas and his wife, Dorothy, drive off in the MVP award Johnny earned in the 1959 championship game. AP PHOTO/ROBERT KRADIN

Moore was pretty happy with the repeat, too. "The 1959 season was icing on the cake," Moore said. "We opened the season in front of a capacity crowd. I'd never been so happy to be back in Baltimore."

The championships cemented Baltimore's emotional ties with the Colts. This was the high point of the team's first decade in existence.

The Colts retired Lenny Moore's No. 24, a testament to the significance of his career in Baltimore. AP PHOTOS

FANCY STEPPING LENNY MOORE

Almost as soon as he joined the Colts as a rookie out of Penn State in 1956, Lenny Moore was nicknamed "Spats" for the white adhesive tape around his high-topped black cleats. It didn't matter much what Moore wore on his feet. Even if he had been wearing army boots, he would have been tough to catch. As quickly as Moore moved on the gridiron, those feet were a blur to would-be tacklers.

Moore was likely the best pure athlete on the early Colts teams. He was an elusive runner, and he could catch passes when split wide as a flanker. At 6-foot-2 and 198 pounds he was big enough to ward off tacklers, and he and quarterback Johnny Unitas developed a sixth sense working together, surpassed only by Unitas' rapport with receiver Raymond Berry. The less-nimble Berry admired Moore's skills. "Lenny has got to be the greatest athlete I've ever seen," Berry said. "He's got all the natural ability anyone could desire."

During Moore's 12-year Hall of Fame career with the Colts, he rushed for 5,174 yards and grabbed 363 passes. He scored 113 touchdowns, including 20 in 1964, and was the stalwart back on the 1958 and 1959 championship teams. "Lenny is so good he gives backs like me an inferiority complex," said Colts halfback Alex Hawkins, who was known more for his wit than his agility.

Born in 1933, Moore was one of eight children in a Reading, Pennsylvania, family where money was tight. At times there wasn't enough food to go around, and he dreamed of being wealthy. When he made as much as $40,000 per year playing football, he considered that to be a good haul.

As a child of the more accepting Northeast, Moore's psyche was bruised when he encountered racism in mid-1950s Baltimore. He was one of about a half-dozen African American players on the Colts at the time. They were turned away from certain bars and restaurants, and they couldn't stay in the same hotels as the rest of the team on Southern road trips for exhibition games. That treatment angered Moore, and at times he spoke up. He was also disappointed that some of his white teammates, so friendly in the locker room, went their own way after practice and games. Moore felt that they didn't defend black players loudly enough in the face of demeaning circumstances.

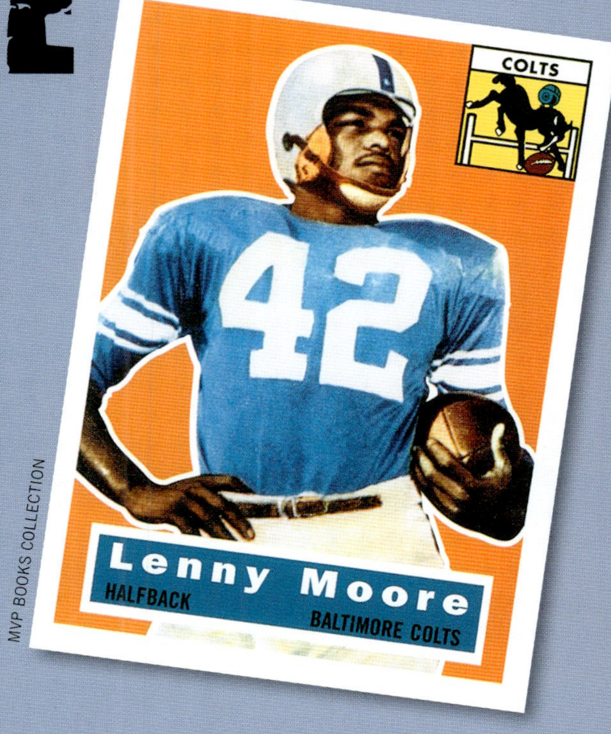

MVP BOOKS COLLECTION

Moore and his white teammates shared in great football accomplishments, but later in life he expressed sorrow that he never knew them as well as he might have as men, because the mores of society kept their socializing to a minimum during his career.

During his playing days, Moore said, only Berry and coach Weeb Ewbank (plus running back Alan Ameche later) seemed to grasp the difficulties faced by the African American athletes. Once, when the team was playing an exhibition game in Austin, Texas, Ewbank recognized the black players were prohibited from visiting many of the finest establishments in town, so he hired taxis to take the African American players to the most popular black-oriented bar, went with them to scope out its safety, and told the owner to take care of his guys before he left. Not many coaches would have ridden that extra mile.

Moore, who retired as a player in 1968, later became a broadcaster.

NEW COACH IN, OLD PLAYERS OUT

All football teams age, and few are able to stay together at their peak. Usually, the coach pays the price when a team unravels. Despite his success, that rule was consistently applied to Weeb Ewbank, who lasted with the Colts through 1962 season.

The 1960 Colts went just 6–6, and Baltimore hired a new coach for the 1963 season, a former defensive back named Don Shula. No one could have imagined that Shula, only 33, was embarking on a career that would make him the winningest NFL coach of all time. There was some concern that he might be too close to the players because he had shared a roster with some of the older ones, but that never materialized as a problem for the youngest coach in the league.

Shula immediately revived the Colts. They were 8–6 in 1963 despite injuries to important players and an overpowering 12–2 in 1964 before being crushed by the Cleveland Browns in the championship game, losing 27–0.

When owner Carroll Rosenbloom, called "C.R." by his friends, investigated Shula, he said the only negative he heard was that the man had a temper. Unitas said Shula distributed his anger fairly and without discrimination. Shula carefully gave due to veterans while deflecting some of the praise he received after his 1964 campaign.

"I wasn't taking over an expansion team," Shula said. "This club had material, guys like [Johnny] Unitas, [Lenny] Moore, [Gino] Marchetti, and [Jim] Parker. All we needed was a little strengthening here and there, and we got it."

The Colts had lost Alan Ameche along the way. He ruptured an Achilles tendon and retired at age 28 after the 1960 season. He played just six NFL seasons, although it was said he could have come back from the injury if he had wanted. Defensive end Don Joyce, a Pro Bowler in 1958, departed in 1960 and played elsewhere through 1962. Joyce was one of the team's most colorful players. He was a professional wrestler in the offseason and once won $100 from Marchetti in a chicken-eating contest. Joyce ate 38 pieces but received no extra credit for the mashed potatoes, gravy, and vegetables he inhaled along the way.

Tight end John Mackey, a future Colts superstar, signs his rookie contract in 1963. General manager Don Kellet and new head coach Don Schula stand behind the newest Colt. AP PHOTO

Fatso Donovan packed it in as well. He retired in 1961, and the Colts threw a celebratory day for their longest-serving player. Iconic Baltimore newspaperman John Steadman once called Donovan "Santa Claus in a helmet," which would have been true if St. Nick guzzled beer like water. Some 54,796 people came out to Memorial Stadium to honor the old defensive tackle on Art Donovan Day, and the big guy broke down in tears. Always a wound-up player, Donovan, who was presented with a Cadillac, declared, "This is worse than playing."

Worse than retiring was death, so the Colts were shocked when Big Daddy Lipscomb died in 1963. Lipscomb had moved on to the Pittsburgh Steelers in 1960 but was still a regular in Baltimore. When the 31-year-old Lipscomb was found dead with heroin in his bloodstream, his friends did not believe the ruling of accidental death. Lipscomb was notoriously scared of needles, was not known to do drugs, and did not seem a ripe candidate for suicide among those who knew him well.

Lenny Moore, Lipscomb's closest friend on the Colts, never believed the official findings and never got over the mystery of Lipscomb's death. Moore said that Lipscomb was so afraid of needles he hid in a corner of the locker room when it was time for the team to get flu shots and, "It literally took six men to hold him down for the doctor to administer the shot." That was one of many unanswered questions, but Lipscomb was gone for good in 1963.

Baltimore's new acquisitions added explosiveness to the offense. Tight end John Mackey was a future Hall of Famer. Receiver Jimmy Orr and halfback Tom Matte were clutch players.

Mackey, in conjunction with Chicago's Mike Ditka, redefined the tight end position. Strong enough to block onrushing linemen, they were also agile

MVP BOOKS COLLECTION

Fans and teammates were shocked when Eugene "Big Daddy" Lipscomb died in 1963. AP PHOTO/NFL PHOTOS

Iconic Baltimore newspaperman John Steadman once called Art Donovan "Santa Claus in a helmet," which would have been true if St. Nick guzzled beer like water.

As if Johnny U needed more weapons, Jimmy Orr emerged as another receiving threat for the Colts in the early 1960s.
AP PHOTO/NFL PHOTOS

enough to go deep for passes and run well after the catch. Mackey was powerful enough to shed tacklers when they caught up to him. Assistant coach Dick Bielski once said, "Once he catches the ball, the great adventure begins. Those people on defense climb all over him. The lucky ones fall off. The others might get trampled."

Bielski's was a pretty good horse analogy given that the 6-foot-2, 225-pound Mackey played for a team named the Colts. Headline writers at newspapers used phrases such as "Colts' Mackey One-Man Stampede" to describe his play. "If I can keep them off my legs, I can continue to run," Mackey said.

One guy who could really run—and resembled a deer when he did so—was Orr. Unitas got acquainted with the lightweight, fleet-footed target in 1961, and Orr caught a team-leading 55 passes for 11 touchdowns in 1962. He grabbed 41 more balls in 1963 and 40 in 1964, emerging as a dangerous complement to Raymond Berry. Berry, meanwhile, was in the process of setting an all-time NFL record for catches, headed toward his career total of 631.

Orr was a free spirit, a guy who would've gotten along famously with Joyce and Donovan if he'd come along sooner. At 5-foot-11, 185 pounds, Orr was built more like a fella you might bump into at the hardware store than on the gridiron. He firmly believed that all work and no play would made Jimmy a dull boy. He liked to take in the sights when he went on the road, and he was not an early-to-bed adherent—Orr was more likely to catch the worm in the bottom of a tequila bottle than on a morning expedition for night crawlers.

Yet Orr was the NFL's rookie of the year with the Steelers in 1958 and a two-time Pro Bowler—once with Pittsburgh and once with the Colts. Between 1958 and 1970 he caught 400 passes for 7,914 yards

Jimmy Orr caught 400 passes for 7,914 yards and 66 touchdowns for the Colts between 1958 and 1970.

and 66 touchdowns. He did it his way. "Training, as far as I'm concerned, is a state of mind," Orr said. "Some athletes find that if they get away from the training routine, it breaks their concentration. Getting away from it only makes me come back to it refreshed. Besides, if I went to bed every night for as long a season as we have, I'd probably go insane."

Although such inclinations seemed to come naturally, Orr also broke into the league with the Steelers when Bobby Layne, who was both a Hall of Fame quarterback and a notorious partier, ran the offense. Orr recalled a story from his rookie year with the Steelers. At a hotel in Chicago before a game against the Bears, he was on his way to bed at 11 p.m. when Layne found him in the hallway and asked him to join him on a saloon excursion. "We went outside and caught a cab, and that night Bobby Layne introduced me to Chicago," Orr said. They did not get back to the hotel until moments before coach Buddy Parker's wake-up call for breakfast and pre-game ankle taping. The duo played on no sleep and hooked up on the winning play, a 66-yard touchdown pass.

Unitas demanded that his receivers play hard, give their best, and produce no matter what they did in their free time. Though he didn't go boozing all night before games, he had no gripes about Orr, who was so fast that Unitas had to adjust his throwing style. "Most receivers run at a controlled speed and turn it on when they make their break," Unitas said. "Jimmy goes downfield at full speed and makes his break at full speed. I don't know how many touchdown passes Jimmy's got, but he's got a lot and most of 'em were big ones. He's a money ballplayer."

Tom Matte was a quarterback at Ohio State but a running back with the Colts. He was not especially speedy and not especially statuesque at 6 feet and 215 pounds, but he was hard to bring down, coming through whenever he was assigned a job. He certainly grabbed attention in 1963 when he rushed for 541 yards and caught 48 passes to lead the team.

Matte is best remembered in Baltimore for his role as an emergency quarterback in the final game of the 1965 regular season. With both Unitas and backup Gary Cuozzo sidelined with injuries, Shula restored Matte to his old college position, with plays written on a wristband. After an initial reaction of "Who, me?" Matte led the Colts to a 20–17 victory over the Rams and a spot in the playoffs. In Baltimore, this is fondly recalled as "The Matte Game."

Bobby Orr tumbles to the ground after making a leaping catch for a touchdown against the Los Angeles Rams in 1968. AP PHOTO/NFL PHOTOS

Tom Matte runs through the Cleveland Browns defense during a game Memorial Stadium in Baltimore.
FOCUS ON SPORT/GETTY IMAGES

Tom Matte was one of the most reliable Colts in team history, doing whatever it took to help his team win. Here, filling in for an injured Johnny Unitas at quarterback, Matte hands the ball to Lenny Moore in a 1965 game against the Packers. AL MESSERSCHMIDT/GETTY IMAGES

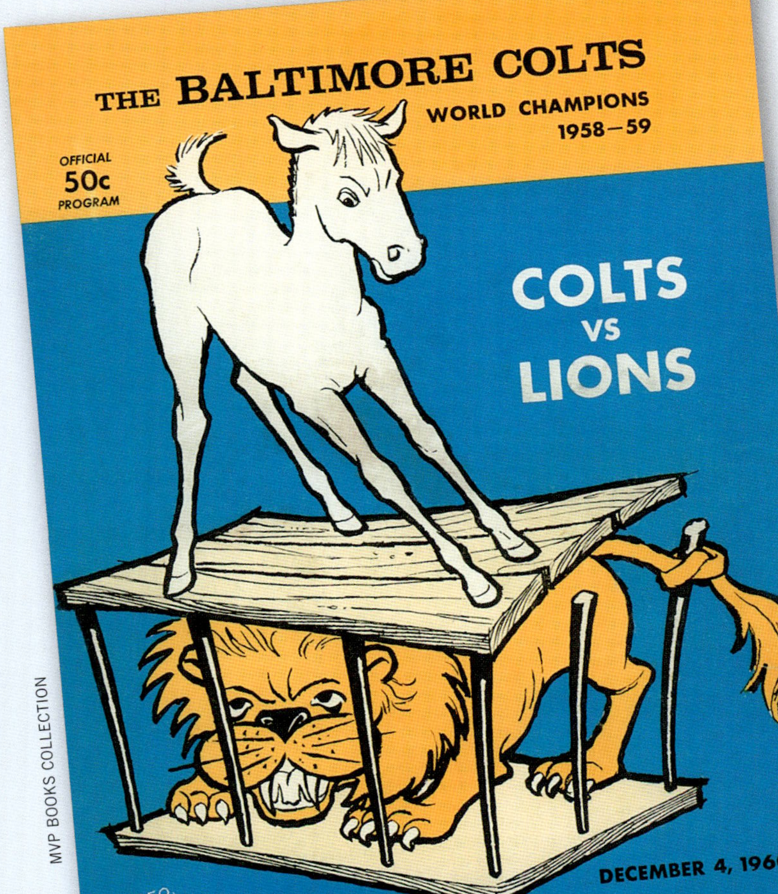

MVP BOOKS COLLECTION

"We had to redesign our whole offense around what I could do," said Matte, who threw only seven passes and completed one against the Rams but ran for 99 yards. "A lot of plays came in from the sideline, and we made up plays in the huddle."

Matte reprised the role in a controversial playoff game against the Packers, which the Colts lost 13–10 in overtime. Green Bay's Don Chandler—the same player who had punted for the Giants in the 1958 overtime title game—hit a field goal that pulled the Packers into a tie to force overtime. Later replays revealed that Chandler had actually missed the kick, and a correct call would have given the Colts the win in regulation.

Matte called the Packers playoff game the high point of his career, not for the way he played, but for the way the team rallied around him. "Thirty-nine ballplayers adopted me that day," he said, "and they weren't going to let anything happen to me. I wasn't hit in the backfield once."

JOHN MACKEY

Tough Man with Soft Hands

John Mackey was a tight end extraordinaire, one of the earliest practitioners to show that a man the size of a lineman could not only block but also catch passes like the lighter-weight split ends or flankers. Mackey did it so well that he was inducted into the Pro Football Hall of Fame.

Mackey joined the Colts in 1963 after a notable career at Syracuse University. At 6-foot-2 and 225 pounds, Mackey was both stronger and swifter than his size indicated. It made him a handful to cover for defensive backs. "He's run over people better than me," said New York Jets safety Jim Hudson before Super Bowl III in 1969.

MVP BOOKS COLLECTION

John Mackey charges toward the end zone after catching a Johnny Unitas pass against the San Francisco 49ers in 1966. BALTIMORE SUN/MCT VIA GETTY IMAGES

Mackey, who caught 331 passes, 38 for touchdowns, was a five-time Pro Bowl choice in a career that lasted through 1972. He was voted the NFL's greatest tight end of its first 50 years of existence. When someone suggested to Baltimore quarterback Johnny Unitas that Mackey was the prototype tight end, he said, "What does that mean? If it means fast, a great blocker, able to run fine patterns, yes, he was that."

Popular with fans, Mackey had some tense moments with Colts management when he held out for more money in contract negotiations and when he became president of the National Football League Players Association in 1970. Mackey battled to bounce back from a severe knee injury to start fresh with the San Diego Chargers in 1972.

Mackey, who unified players in the union following the merger between the NFL and the AFL, sued the league two years after his retirement, seeking to overturn the "Rozelle Rule" that required compensation for departing players. The Mackey case nullified that rule and opened the door to true free agency for pro football players.

Bitter when the Colts relegated him to being a part-time player in 1971, Mackey wanted to prove his worth with another team and did so with the Chargers after he was placed on waivers. A last season with San Diego concluded his on-field career. "I've had 10 great seasons," a mellower Mackey said when he stowed his cleats, "and everybody can't say that. And I walk away healthy."

It took a surprising two decades for Mackey to be enshrined in the Hall of Fame, and there were suggestions that the missing votes represented reprisals for his labor union activity, a form of blackballing, in a sense. "Well, there have been rumors that I was [blackballed]," Mackey said at the time of his induction, "but I don't really know. I didn't try to figure out the process or do any investigation of what was going on."

Later in life Mackey became one of the symbols of the NFL's failure to provide large enough pensions to its older players and a demoralizing example for those who may have suffered long-term ill effects in the sport. Although at the time he believed he retired healthy, later problems suggested that was not so. Mackey had to fight for disability income, and eventually he died from frontotemporal dementia at age 69 in 2011.

John Mackey was an excellent all-around tight end—willing to block, but more than capable of catching and running as well. AP PHOTO/NFL PHOTOS

SUCCESS ALL OVER AGAIN

Tight end John Mackey (88) and flanker Willie Richardson (87) formed a formidable receiving duo for Baltimore in the late 1960s. AP PHOTO/NFL PHOTOS

As a two-time champion, Weeb Ewbank was a tough act to follow. But young Don Shula built the Colts back into consistent winners in the mid-to-late 1960s.

The 1967 team finished 11–1–2 and seemed to be a Super Bowl contender. The offense steamrolled opponents, and the defense intimidated them. Johnny Unitas was still Unitas, throwing for 3,428 yards and 20 touchdowns. Willie Richardson caught a team-high 63 passes. Tackle Fred Miller and end Ordell Brasse were all-pros on a defensive unit that held foes to 198 points in 14 games. The Colts jumped on teams early, out-scoring them 78–26 in the first period during the regular season. This was definitely a championship-caliber team.

Yet the Colts did not advance to the playoffs. Posting the same record as the Los Angeles Rams, Baltimore lost 34–10 to L.A. in the final game of the season at the Los Angeles Coliseum, losing the tie-breaker and allowing the Rams to advance. "They exerted a great amount of pressure on Unitas, and he had trouble throwing the ball," said Shula, who admitted great disappointment at the small differential in a long season between going undefeated and being shut out of the playoffs altogether.

The 1967 failure was turned into angry motivation for the 1968 season. The Colts had played tremendous football and received no reward. They returned with a vengeance, indeed even raising their quality of play to a rare level seen in league history—and without Unitas.

Unitas was out with an injury for nearly the entire season, and the Colts' offense was turned over to Earl Morrall. Hired primarily as an insurance policy, Morrall remarkably proved to be as outstanding as Unitas had been. Throughout his career, for four different teams between 1956 and 1968, Morrall had shown sporadic greatness mixed with bad luck and sometimes erratic play. He threw 24 touchdowns for the Detroit Lions in 1963 and 22 for the New York Giants in 1965. Before and after those sterling seasons, he suffered an injured shoulder and was used only part time. Morrall was already 34 when he joined the Colts, arriving in Baltimore with unwanted nicknames such as "The Understudy," and "Mr. Inconsistent."

But when Unitas went down in 1968, Morrall stepped in seamlessly. He threw for 2,909 yards and 26 TDs, was chosen for the Pro Bowl, and was voted MVP of the NFL—stunning honors and accomplishments for someone who began the year on the bench.

"Never in my wildest dreams did I think anything like this would develop at the time of the trade," said Morrall, who was just hoping to play from time to time in relief of Unitas. "This is certainly the biggest personal honor I've ever received."

Losing a quarterback like Johnny Unitas for a season usually spells disaster—look no further than the 2011 Colts for proof. But in 1968, Earl Morrall was excellent while filling in for an injured Johnny Unitas. Here, he leads the Colts to a 16–3 victory over the Packers at Lambeau Field. VERNON BIEVER/NFL/GETTY IMAGES

"Never in my wildest dreams did I think anything like this would develop . . . . This is certainly the biggest personal honor I've ever received."—Earl Morrall after winning the league's MVP award in 1968.

Earl Morrall laughs with Mike Curtis after a victory in December of 1968. AP PHOTO

Just as in 1967 the Colts were again overwhelming on both sides of the ball—even more so. They finished 13–1 while scoring 402 points and surrendering a stingy 144. Middle linebacker Mike "The Animal" Curtis, cornerback Bobby Boyd, and tackle Fred Miller were all defensive all-stars. Between 1960 and 1968 Boyd set the team mark with 57 career interceptions. Actually, Boyd was briefly considered as the fill-in quarterback when Tom Matte handled the role.

Remembering the rare occasion he got burned for a long-yardage touchdown,

Billy Ray Smith (left) was not a small man—he just looked that way next to Bubba Smith, a massive presence on the Colts defensive line. FOCUS ON SPORT/GETTY IMAGES

"I like to sit on quarterbacks. It gives me pleasure." —Bubba Smith

Boyd maintained the philosophy into retirement that the cornerback is the most important defensive man on the field. "I still think cornerback is the key position on defense," he said. "Those two backs can make or break the defense."

Boyd was one of the veterans of the defense. One of the more recent additions was a mammoth defensive end who had become as popular as any Colt. Bubba Smith, a two-time All-American at Michigan State, was the team's No. 1 draft choice in 1967. Smith stood 6–7 and weighed between 280 and 300 pounds, depending on his mood. He was a scary pass rusher who was still improving in the late 1960s.

"I like to sit on quarterbacks," Smith said. "It gives me pleasure."

At the end of the 1968 season, Ogden Nash—a popular poet who wrote light-hearted verse during most of an adult life spent in Baltimore—penned a collection of funny pieces about members of the Colts for ***Life*** magazine, including one on Smith. It read in part, "When hearing tales of Bubba Smith/You wonder is he man or myth./He's like a hoodoo, like a hex/He's like Tyrannosaurus Rex." Nash also wrote an appropriate ditty about Matte's appearance at quarterback, asking, "Is there a Baltimore fan alive/Who's forgotten Tom Matte in '65?/The Colts by crippling injuries vexed/ Unitas first and Cuozzo next—What would become of the pass attack?/Then Matte stepped in at quarterback."

The personable Smith became an actor after his nine-year football career, appearing mostly in comedic movies or lighthearted TV shows with his size employed as a foil for jokes. On the field, his size enabled him to become acquainted with many quarterbacks, though he didn't make many friends in the process. Off the field, Smith clearly enjoyed people, and his demeanor showed it.

"I have to be casual because of my size," Smith said. "You know, to cope with people. They know what I could do to them. Me being casual puts people at ease. Whereas if I came on mean, people would withdraw from me."

Just like those quarterbacks.

There were occasional suggestions that Bubba was not mean enough on the field, but no one ever said that about one of his fellow defensive linemen, the 6-foot-4, 240-pound Billy Ray Smith, who played with the Colts between 1961 and 1970. Smith won six Arkansas Golden Glove boxing titles. When he was joined by the younger Smith, Billy Ray said, "Hubba, hubba, hubba, here comes Bubba!"

And here came the Colts with a sensational season that figured to be capped by a cakewalk through the playoffs—but winning the NFL title was no longer the ultimate goal. With a merger between the NFL and the AFL percolating, the leagues announced the Super Bowl—a new inter-league event to determine pro football's champion. In the NFL playoffs the Colts polished off the Minnesota Vikings 24–14 and the Cleveland Browns 34–0 for the right to meet the AFL's New York Jets win the big game.

Two Super Bowls had been played to date, and the Green Bay Packers had won both, manhandling first the Kansas City Chiefs in 1967 and then the Oakland Raiders in 1968. Although fans, especially those of the AFL, thought it was pretty cool that there was a showdown, the NFL did not believe the younger league had yet reached parity. The prevailing thought was that the Colts' toughest games were behind them.

Earl Morrall (15) led Baltimore to a 34–0 win over the Cleveland Browns in the NFL championship game on December 29, 1968, earning the Colts a trip to Super Bowl III in Miami. FOCUS ON SPORT/GETTY IMAGES

From Understudy to MVP

EARL MORRALL, 1968

182 completions for 2,909 passing yards

26 Touchdowns

93.2 Passer Rating

Led the Colts to 13 regular-season wins and a berth in Super Bowl III

Selected to the Pro Bowl and named the NFL's MVP

BUBBA SMITH

Scaring QBs Silly

"Kill, Bubba, Kill!" was the chant created by hometown fans when Bubba Smith was an All-American defensive star for Michigan State. The chant followed him from East Lansing to Baltimore, into his pro career with the Colts.

In real life, Smith was a much gentler man than the dramatic phrase implied, but he had a killer instinct on the field that enabled him to separate man from ball and quarterback from senses. Smith was a supreme pass rusher who stood 6-foot-7 and at his largest weighed nearly 300 pounds. He could intimidate opponents with a glower.

Bubba Smith crushes Rams running back Dick Bass at Memorial Stadium. FOCUS ON SPORT/GETTY IMAGES

One of the most colorful players of his era, Smith joined the Colts in 1967. Although he never quite dominated the NFL the way he had the Big Ten, Smith was a two-time all-pro and had to be double-teamed to avoid disrupting foes' game plans.

Size made Smith imposing, but he said the game of football is 80 percent mental. "If I'm in the right frame of mind," he said, "I can handle anybody. If I'm not, I might as well stay in the locker room. It's not something I can turn on. I have to feel it." The more experience he gained, the more Smith felt it. He improved each season and was a member of the Colts' 1971 Super Bowl champion team. He lost weight and gained strength.

"I figure with my size I've got a chance to be the best at my position in pro football," Smith said. "Nobody likes to get to the passer and dump him more than I do. You know how that feels? To a lineman, it's the defensive equivalent of scoring a touchdown."

But injuries derailed Smith's career, and he retired after just nine seasons. In 1972, Smith ruined a knee in a preseason game in Tampa and sued the Buccaneers for $2 million for negligent handling of the down marker that tripped him up. Smith limped to the end of his career with Oakland and Houston. "There's not enough money in the world for the pains suffered mentally and physically," Smith said. "The mental anguish almost drove me crazy."

After retiring in 1976, Smith became famous in a different way.

BUBBA SMITH
COLTS
DEFENSIVE END

MVP BOOKS COLLECTION

He became an actor and played roles in several comedy films, including the *Police Academy* series, and he appeared on many TV shows as well. He also was renowned for working on Miller Lite beer commercials that featured retired pro athletes. One Smith appearance was regarded as an unforgettable classic. When extolling the virtues of the beverage, Smith ripped off the tops of cans bare-handed and proclaimed, "I also like the easy opening cans."

However, Smith stopped making the beer commercials when he visited his alma mater and heard students shouting back and forth "Tastes great" and "Less filling" instead of cheering for the Spartans. He didn't want to be a pitchman anymore if it meant contributing to young people starting to drink. Smith, who wrote a book about his various experiences, died suddenly at 66 during the summer of 2011, shocking Colts fans. An autopsy revealed that the cause of death was acute drug intoxication from an overdose of diet pills. The giant man was apparently trying to reduce.

COLTS BECOME HUGE UPSET VICTIMS

It came as somewhat of a shock to the Colts and the rest of the football world that the New York Jets had the audacity to see themselves as true competitors in the Super Bowl. The Jets refused to believe they were going to the Orange Bowl in Miami to simply line up and fall down.

Three days before the January 12, 1969, game that was the first to be officially termed the "Super Bowl," the flashy Jets quarterback Joe Namath appeared at the Miami Touchdown Club. He didn't bother to couch his emotions in platitudes. "We're going to win Sunday," said the shaggy-haired former Bear Bryant quarterback from Alabama. "I guarantee it."

In those innocent days of sport, only two athletes were known to issue such bold statements—wrestling's Gorgeous George (and everyone knew how meaningless that was) and heavyweight champ Muhammad Ali. Namath ignited a firestorm. The Colts never believed the boast for a minute, but the Jets certainly believed in themselves.

And on game day, it was the upstart Jets, not the supposed team-for-the-ages Colts, who prevailed 16–7. The Jets were the Jets all of the way. The Colts were not the Colts that everyone had seen. Earl Morrall couldn't generate offense, and Johnny Unitas replaced him late—but too late. The Jets' triumph was perhaps the greatest big-game upset in football history.

"I think you have to give Namath the majority of the credit," Don Shula said. Calling the defeat "a bitter loss . . . for me to swallow," Shula later admitted, "Yes, we did blow it."

Morrall was the hero of the season, except for one day versus the Jets, when he was just 6-for-17 for 71 passing yards. "I can't account for it," Morrall said after the loss. "They just made the plays and we didn't. My protection was good."

Billy Ray Smith was as unhappy about the loss to the Jets as any Colt. "Money, marbles, or chocolate, I hate to lose," he said.

Oh, that loss did rankle—for the players, the fans, and the organization—and it remains one of the most famous games in NFL history. The Jets' victory changed history, establishing the credibility of the AFL and altering the course of a powerful Colts team. Coach Shula said his relationship with owner Carroll Rosenbloom was never the same after the defeat, which made it easier for him to entertain an offer from the Miami Dolphins that resulted in his departure to become coach and part owner of the team.

"Money, marbles, or chocolate, I hate to lose." — Billy Ray Smith

Colts owner Carroll Rosenbloom consoles a dejected Earl Morrall after the team's loss in Super Bowl III. MVP BOOKS COLLECTION

A frustrated Tom Matte watches from the sideline during the Colts' 16–7 loss to the Jets in Super Bowl III. FOCUS ON SPORT/GETTY IMAGES

PRO FOOTBALL'S BIGGEST UPSET

SUPER BOWL III

NEW YORK JETS 16 — **BALTIMORE COLTS** 7

	1	2	3	4	Total
NEW YORK JETS	0	7	6	3	16
BALTIMORE COLTS	0	0	0	7	7

The Baltimore Colts were 18-point favorites over the New York Jets for Super Bowl III, played at Miami's Orange Bowl on January 12, 1969. Some people felt the bruisers representing the National Football League might run the score into the stratosphere, with the final margin being something like 56–0.

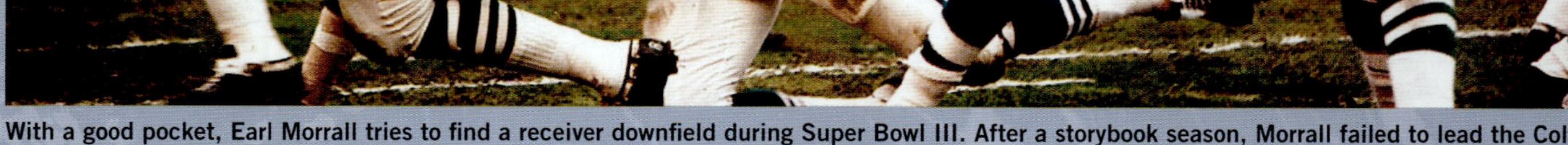

With a good pocket, Earl Morrall tries to find a receiver downfield during Super Bowl III. After a storybook season, Morrall failed to lead the Colts on a successful scoring drive in the big game. AP PHOTO

COLTS BECOME HUGE UPSET VICTIMS

It came as somewhat of a shock to the Colts and the rest of the football world that the New York Jets had the audacity to see themselves as true competitors in the Super Bowl. The Jets refused to believe they were going to the Orange Bowl in Miami to simply line up and fall down.

Three days before the January 12, 1969, game that was the first to be officially termed the "Super Bowl," the flashy Jets quarterback Joe Namath appeared at the Miami Touchdown Club. He didn't bother to couch his emotions in platitudes. "We're going to win Sunday," said the shaggy-haired former Bear Bryant quarterback from Alabama. "I guarantee it."

In those innocent days of sport, only two athletes were known to issue such bold statements—wrestling's Gorgeous George (and everyone knew how meaningless that was) and heavyweight champ Muhammad Ali. Namath ignited a firestorm. The Colts never believed the boast for a minute, but the Jets certainly believed in themselves.

And on game day, it was the upstart Jets, not the supposed team-for-the-ages Colts, who prevailed 16–7. The Jets were the Jets all of the way. The Colts were not the Colts that everyone had seen. Earl Morrall couldn't generate offense, and Johnny Unitas replaced him late—but too late. The Jets' triumph was perhaps the greatest big-game upset in football history.

"I think you have to give Namath the majority of the credit," Don Shula said. Calling the defeat "a bitter loss . . . for me to swallow," Shula later admitted, "Yes, we did blow it."

Morrall was the hero of the season, except for one day versus the Jets, when he was just 6-for-17 for 71 passing yards. "I can't account for it," Morrall said after the loss. "They just made the plays and we didn't. My protection was good."

Billy Ray Smith was as unhappy about the loss to the Jets as any Colt. "Money, marbles, or chocolate, I hate to lose," he said.

Oh, that loss did rankle—for the players, the fans, and the organization—and it remains one of the most famous games in NFL history. The Jets' victory changed history, establishing the credibility of the AFL and altering the course of a powerful Colts team. Coach Shula said his relationship with owner Carroll Rosenbloom was never the same after the defeat, which made it easier for him to entertain an offer from the Miami Dolphins that resulted in his departure to become coach and part owner of the team.

"Money, marbles, or chocolate, I hate to lose." — Billy Ray Smith

Colts owner Carroll Rosenbloom consoles a dejected Earl Morrall after the team's loss in Super Bowl III. MVP BOOKS COLLECTION

A frustrated Tom Matte watches from the sideline during the Colts' 16–7 loss to the Jets in Super Bowl III. FOCUS ON SPORT/GETTY IMAGES

PRO FOOTBALL'S BIGGEST UPSET

The Baltimore Colts were 18-point favorites over the New York Jets for Super Bowl III, played at Miami's Orange Bowl on January 12, 1969. Some people felt the bruisers representing the National Football League might run the score into the stratosphere, with the final margin being something like 56–0.

SUPER BOWL III

NEW YORK JETS 16 — **BALTIMORE COLTS** 7

	1	2	3	4	Total
NEW YORK JETS	0	7	6	3	16
BALTIMORE COLTS	0	0	0	7	7

With a good pocket, Earl Morrall tries to find a receiver downfield during Super Bowl III. After a storybook season, Morrall failed to lead the Colts on a successful scoring drive in the big game. AP PHOTO

Bubba Smith gets after Joe Namath in Super Bowl III. Unfortunately, Bubba and Co. couldn't keep Namath from making good on his guaranteed victory.
AP PHOTO

None of those people wore the green uniforms of the New York Jets, representatives of the American Football League. The man who wore the green No. 12 jersey was a brash, young quarterback named Joe Namath. He wore his hair long and his shoes white, and he kept his mouth going 100 miles per hour. His words before the third Super Bowl stamped him as cocky, a seer, and purveyor of words worthy of *Bartlett's Familiar Quotations*.

Joe Willie Namath, formerly of the Bear Bryant Crimson Tide in Alabama, guaranteed that his upstart New York Jets, the champions of the AFL, would defeat the established, awesomely powerful Baltimore Colts of the NFL.

On their way to a complete merger, the NFL and AFL had begun playing a world championship game two years earlier. In the first postseason encounter in 1967, Vince Lombardi's Green Bay Packers had disposed of the Kansas City Chiefs with a wave of the hand. In 1968, the Packers had brushed away the Oakland Raiders. These results supported skeptics who felt that the younger league had not attained parity with the NFL.

Now came a Colts team with a 15–1 record, deemed to be as well-rounded a power as had been seen in ages. The Colts could run and pass on offense, and their defense was fearsome. It was the season that Earl Morrall stepped in for an injured Johnny Unitas at quarterback, one flat-top haircut subbing for another, throwing 26 touchdown passes on his way to the Pro Bowl. He was one of eight Colts selected. That didn't stop Namath, who drew media attention like a moth to a flame, from announcing that there were at least five quarterbacks in the AFL better than Morrall.

Later, after the game was over, Baltimore coach Don Shula admitted that the Colts were overconfident. They believed in their own abilities and were not that impressed with the film they'd reviewed of the Jets. All around them, newspapers and television sportscasters opined that the Jets didn't belong on the same field as the Colts, except perhaps to pick up their discarded towels. "Their defense seemed awfully weak," Shula said. "During all of the time we were in Miami there was the feeling that the AFL and its representative, the New York Jets, weren't qualified to play us in a Super Bowl and that it shouldn't be much of a game at all."

Shula fell under the spell of that hype, too. So did Colts owner Carroll Rosenbloom, who had invested a considerable sum of money in arranging for a major party to celebrate victory after the game. Yet the impossible came to pass: the sun rose in the west, the egg came before the chicken, and the Colts lost 16–7. Joe Namath was a prophet, and the Colts were humiliated.

The architect of the Colts' defeat was their old coach Weeb Ewbank, whom a decade earlier had led them to championships. He was apparently not washed up, but he was freshly washed—his team threw him into the shower after the win, against his wishes. In the locker room before the game, he told his team he knew it would win the game. He also asked not to be carried off the field due to an aching hip. Namath felt that Ewbank "didn't make a bad call" all game.

President Richard Nixon, Vice President Spiro Agnew, and a slew of other politicians attended. It looked as if the group had taken a wrong turn on their way to a political convention.

The game was scoreless through the first period, and the 75,377 spectators noted only a few indicators that added to the building suspense. The Jets took a 7–0 lead into the locker room at halftime—already an upset. The only first-half score was on a four-yard run by New York fullback Matt Snell. A mix

The scoreboard read 16–0 in the fourth quarter when the Colts replaced a struggling Earl Morrall with Johnny Unitas. Not even Johnny U could mount a comeback that day. WALTER IOOSS JR./SPORTS ILLUSTRATED/GETTY IMAGES

of Snell short bursts and Namath passes, some to Bill Mathis but mostly to George Sauer Jr., steered the Jets 80 yards for the score. Meanwhile, the Colts had squandered their best chances.

"I think the game could have turned around completely," said Colts defensive end Bubba Smith. "We just blew 21 points in the first half. If we had scored, they would have had to play our game." The Colts moved the ball pretty well but committed turnovers to truncate drives. Morrall sought to regain his regular-season magic, but while aiming for receiver Willie Richardson, he was intercepted by Johnny Sample. Sample was the type of player who strutted in his walk and talked as good a game as Namath. He was an ex-Colt at the end of his career who later gained fame for writing a book titled *Confessions of a Dirty Ballplayer*.

Much like Namath, Sample had been a lightning rod for anyone with a pen or a microphone leading up to the big game. He said he had been blackballed from the NFL for being outspoken about its racist ways, and he said that these Jets, not the two-time champion Colts he played for in 1958 and 1959, made up the best team he had ever been on. "This is the biggest ballgame of my life, high school, college, grade school, pros, whatever," Sample said. "I've been in three championship games, but this is the Super Bowl game, and it means more to me than any game I've ever played in my life, more to me than anything I've ever done." That was a sample of Sample at his most candid.

After a subdued halftime discussion, the Colts were determined to take over in the third period. But they couldn't. Halfback Tom Matte fumbled on Baltimore's first possession and Ralph Baker recovered. The Jets added to their lead with field goals of 32 and 30 yards from Jim Turner in the third quarter.

Leading up to the game, Unitas had met with Shula and told him he believed he should start. He was healthy again, and after all he had done for the Colts he felt he deserved the shot. Instead, Shula chose to dance with Morrall, the man who had brought him this far—until desperation beckoned. While Turner was hitting a third field goal from the 9-yard line to make the score 16–0, Unitas was limbering up for a miracle. He did drive the Colts to their only touchdown in the fourth period, but there wasn't enough time to wrest the ball away from the Jets and mount a true challenge. It was too late.

"I just wanted to get something going," Shula explained about why he made the switch to Unitas. "Everything Earl was doing backfired." Four interceptions worth of backfiring, plus a Matte fumble, did the Colts in.

The more experienced and respected Colts went up in flames, and it was not an easy thing to digest. Namath sported a wider smile than Miss America. He had opened his big mouth, but then he put his strong, quick-release arm where his words were. He bragged and backed it up. "Eighteen-point underdog," Namath said afterward. "Gee whiz."

The Colts felt they had let something precious slip away, and they felt they had let down the entire league. The NFL's Green Bay Packers had upheld their part of the bargain, beating the AFL in the previous two championship games.

Later that night at the hotel the Colts almost lost something else. Defensive back Rich Volk went into convulsions and it took emergency action to save him. "It was the darkest day of my coaching career," Shula said, "the earthshaking loss to the Jets together with one of my players almost dying."

MVP BOOKS COLLECTION

MVP BOOKS COLLECTION

NO FEAR MIKE CURTIS

MVP BOOKS COLLECTION

Given his reputation and the variety of nicknames affixed to his real name, such as "The Animal," or "Mad Dog," some people were surprised to see Mike Curtis calmly eating in an establishment called The Golden Arm, owned by Johnny Unitas. Curtis was sworn to knock most quarterbacks out.

The Colts kinship was probably all that stood between the chef being sacked by Curtis. He had already announced that it was his mission in life to clobber quarterbacks, and anyone who had seen him line up on the gridiron for Baltimore had no doubt that he was sincere about it. "They're all a bunch of kittens," Curtis said of NFL quarterbacks. "'Cept John, of course."

That was polite of Curtis to acknowledge the restaurant's owner in such a friendly fashion, but the 6-foot-2, 235-pound linebacker was the mortal enemy of anyone who lined up at the position who didn't wear blue and white. A four-time Pro Bowler and the league's 1970 defensive player of the year, Curtis suited up for the Colts between 1965 and 1975 and stayed in the league until 1978. He repelled all incursions into his territory and was the type of hardcore player who gave opposing ball carriers nightmares the night before games—and the night after them, too.

Mike Curtis is down and ready for action against the Pittsburgh Steelers during a 1971 tilt in Baltimore. FOCUS ON SPORT/GETTY IMAGES

It was said of one-time fastball pitcher Early Wynn that he would dust his mother with a high, hard one if she dug in at the plate. It was said likewise that Curtis would deliver a forearm shiver to Mom if she dared run over the middle. And don't get him started on quarterbacks. "Quarterbacks always think they are more valuable than anyone else," Curtis said. "They're not."

Curtis played in an era when sacks were not an official NFL statistic, so it is unclear how many times he squashed quarterbacks. He did intercept 25 passes.

He graduated from buttoned-down Duke and became a Colt with a 14th-round draft pick, and the headlines that accompanied Curtis' career imply that he was one of the meanest men in football history. "Don't mess around with that man Curtis," read one. "Curtis Loves To Belt 'em," read another.

During the 1971 season Curtis played with a broken arm, and foes claimed his cast was a lethal weapon. Put it this way—it wasn't as if wearing the arm protection made Curtis gun-shy. Sometimes he led his tackling with the injured arm, and his general philosophy was that it would hurt them more than him.

That same season Curtis decided to dispense justice on his own when an interloper ran onto the field during a home game and attempted to steal the football. Before the uniformed gendarmes could haul the transgressor off, he encountered a vigilante response from Curtis, who treated the unwelcome visitor like just another quarterback. He sacked him. "The way I looked at it is that this man was interfering with my profession," Curtis said. "He was disrupting my life." When he hit the fellow he fumbled—just a routine sack—and the ball was returned to the line of scrimmage.

SUPER BOWL VENGEANCE SOOTHES THE SOUL

Falling to the New York Jets in Super Bowl III hurt for a long time. There are no do-overs in the NFL. There are second chances, though, and the only way to assuage the pain of defeat is to replace it with the joy of victory.

In Don Shula's stead came Don McCafferty. McCafferty played just one year of pro ball, for the Giants in 1946, but was Weeb Ewbank's offensive coordinator starting in 1962 and had stayed on for Shula's tenure. When Shula left after the 1969 season, McCafferty was promoted and inherited a very talented roster. In 1970, his first season as head coach, McCafferty guided the Colts to an 11–2–1 record and the world championship that had eluded them two seasons earlier.

The Colts, now playing in the realigned American Football Conference, topped Cincinnati and Oakland in the playoffs to reach a Super Bowl V showdown against the Dallas Cowboys. Played in Miami on January 17, 1971, some may think it was the worst championship game ever played. The Colts won 16–13, but the teams combined for 10 turnovers, and slick offensive plays were almost nonexistent. Surreally, the Most Valuable Player award went to a linebacker, Chuck Howley, from the losing team. It was a stark contrast with "The Greatest Game Ever Played."

Dallas led 13–6 at halftime. The Colts had a fourth down with two yards to go near the Cowboys' goal line as the half wound down, but McCafferty took the risk of going for a touchdown instead of a field goal. The play failed.

"If we had lost it, it would have been the worst decision I could have made," McCafferty said, "but someone had to make the decision. I made it, and it turned out to be a bad one. But if we had made it I'd have been a helluva hero. The turning point had to be [Mike] Curtis' interception."

The Colts shut out the Cowboys in the second half and scored 10 points in the fourth period. It was 13–13 with slightly more than a minute remaining in regulation when Baltimore linebacker Curtis intercepted a Craig Morton pass and ran the ball back to the Dallas 28-yard line. The play set up the winning 32-yard field goal from Jim O'Brien after the Colts had scored touchdowns by John Mackey (a 75-yard pass play from Johnny Unitas) and on a two-yard run by fullback Tom Nowitzke.

For Nowitzke, a seven-year pro, it was the biggest play of his NFL career. Before the game he said, "This will be the biggest game I have ever played in. I was unemployed on the Tuesday before the opening game of the season."

O'Brien was feted as the hero, although Earl Morrall did relieve an injured Unitas and carried the club in the late going. Winning a title with a field goal is akin to a batter hitting the game-winning home run in the bottom of the ninth in the World Series for a place kicker. Not many athletes get to do either.

"It was the same as any other kick," O'Brien said. "Earl [Morrall holding] told me to kick it straight and through. You can't worry. You must concentrate."

Jim O'Brien leaps in celebration after kicking the game-winning field goal in Super Bowl V on January 17, 1971. FOCUS ON SPORT/GETTY IMAGES

ROSENBLOOM TRADES THE WHOLE DARNED TEAM

By the early 1970s, Carroll Rosenbloom was itching for change to a warm-weather climate. The savior of pro football for Baltimore wanted more sunshine in his life, and at the least he wanted the city that had backed his championship club to provide more support for him.

Memorial Stadium was an iconic structure for football fans in Baltimore—but it wasn't an owner's dream come true. Peeved that he was unable to secure public funding for stadium improvements, Carroll Rosenbloom packed for Los Angeles. AP PHOTO

Lydell Mitchell carries the ball against the Rams in 1975. AP PHOTO/NFL PHOTOS

He viewed Memorial Stadium, the home of the Colts, as an outdated playing field that needed dramatic upgrading, at minimum. He preferred that Baltimore show its love for him and his team by building a new stadium. The era of luxury boxes and owners convincing communities to pay for the privilege of having a pro franchise was still on the horizon.

Rosenbloom was definitely flirting with other cities that he felt could make him a good deal if he chose to move the Colts. Instead, he found a compromise that would make him happy and kept the team from abandoning Baltimore—supposedly. Rosenbloom engineered a trade of teams with Robert Irsay, taking the Los Angeles Rams off of Irsay's hands in exchange for the Colts.

That deal was consummated in 1972, and after two decades the Colts were no longer Rosenbloom's concern. He had presided over the growth of a team from a shaky entity into a two-time champion in the 1950s and a juggernaut in the early 1970s that gave Baltimore a Super Bowl champion—now he wanted to relocate to surf and sun. He found a way to leave without becoming a lightning rod for ill will and remained an NFL team owner as well.

Rosenbloom was out of the picture, but the rumors that the Colts were bound for another city under new owner Irsay were intense. Baltimore sports fans reeled as newspapers reported the latest of what seemed to be too-good-to-be-true offers from cities trying to poach not only the Colts but the Orioles as well.

While the teams professed their desire to stay in Maryland, they also clamored for government and taxpayer help to build new, state-of-the-art stadiums. The Colts asked, but the city did nothing. Fans likely felt that the team would never depart and that ownership demands for a new stadium were grandstanding more than anything.

John Steadman, a one-time public relations man for the Colts who then established himself as a sports editor of the ***Baltimore News-American***, seemed to take the threats to the Colts' longevity more seriously. In a milestone article, Steadman reported that there was indeed genuine interest in swiping the Colts and the Orioles, from growing cities around the country that had no professional sports teams. Steadman called these communities "vultures on a fence" for the way they eyed Baltimore's teams.

But it had gone beyond that. This was not all wishin' and hopin' with no action. Tampa, Seattle, and Phoenix, all cities that would eventually obtain professional football and Major League Baseball teams, put stunning offers on the table for Baltimore teams.

Each of those cities declared that it would provide stadium rental for $1 per year, free practice facilities, and parking and concession sales money to the teams if the Orioles and Colts uprooted themselves. Cities also offered various deals providing guaranteed minimum ticket sales. It was wise to recall that the Colts themselves were able to replace the old Dallas Texans because Baltimore stepped forward with 15,000 season-ticket buyers.

Colts quarterback Bert Jones talks things over with head coach Ted Marchibroda.
AP PHOTO/NFL PHOTOS

What team wouldn't swoon at such offers? Much of their costs beyond salaries would be covered. Tampa Bay had already built Tropicana Field, which was sitting empty, as a lure to a professional team willing to make the jump to the Sunshine State.

At that time the National Football League was also fielding feelers from Orlando, Jacksonville, Memphis, Honolulu, and Birmingham. Though these communities were lobbying for expansion teams, they were quite willing to accept a team on the move instead. The Orioles were also being pursued by New Orleans as a tenant for the Superdome, and the new Washington Redskins stadium, which was less than an hour down the turnpike, was also being discussed as a baseball destination.

The Maryland Sports Authority had already conducted a feasibility study to determine how much it would cost to revamp and upgrade Memorial Stadium to make the Colts and Orioles happy and concluded the cost would be in the neighborhood of $47 million. At that point the stadium would seat 70,000. There was much discussion about whether it was worth it to bother renovating the stadium that had been built in 1953, or if it made more sense to build new. What was always at issue was who was going to foot the bill.

Governor Marvin Mandel pledged that Baltimore could build a new stadium and that such a massive construction project could be accomplished without taxpayer money. That was certainly the politically correct thing to say, but there was skepticism that such a plan would ever come to fruition.

It did not help the Colts' image at that time that Irsay was a newcomer owner and that he hired the abrasive and impatient Joe Thomas as general manager. Thomas

MVP BOOKS COLLECTION

kicked butt and took names, and he didn't care what anybody's name was. While the Colts were trying to get a new stadium built, Thomas was ripping up the team's heritage by dumping revered players of the past. He even exiled Johnny Unitas to San Diego, sending the clear message that no one was safe.

Thomas was a public relations nightmare. He didn't know how to temper his blunt nature. He created a firestorm when he let Unitas go and seemed surprised when the reaction was extreme.

"Everyone talks about the way it was handled here," Thomas said. "They say we could've been nicer about it. You have to realize that I had about one to one-and-a-half hours to locate John and tell him. I mean, because of what he's meant to the club, I didn't want him to find out from the press. Unitas was 40 . . . he wasn't gonna stay around that long."

Sensitivity was not Thomas' middle name.

Unitas soon made it clear that Thomas was not his favorite person in the world. In 1970, Unitas had signed a 10-year contract with the Colts under Rosenbloom that was intended to link him to the

MVP BOOKS COLLECTION

MVP BOOKS COLLECTION

MVP BOOKS COLLECTION

The Colts had Elway penciled in as the next great quarterback to wear the helmet with the horseshoe on the side—Elway had other thoughts.
AP PHOTO/PAUL SAKUMA

team well beyond his playing days. But when Irsay took over and installed Thomas, Unitas charged that the team abrogated the deal. So he sued the Colts, claiming that from October 1972 on, Thomas "engaged in a course of conduct which was designed to and did, in fact, embarrass and humiliate Unitas and otherwise make it impossible for Unitas to carry out his obligations under the agreement."

What an unseemly picture that was—an all-time legendary star suing his former team for $225,000 in compensatory damages and $500,000 in punitive damages.

The atmosphere surrounding the Colts at that time was definitely toxic, but good times were not that far away. Under coach Ted Marchibroda, with young Bert Jones at quarterback and Lydell Mitchell as a showcase running back, the Colts ran off three straight division titles between 1976 and 1978. This was the high point of the Irsay era in Baltimore. However, when Jones got hurt in 1979, the Colts flopped and went into a long-term tailspin under Mike McCormick and Frank Kush. In 1982, when the NFL endured a two-month strike that interrupted the season, attendance plummeted. Whereas once the Colts had been among the most popular franchises in sports, the combination of several losing seasons, the league-wide labor action, and unpopular owner Robert Irsay's demands for a new stadium, after years of blind allegiance many Baltimore fans were turned off.

The Colts owned the No. 1 pick in the NFL draft in 1983, and they selected Stanford quarterback John Elway, envisioning that he would resuscitate the franchise. It was the right instinct, because Elway later ended up in the Hall of Fame. But Elway did not want to play for the losing Colts or the hard-nosed Kush and pretended he would stick with baseball after spending two seasons in the minors with the New York Yankees. He demanded a trade, and after much wrangling, Irsay gave in. Elway was out the door, on his way to becoming a nine-time Pro Bowler and the winner of two Super Bowls with the Denver Broncos.

With the 1st pick in the 1983 NFL Draft, the Colts selected Stanford quarterback John Elway—but the future Hall of Famer wanted nothing to do with the Colts.

In an unfathomable scenario for Baltimore fans, 1983 would not only mark the end of Elway but also the end of the Colts' stay in the Charm City. A decade after he assumed ownership of the team, no new stadium had been built, and no new stadium was on the horizon. Relations between Irsay and local government officials grew more acrimonious as nothing was resolved. A threshold had been crossed. The Maryland legislature was acting to give governmental authorities the right to seize the Colts by eminent domain.

Fearful that such a nightmare scenario would unfold and that he would become entangled in years of litigation to regain complete autonomy in running the club as he saw fit, Irsay bargained behind closed doors with enthusiastic representatives of Indianapolis. After the 1983 season the Colts did not announce a plan to sell season tickets for the 1984 campaign. Those who realized that fact became increasingly suspicious that the team had some kind of departure trick in mind.

MVP BOOKS COLLECTION

CHUCK SOLOMON/NFL/GETTY IMAGES

BERT JONES

Second-Generation NFL Star

Yes, the Baltimore Colts did have at least one outstanding quarterback between the Johnny Unitas and Peyton Manning eras. Bert Jones grew up in a football household and eclipsed his father's fame as a pro with a new generation of football fans.

Son of Dub Jones, the one-time Cleveland Browns star, Bert Jones was an All-American at Louisiana State after growing up in Ruston, Louisiana. He was a late bloomer for the Tigers, hardly starting until his senior year. But he was the Colts' No. 1 pick in 1973, the second player selected in the draft, and he was chosen with the idea of replacing Unitas. "When you have the opportunity to get a quarterback of his stature, you have to take him," said Colts general manager Joe Thomas.

There was a lot of pressure and there were growing pains, but in 1976 Jones threw for 3,104 yards and 24 touchdowns and was voted the NFL's Most Valuable Player. He was an all-pro that year, though he never quite matched that performance again. A shoulder injury ruined his 1978 and 1979 seasons after he led the Colts to three straight division titles.

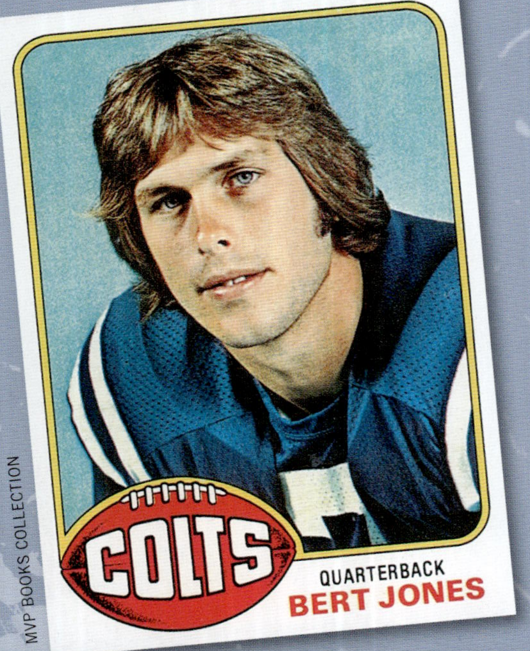

MVP BOOKS COLLECTION

Bert Jones huddles the Colts offense during a 1976 game against the Tampa Bay Buccaneers at Memorial Stadium. GEORGE GOJKOVICH/GETTY IMAGES

Jones did have football in his genes. Dub Jones played running back and flanker for some of the great Browns teams of the 1950s, spending 10 years in the pros. The elder Jones once scored six touchdowns in a single game, still the NFL record. When he was only in second grade, about age six, Bert Jones said a teacher asked what he wanted to be when he grew up. At that age most kids pick fireman or policeman. "A professional football player," he announced. Indulgently, the teacher asked what he would do if he couldn't be a football player. Jones replied, "I wouldn't want to be anything." Jones lived up to his dream when he grew to 6-foot-3, 205 pounds, and developed a powerful arm.

There were some early struggles to attain the Colts' starting job, as there are with most young quarterbacks, but Thomas never wavered. "I wouldn't trade Bert Jones for any quarterback in football," he said.

Jones compared football to calculus. "Until somebody tells you how to solve a problem, you can't do it," he said.

An outdoorsman of many stripes, Jones also was a downhill skier and flew his own plane—he even hosted an outdoors show on ESPN. When still an active player, Jones took a trip to a remote area of Honduras where he camped and lived off the fish he caught. There happened to be a bunch of sharks in the neighborhood, and although they did not menace him any more than the average defensive lineman had, Jones admitted that he viewed them with a mix of fear and fascination.

Jones led the Colts to some significant triumphs, but injuries cut his career short. When he switched to the Los Angeles Rams in 1982, he got into only four games. Then a neck injury ended Jones' career early.

LYDELL MITCHELL

Just Like the Other L.M.

MVP BOOKS COLLECTION

In some ways Lydell Mitchell was the second coming of Lenny Moore in 1972. Just like Moore before him, he came out of Penn State to join the Colts.

Mitchell teamed with Bert Jones to create an effective offensive punch for the Colts. Opponents could not key on Mitchell's running with Jones throwing, and they could not focus on Baltimore's passing game with the explosive Mitchell coming out of the backfield. In the mid-1970s, Mitchell was a three-time Pro Bowl selection, and he rushed for more than 1,000 yards three straight years, too.

As further proof of the 5-foot-11, 205-pound Mitchell's versatility and skill, he led the league in pass receptions twice, in 1974 (72 catches) and 1977 (71). At Penn State Mitchell partnered with fullback Franco Harris in the backfield, and decades later the two men are business partners in a bakery in Baltimore.

"I can do anything on the football field," Mitchell said in 1975 when he was at the peak of his game. By then it was okay for Mitchell to sound cocky. He was irritated that he had been a No. 2 draft pick, not a No.1, and it bothered him during his rookie year that the Colts first relied on Don Nottingham and Don McCauley before making him the starter. Gradually, he proved himself to be clearly better than those alternatives.

Mitchell had the speed to run around the corner, the power to duck between the tackles, and the good hands to grab passes thrown to him in the flat. He also possessed terrific peripheral vision, allowing him to evade would-be tacklers long enough to miss their best, hardest shots. "I see well all around me, and I can sense when I'm about to get hit," Mitchell said. "So I protect myself. It's very seldom that anybody gets a real solid, head-on shot on me. That's where runners get hurt. I take the shot on my arm or my side."

During that 1975 season Mitchell rushed for more than 100 yards in a game six straight times, a club record. The amazing thing was that 25 years after the franchise was founded, and despite fielding such luminaries as Alan Ameche and Moore in the backfield, Mitchell was the first Colt to run for more than 1,000 yards in a season.

"Don't give me the credit for the running," said Mitchell, who compiled 6,534 yards on the ground during a career that ended in 1980. "The offensive line has let me run, and I feel because of their blocking I'm moving better than in a long time."

Mitchell loved playing for coach Ted Marchibroda, a former NFL quarterback who trained for his first head coaching job with the Colts as offensive coordinator of the Washington Redskins. "We believe in him, and he believes in us," Mitchell said. "He gives all of us a lot of confidence. The guy does a tremendous job preparing us."

Lydell Mitchell tries to elude a would-be tackler during the Colts' 28–27 victory over the Cincinnati Bengals in 1976 at Memorial Stadium.
AP PHOTO/NFL PHOTOS

THE NIGHT OF RECKONING

With only a few confidantes aware of his plans, Robert Irsay had secretly committed the Colts to take up residence in Indianapolis. He had leveled the death penalty on Baltimore.

There was a lot of finger pointing and animosity between Robert Irsay and the Baltimore media. Here, Irsay vehemently denies an alleged plan to move the team to Phoenix. AP PHOTO/BILL SMITH

Irsay worried that if word leaked out, drastic local government action would be taken to halt him. So Irsay made the choice to move the Colts—lock, stock, and locker room—out of Baltimore. It happened under cover of darkness, with no warning to city officials, fans, or players. March 28, 1984, will forever live in infamy for Baltimore's football fans.

All proof that the Colts were changing cities was kept hush-hush until the last possible minute. It was the offseason, so head coach Frank Kush, who had come to Baltimore from Arizona State, was at the home he had maintained in Tempe, Arizona. Kush was working in his yard when Irsay called him personally and told him to jump on a plane and return to Baltimore. The Colts were going elsewhere, he told him, but Irsay did not even inform Kush where the club was headed.

Everyone working at the Colts' offices, including as many coaches who could be rustled up, was ordered to gather for a staff meeting at 5 p.m. That is how most employees found out that they were going to be switching homes. At almost the same time the Colts telephoned David Frick, who had represented Indianapolis Mayor William Hudnut III in negotiations to bring the Colts to the Midwest. He was told that he had a deal to obtain the Colts.

Everyone was surprised that things were being packed up for a quick exit—that night— but Irsay and those around him felt the eminent domain clause that the legislature conjured up was going to be applied before the next day was over. So that lent urgency to the departure.

The day the music died in Baltimore—Mayflower moving trucks leave the Colts' facilities in the dark of night. Next stop: Indianapolis.
BALTIMORE SUN PHOTO BY LLOYD PEARSON

Despite all efforts at secrecy, word began to leak out, and TV stations reported the developments on their 10 p.m. news reports. Yes, they said, the Colts were leaving town. Radio stations began reporting the same news. Longtime Colts fans telephoned one another, asking each other whether the news was true. Some fans ran to their cars and drove to Colts headquarters and gathered outside of chain-link fences. What they saw dismayed them.

Taking no chances, Colts officials in the know had worked quietly to line up the Mayflower moving company for this delicate move. Stressing the need to move with dispatch but also be low-key, it was decided that the company would take on the big job but would not use trucks based in the Baltimore area. No one wanted a revolt from workers who might be sympathetic to the Baltimore fan cause—or worse. No one wanted any sabotage. Even the supervisor brought in to oversee the job was not initially told where the trucks were headed.

Players found out what was going on the same way the public did—from radio, TV, or word of mouth. They had no belongings to pack because it was the offseason, so they were kept out of the loop.

It was alternately sleeting and snowing when a fleet of Mayflower moving vans set out for Colts headquarters in Owings Mills, Maryland. There they loaded up all of the team's possessions and hauled them away, heading west 600 miles to Indiana. There were 11 vans, all 18-wheelers, with 15,000 pounds of Colts items packed inside.

For those who watched the trucks roll and for those who had just heard about it secondhand, the entire scene seemed surreal. The next day broadcast media interrupted local programming to fill the airwaves with tributes to the Colts and reports on their sad departure. It was a day's worth of news bulletins, approached as if a national figure had died.

A love affair with one city, an era that had witnessed championships and individual greatness, had come to an end—and at the same time, the history and tradition of Colts football was about to continue under the banner of another community.

It sounded alien at first—the Indianapolis Colts. But more than a generation has passed and entire families have come of age without hearing the words "Baltimore Colts." To anyone under 25 who is not up on his NFL history, hearing that team name sounds peculiar. He might not even know the Colts ever belonged to Baltimore, a city they proudly represented for three decades.

11 Mayflower vans, all 18-wheelers, were packed with 15,000 pounds of Colts items. Baltimore's team pointed its compass toward Indianapolis.

FOOD IS NOT THE MAIN DRAW AT THIS *DINER*

Diner is not really a football movie, and yet it is. Directed by Baltimore-born Barry Levinson, the1982 film tells the story about the city he grew up in and a group of 20-something friends who reunite back home for a wedding—and it's also about the Colts.

The movie takes the viewer back to 1959 when the Colts had the world at their fingertips. They won the National Football League title in 1958, but the characters didn't need that level of success to reward their allegiances. They were Colts fans growing up, even in the years when the Colts were nothing special.

Ostensibly, the movie is about young men who have headed out into the world without leaving their pasts behind. They reminisce about their late nights at the diner, and not more than a few minutes goes by without talk turning to the Colts.

The subplot that distinguishes *Diner* for its reverence for the Baltimore Colts is the task that the groom has set out for his fiancée. He is such a passionate Colts fan that he cannot imagine marrying a woman unless she knows a certain amount of trivia about his other love. So the groom announces he cannot go through with the marriage unless his wife-to-be passes the equivalent of a Colts SAT. Eddie designs a 140-question examination that fiancée Elyse must conquer. As the movie moves toward the scheduled wedding, there is considerable speculation about whether or not the hard-studying Elyse will pass the test.

Eventually, Elyse's showdown comes. Six questions are asked on screen. They are not gimme questions, either. The moviemakers went to the Colts' front office and enlisted then-assistant general manager Ernie Accorsi's aid to give the quiz credibility.

Among the questions: Buddy Young played for a team that no longer exists. What was the name of that team? (Answer, New York Yankees). What was the longest run from scrimmage by a rookie in his first game? (Answer, Alan Ameche's first-play, 79-yard touchdown run in the 1955 season opener.)

Elyse flunks the test by two points, but Eddie decides he loves her too much anyway to let her go.

Diner, which received an Academy Award nomination for Levinson for best screenplay and was his first directing job, features an extraordinary cast of young actors, including Steve Guttenberg, Daniel Stern, Mickey Rourke, Kevin Bacon, Paul Reiser, and Ellen Barkin. Levinson later gained additional fame for making *Rain Man*; *The Natural*; *Avalon*; *Good Morning, Vietnam*; and *Bugsy*. *Diner* made it as far as a television pilot for the small screen and was scheduled to be converted into a Broadway musical in 2012 with Levinson penning the book and Sheryl Crow writing the songs.

On the sports front, Levinson became a minority owner of the Baltimore Orioles.

MGM STUDIOS/COURTESY OF GETTY IMAGES

COLTS FEEL THE LOVE FROM INDY

As sad as Baltimore was, Indianapolis was ecstatic to have the Colts. Only five years earlier, seeking a way to boost tourism and develop a better and growing business climate, the Indiana Sports Corporation had been created. The goal was to make Indianapolis a destination city for sports of all sorts.

The organization started small, reaching out to college conferences and luring their nonrevenue sports championships that attracted minimal numbers of fans. But the group grew increasingly ambitious, and with the backing of Mayor William Hudnut, and his determination, the acquisition of the Colts was a game-changer. The image was important to city fathers.

"I was saying for eight years we were in the process of becoming major league," said Hudnut, who served as mayor for 16 years and spearheaded the sports tourism market plan for the city. "Now, we can say, I think without grandiose pomposity, that we are a major-league city."

The Hoosier Dome (later called the RCA Dome) was a leap of faith for Indianapolis. Indeed, the city took a major risk when it invested in a costly domed convention center without a cornerstone tenant—and the dome was a major part of the $77-million-plus cost.

Going pro had not been the goal at first, but it was the byproduct of building a foundation on sports that turned Indianapolis' downtown around. Basketball had always been huge, and the Indiana boys' state basketball tournament generated a fevered atmosphere summed up as "Hoosier Hysteria." Indianapolis was also home to the most famous automobile race in the world, the Indianapolis 500, as well as the National Basketball Association's Pacers. But to many, Indianapolis was just another wannabe big-time city, competing with Memphis, Jacksonville, and other cities in Florida for an NFL team.

Suddenly Indianapolis, with its population of 1.2 million people in the metropolitan area, was big league. "Big league." Hoosiers loved the sound of that description rolling off their tongues, and Hudnut loved what he had wrought. If it sounded as though he was gloating when Indianapolis was selected by its new best friend Bob Irsay as the home of the Colts, he wasn't alone.

Tom Moses, who chaired the committee that led the fight to bring the Colts to town, said he recalled being ridiculed for the effort, reminded often that the city of 725,000 people was casually relegated to small-town stature.

"We were always the racetrack in the cornfield," Moses said of the community being identified so closely with the Indianapolis Motor Speedway and nothing else. "Everyone thought we couldn't do it. Now we can say, 'Ha, ha, ha.'"

The new Hoosier Dome in downtown had a tenant, and the NFL's trademark was a stamp of approval without equal in the sports business. Restaurants and hotels sprang up all over the downtown area, making for a fan-friendly core business district.

Indianapolis had made some guarantees to Irsay if the city did not prove to be as hospitable as expected. A few years before the Colts left Baltimore, they endured a season where average attendance dipped below 17,000 for home games. That was unheard of and unacceptable in the modern NFL era. In attracting the Colts, Indianapolis officials guaranteed that attendance would exceed 40,000 per game or else the city would make up the revenue

Happier days for Robert Irsay, celebrating after the NFL announced it would not block the Colts' move to Indianapolis. AP PHOTO

to the team. Indy needn't have worried. The Indianapolis Colts brought in 60,000-plus fans per game from the start and had 143,000 season-ticket applications. The team held out 3,000 seats per home game for individual sales.

When Irsay made his move, the days of $1 specials from zealous cities campaigning for the Colts were long gone, or so it seemed. Indianapolis did fork over in a variety of ways to make the move irresistible to Irsay. At the same time he was feeling unappreciated in Baltimore, Irsay was offered this package from Indianapolis: a guarantee of $7 million in revenue for 12 years, a $12.5 million loan, and a commitment to building a $4 million training facility. Irsay wasn't from Baltimore, did not have long ties to the community that other Colts did, and didn't feel he had the respect or ear of Baltimore or Maryland governmental officials. Taking the Indianapolis deal seemed logical to him.

The Hoosier Dome offered luxury boxes, something Memorial Stadium never had. The private suites era was upon the NFL, and they paid off. Suite owners were the wealthiest patrons paying the highest prices to watch the team. The Hoosier Dome had 97 suites. The concept of suites hadn't even been incubating in anyone's imagination when Memorial Stadium was constructed.

The arrival of the Colts provided Indianapolis with income from stadium rentals, a 5 percent tax on tickets, suite licenses, and 41 percent of the concession income with 59 percent of that income going to the team. It was calculated that in 1984, the Colts' first season in Indianapolis, the city reaped an extra $100,000 of income from its hotel-motel tax alone.

Gloom descended on Baltimore football fans, who have never forgiven Robert Irsay. Some fans fought back on more than one front. Strong appeals were made to NFL commissioner Pete Rozelle to rule the move out of bounds. Fans believed that, at the very least, Baltimore should have been rewarded with another professional team.

Rozelle, as the apparent supreme authority of the NFL, had frowned on Oakland Raider owner Al Davis' relocation of that team from its ancestral home to Los Angeles in 1982. Rozelle fought for Oakland's fans, but Davis refused to buckle to Rozelle's orders. The ensuing court battle went to the U.S. Supreme Court. Lower courts ruled that the commissioner had only limited power to invoke a league clause referred to the overall "good of the game." When it came to interfering with a private businessman's handling of his team, the courts drew a line.

In November of 1984, the Supreme Court took up the ruling and let it stand. That effectively gave owners the legal right to move their teams around as they saw fit, regardless of whether the commissioner or other owners approved. Davis, who died in October 2011, kept the Raiders in Los Angeles until 1994 and then brought them back to Oakland on his own.

The decision set a precedent, and the legal briefs made it clear that Baltimore could not successfully sue for the return of the Colts. Football fans had to count on expansion sometime in the future. That remedy was never applied by Rozelle, but in a roundabout way the court decision helped Baltimore. Eventually, another owner, looking for fresh territory to conquer, pulled his team out of his longtime host city and moved it to Baltimore. Art Modell hired moving vans of his own to bring the Cleveland Browns to Baltimore, where they became the Ravens in 1995.

The Colts players who had brought glory to Baltimore on the field and represented the Baltimore Colts when they were enshrined in the Hall of Fame did not transfer their allegiance to Indianapolis. They stood shoulder-to-shoulder with the jilted, disappointed fans and never supported the Colts again. It was their grudge against Robert Irsay that came to the fore. They didn't hate the Colts of Indianapolis; they just didn't care about them. And those old-time players were just as happy for Baltimore when the Ravens appeared as the fans were.

It took until November 1998 for the schedule to bring the Indianapolis Colts to Baltimore to face the Baltimore Ravens for the first time. Johnny Unitas, the human face of the old Colts, made it clear where he stood. He said he was going to be cheering for the team from Baltimore, not the one from Indianapolis.

"I back the Ravens now," Unitas said. "Baltimore is my hometown, and I cheer for the home team. Sure I was upset that we lost a franchise. But the thing that really gets me is that they continue to use our records in their press guide."

The Colts are still the Colts in the eyes of the NFL, and that makes sense whether Unitas felt that way or not. After all, the Ravens were previously the Browns, so they have their own history.

Even if Unitas didn't want to change planes in Indianapolis ever again, Indianapolis embraced the Colts and made friends with the team.

Evidence abounded in every way that Mayor Hudnut was correct in saying that the Colts lifted his city into the big time. The Colts very quickly served as catalysts to revitalize the downtown, and it happened more quickly than anyone predicted. Within 20 months of the Colts' move to the Midwest, Indianapolis saw the addition of 19 new restaurants to the immediate area surrounding the Hoosier Dome. That was a startling rate of development, and the Colts were clearly the reason why it happened.

And the Colts drummed up all that excitement without even playing well. Their rise to becoming one of the winningest teams in the league was still years away. Still, the Indianapolis Colts

The Indianapolis Colts were an immediate hit, selling 57,000 season tickets in 1984—just one year after the Baltimore Colts sold 23,000.

MVP BOOKS COLLECTION

were an immediate hit, selling 57,000 season tickets in 1984—just one year after the Baltimore Colts sold 23,000.

Tickets were sold at a higher price, too, for $21, $17, and $10, compared to the Baltimore fees of $14, $13, $9, and $7. It seems remarkable that as late as the mid-1980s NFL tickets could be had for such low prices. In 2011, the Indianapolis Colts' cheapest ticket went for $60.

Although Irsay may not have spoken with tact when he informed fans that the Colts belonged to him, not to Baltimore or Indianapolis, he did draw an audience of gleeful fans numbering about 20,000 to hear him make his thanks-for-having me-in-Indianapolis debut speech at the Hoosier Dome. It was hard to convince the football fans of Indianapolis that these were not their Colts. They were in love from the sighting of the first horseshoe.

"We didn't steal the Colts. The city of Baltimore lost them."—Mayor William Hudnut

A decade later, when journalists revisited Baltimore to gauge the level of bitterness that remained from the Colts' slippery departure, they discovered that feelings were still raw. But there were no regrets in Indianapolis, no second thoughts, and really, not a whole lot of sympathy for Baltimore. The Colts belonged to Indiana, and that was that.

Hudnut, who was mayor until 1992, was as proud as ever about the transfer of the Colts to Indianapolis—his city—on his watch, when interviewed in 1984.

"We didn't steal the Colts," Hudnut said of shrinking attendance in Baltimore at the time. "The city of Baltimore lost them."

In the end, the Colts' move from Baltimore to Indianapolis was like any divorce, with two sides to the story. As is often the case, the Colts were loved by two parties but could only choose one. Their love affair with Baltimore ended in early 1984, and their love affair with Indianapolis began immediately.

BALTIMORE COLTS RECORDS, 1947–1983

Year	Record
1947	2–11–1*
1948	7–7*
1949	1–11*
1950	1–11*
1953	3–9
1954	3–9
1955	5–6–1
1956	5–7
1957	7–5
1958	9–3
1959	9–3
1960	3–9
1961	3–9
1962	5–6–1
1963	5–7
1964	7–5
1965	9–3
1966	9–3
1967	11–1–2
1968	13–1
1969	8–5–1
1970	11–2–1
1971	10–4
1972	5–9
1973	4–10
1974	2–12
1975	10–4
1976	11–3
1977	10–4
1978	5–11
1979	5–11
1980	7–9
1981	2–14
1982	0–8–1
1983	7–9

*Pre-1950: All-America Football Conference

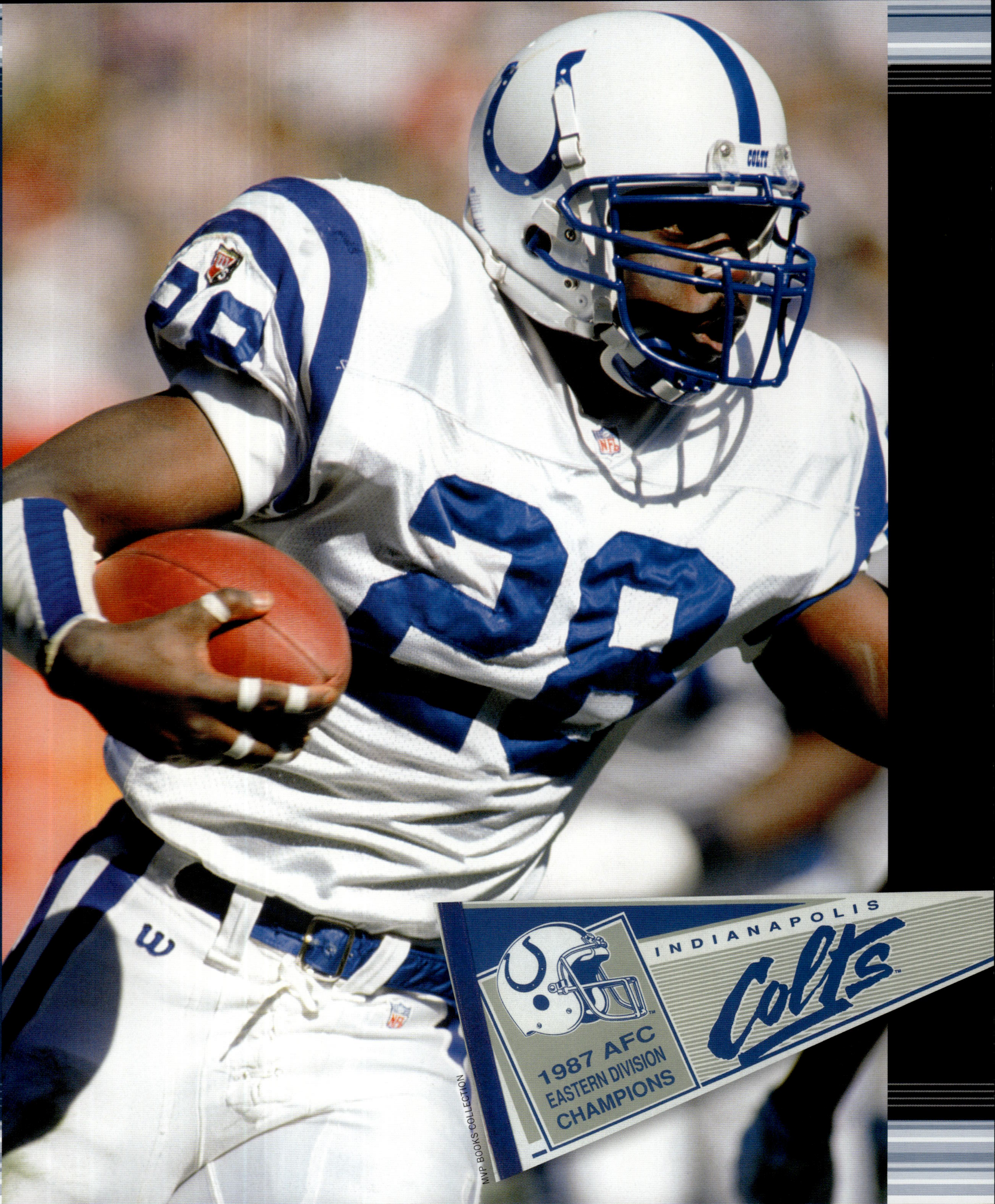

MVP BOOKS COLLECTION

Part II

1984-1997

Baltimore was outraged, but Indianapolis was overjoyed. For a city that had hoped and dreamed, hustled and planned, the arrival of a National Football League franchise was a special stamp of approval for the capital of the state of Indiana. Home previously to just one major-league franchise, basketball's Indiana Pacers, the Colts heralded a brand-new era of growth and pride in a city that had cast its lot behind a vision of itself as America's sports capital and built a spanking new stadium on spec.

The greatest early achievement of the Colts in Indianapolis was simply their existence. Progress on the field came only in fits and starts, very gradually. It took years to reach the playoffs and years more to actually win a playoff game.

Initially, owner Robert Irsay, the man who uprooted the Colts from Baltimore, was one of the biggest sports heroes in town. Eventually, he gave way to running back Eric Dickerson, quarterback Jim Harbaugh—a.k.a. "Captain Comeback"—and Marshall Faulk.

The Colts were granted a honeymoon period as they made themselves at home in Indianapolis, but they fell to the depths of the NFL standings before making the personnel move that transformed the franchise into a perennial playoff team. The Colts built from the ground up, and it was a job that took more than a decade to complete.

The next era of Colts football unfolded in a new city and saw two excellent running backs churning out yards for Indianapolis—Eric Dickerson (29) and Marshall Faulk (28). (RIGHT) RICK STEWART / ALLSPORT/GETTY IMAGES; (OPPOSITE) GEORGE ROSE/GETTY IMAGES

NOT MUCH TO WORK WITH

After slipping away from Maryland's snowfall in the dead of night, the Baltimore Colts woke up in the Midwest as the born-again Indianapolis Colts, putting their decades-old ties to the All-America Football Conference and their early days in the National Football League behind them. With Indianapolis Mayor William Hudnut stretching his arms the widest, the entire city offered hugs to the Colts.

MVP BOOKS COLLECTION

It was the beginning of a new era, and at first blush these Colts looked as if they might be able to play a little bit of football. Indianapolis had been willing to settle for an expansion team, which would have taken years to turn into a winner. Instead it got the Colts, who had gone 7–9 the previous season under coach Frank Kush—not playoff ready but not bad.

The most likely new offensive star for the Colts' first year in Indianapolis was Curtis Dickey, a burly back who rushed for 1,122 yards in 1983. The Colts drafted the former Texas A&M standout in the first round of the 1980 draft, and he seemed to be emerging as an all-pro prospect after scoring11 touchdowns as a rookie. The man was a bullet in pads. In college he won the NCAA indoor 60-yard dash three times. If he could break through the line of scrimmage, Dickey was hard to catch from behind.

What no one could know was that 1983 would be the high point of Dickey's career. Although he rushed for 523 yards in 1984, injuries wrecked Dickey's chances to shine in Indianapolis. He started just nine games in '84 and had only 11 rushing attempts in 1985. A year later he was gone to the Cleveland Browns, and a year after that he retired.

MVP BOOKS COLLECTION

The promise and disappointment of Curtis Dickey seemed to symbolize the Colts' early years in Indianapolis. One minute things looked great; the next minute they looked shaky. Highs and lows, comings and goings, all made for a rocky start in front of fans longing to love their Colts.

Coach Kush was a famous, near-legendary coach at Arizona State, compiling a 176–54–1 record with the Sun Devils between 1958 and 1979. Arizona State was a perennial college power, winning five straight Western Athletic Conference titles in the days before the school became part of the Pac-10. In one stretch, they won the Peach Bowl and the first three Fiesta Bowls. In 1974, Arizona State finished 12–0.

Head coach Frank Kush and quarterback Mike Pagel were both holdovers from the Baltimore era. DIAMOND IMAGES/GETTY IMAGES

"It's a severe, severe addiction," Schlichter wrote in his candid autobiography. "It's kind of like crack cocaine in that it takes away your soul and your character. I know I'm only one step away from imprisonment, insanity, or death."

With Schlichter sidetracked, Mike Pagel, who essentially had been drafted from Arizona State to be the backup, became the starter. Pagel beat out Purdue's Mark Herrmann for the starting job in the 1983 season. Although rough around the edges, Pagel did help the Colts win games by throwing for 2,353 yards and 12 touchdowns. In 1984 Pagel shared the role with Schlichter and took the majority of the snaps. When Schlichter again gambled himself off the team in 1985, Pagel was the main guy with 14 touchdown passes and 2,414 yards passing.

Pagel was familiar with Kush's run-first offense, having played under him in college. "One big key to our running game is that we use two different sets," Pagel said, and it was imperative that Dickey be healthy. "We run inside and outside from both of those sets."

Disappointed in the weak offensive line in '82, Kush stuck to his guns in believing that the Colts should be a power team. "I think we've proved that we can play with the bulk of them," he said. "If we play well. We've got to be physical. We've got to kick the hell out of them, that's all. That's what we've got going for us."

Despite their poor performance, the Colts sold out 19 of their first 21 games in Indianapolis, putting more than 60,000 fans into the Hoosier Dome each time.

Jack Trudeau huddles the offense during a game at the Hoosier Dome. Trudeau replaced Mike Pagel in the mid-1980s, but neither signal caller had much success in Indianapolis. GEORGE GOJKOVICH/GETTY IMAGES

Despite ample opportunity, Pagel could not nail down the starting job, and by 1986 that position belonged to Jack Trudeau, another Ohio State alum. Pagel was shipped to the Browns and spent 12 years in the NFL, mostly as a backup.

Despite their poor performance, the Colts sold out 19 of their first 21 games in Indianapolis, putting more than 60,000 fans into the Hoosier Dome each time. From the mayor's office to the nosebleed seats, the prevailing outlook was that having the team in Indianapolis was a great start. Making it a winner would follow.

"It's a lot better being inside the NFL wishing you were winning rather than being outside, wishing you were in," Hudnut said.

The Colts defense gangs up on a Dolphin ball carrier during a 1984 loss in Miami. AL MESSERSCHMIDT/GETTY IMAGES

MAKING INDIANAPOLIS BIG TIME

On April 2, 1984, negotiator David Frick, Indianapolis Mayor William Hudnut, and Colts owner Robert Irsay were welcomed to the city and cheered on for bringing the NFL to Indiana.
BETTMANN/CORBIS

Stealing the Colts from Baltimore was part of a master plan for Indianapolis and Indiana as the first city and state in the United States to recognize how valuable sports tourism could be to the local economy.

The Indiana Sports Corporation was founded in 1979 with the basic mission of making Indianapolis the capital of amateur sport. At the time there was virtually no competition to become hosts of sporting events that were not of the highest absolute profile, such as the Super Bowl or the NCAA Basketball Tournament. Even the most lucrative events were not seriously sought after.

In 1979 no one really thought about playing a Super Bowl anywhere but Miami, Florida; Pasadena, California; or New Orleans, Louisiana. The Super Bowl was all about warm-weather destinations. The Final Four was still being contested in 15,000- or 20,000-seat arenas that served as a home base for a college or NBA basketball team. No cities were aggressively chasing events such as non-revenue sports conference championship meets. In Indiana, however, there was vision. There was recognition that money could be made by attracting competitors and their close relatives to a site. The athletes and their families spent money on hotel rooms, food, and souvenirs.

The Sports Corporation started small. The very first college championship event lured to Indianapolis was the Midwestern Collegiate Conference cross-country running championships in fall 1979. That league no longer even exists; it was a forerunner of the Horizon League. That was a modest beginning. Soon, Indianapolis was wooing other gymnastic, bicycling, and swimming events that had limited attendance followings. One after the other they took up residence in Indianapolis. Athletes, coaches, movers and shakers in their sport, and their fans returned home and talked about how they were treated well, how the city embraced them, how Indianapolis was a great place for their competition.

It was not as if other cities were hungry to host them, either. Indianapolis was far ahead of the curve, making itself into a sports destination long before anyplace else even pondered the idea. That head start paid off on several fronts as Indiana went hunting for bigger game.

When it became apparent that the Colts were wavering in their allegiance to Baltimore, Indianapolis went after the pro football team. Home to just one other major-league franchise, the NBA's Indiana Pacers, these Hoosiers sensed this was a team ripe for the plucking, that represented a chance to turn the city into a bigger dot on the map. Mayor William Hudnut III, who served in office from 1976 to 1992, was ready with a proposal to land the Colts if they were receptive to fleeing Baltimore. They were, and Indianapolis just kept rolling, building on its sports résumé.

In 1982, Indianapolis hosted one of the prime American amateur sporting competitions. Called the U.S. Sports Festival, the now-defunct event was looked at as a United States Olympics, pitting teams from the East, West, South, and North in Olympic-style events. A mix of the country's best athletes and best prospects competed. It was good practice for a city with grand aspirations.

Typical of Indiana's aggressiveness was how the state acquired the right to conduct the 1987 Pan American Games. The Olympics of the region was a huge step up in class from small-conference swimming events to bringing in what seemed to be half of the world. There were 4,300 athletes from 38 countries in the hemisphere competing in 30 sports at 23 venues. There was a certain amount of serendipity and a certain amount of making its own luck involved in Indianapolis being awarded the games. Originally, Santiago, Chile, had been chosen as the site. But that city withdrew because of political unrest. Indianapolis wasn't even the second choice. Quito, Ecuador, was supposed to fill in but also withdrew. "We'll do it," said Indianapolis. It was a huge coup staging the complicated event, but fixing a problem that was becoming embarrassing engendered goodwill in the international sports community.

Whereas once the philosophy was that no sporting event was too small to host, Indianapolis made the transition to believing no sporting event was too large to chase. The entire sports development effort was designed to boost the fortunes of a sleepy downtown better known for its state government buildings than as a tourist destination.

When it was proved that the model could work—athletes, plus fans, equals cash—Indianapolis showed little reluctance to increase its own investment. The Hoosier Dome and then Lucas Oil Stadium were both built for football, and the lavish Conseco Fieldhouse went up for NBA basketball.

Downtown transformed. Hotels, restaurants, and nightclubs sprang up near the new sports palaces. In a concentrated, several-block area fans could park their cars at their hotels and never move them again during a weekend of fun that included eating, drinking, and ballgames, all within walking distance.

In 1999, Indiana trumped itself by convincing the NCAA to move its headquarters from Overland Park, Kansas, to Indianapolis. The governing body of intercollegiate sport became a major employer in downtown.

Indianapolis' downtown and its appetite for attracting big-time sporting events only grew. The combination of facilities and convenience led to suggestions that Indianapolis should become the permanent home of the coveted (partially because it is worth $50 million to a local economy) men's Final Four. Indianapolis worked hard to wrest Big Ten basketball championships from Chicago (at least on a semiregular basis), and the first Big Ten football championship game in December 2011 was staged at Lucas Oil Stadium.

All of this was prelude to Indianapolis hosting the Super Bowl in February 2012, the granddaddy "get" of all sporting events with the possible exception of the Olympic Games themselves. If the Baltimore Colts had never bolted for Indianapolis, Lucas Oil Stadium would not exist, and Indianapolis would not have become a Super Bowl site.

More than a quarter of a century later, Mayor Hudnut's comment that the Colts coming to town was "one of the greatest days in the history of the city" was accurate.

Seen here with a packed crowd in 1985, ground was broken on the Hoosier Dome in 1982 and was ready to welcome the Colts when they arrived in Indianapolis for the 1984 season.
GEORGE GOJKOVICH/GETTY IMAGES

OUT WITH THE OLD; TIME TO START FRESH

Frank Kush left Colts at the end of the 1984 season, actually quitting with one game left in the regular season to accept a long-term deal with the Arizona Outlaws of the United States Football League. He was replaced by Rod Dowhower, who led the Colts to 5–11 and 3–13 records in 1985 and 1986, respectively. Actually, Dowhower was ousted after 13 straight losses to start the 1986 season, so he can't claim credit for those three wins.

A one-time quarterback at San Diego State, Dowhower was a longtime college and pro assistant who came to the Colts after being offensive coordinator for the St. Louis Cardinals. It was a short reign with poor results.

"Rod was a real talented guy," said Colts general manager Jim Irsay, the son of the owner. "I feel sorry for Rod in a way because on paper he was ready, but unfortunately there is no school for head coaches in this league. He came in a bright guy, but he didn't really know what he was getting himself into."

Nor did Dowhower recognize the folly in counting on Schlichter as his starting quarterback. Schlichter was still too distracted by gambling to be a team leader, and Dowhower had to cut him.

In an embarrassing and strange incident, Dowhower also cut his pants. So engrossed in a close game against the Miami Dolphins, Dowhower began hyperventilating and fell to the field, splitting his pants. Sheepishly, Dowhower explained, "I kind of overexposed myself to 60,000 fans."

Sports Illustrated had a biting comment to make on the material Dowhower was given to work with by Robert Irsay. "They say he made a ton of money in his first season in the new town last year," one story went, "but why should he spend it frivolously, like on players?"

It was during the 1986 season of ineptitude that some people began referring to the Colts as the Dolts. The sarcastic name was often coupled with the speculation that the team could take a run at the all-time worst NFL streak of 0–26 set by the Tampa Bay Buccaneers in the 1970s. At one point Dowhower was asked to sum up Indianapolis' season to date in one word. He said, "One word. Not good." Actually four words, but who's counting? "Seriously," he added, "we've had some things happen to us that would be upsetting to any football team."

Surprisingly, after Dowhower was fired, the Colts won their final three games of the season under Ron Meyer. The inexplicable rise of the Colts earned Meyer a full-time shot at the job.

Head coach Rod Dowhower chats with 49ers coach Bill Walsh prior to their game at Candlestick Park in 1986. GEORGE ROSE/GETTY IMAGES

RON MEYER TO THE RESCUE

The Indianapolis Colts were 0–13 during the 1986 season when Ron Meyer was summoned to become head coach. Meyer was not an interim hire. He was brought in not only to prevent the ship from running ashore but also to steer a proper course across the seas in the future.

Meyer was a prominent college coach at Southern Methodist between 1976 and 1981, pretty much the last time any boss had much success at SMU, and he displayed the type of enthusiasm that rubbed off on people. As awful as the Colts were when he arrived, Meyer somehow coaxed three straight wins out of the team.

Meyer certainly seemed like a long-term solution when the Colts followed up that eye-catching finish by making the playoffs in 1987 and winning the AFC Eastern Division. A loss to the Cleveland Browns marked the first playoff game for the club since moving from Baltimore. In a season cut a little short by labor problems, Indianapolis finished 9–6, and Meyer was named AFC coach of the year.

Although hopes were raised, the Colts went 9–7 in 1988 in a tumultuous campaign fraught with personnel problems and did not qualify for the playoffs. Gary Hogeboom was not the quarterback of the future, and juggling players was not the answer to a great run.

Meyer was outgoing and could be witty and entertaining for reporters, but he didn't always get his analogies right. Sometimes he missed a word trying to make a point. In a famous case, he talked about how "Moses had come down off the mountain with the tabloids." Presumably, these were the Ten Commandments that God handed down to Moses on tablets. Meyer might have benefited if someone with greater knowledge had handed down 10 plays for his offense.

"Tabloids" was a speech accident. Meyer's candid assessment of one of his players was not. In perhaps the greatest single succinct scouting report ever issued by a football coach, Meyer said of defensive end Mel Agee, "He looks like Tarzan, plays like Jane." Top that, John Madden.

Ron Meyer found a way to get the most out of the Colts in his first two seasons as head coach. DON LARSON/NFL/GETTY IMAGES

What neither Meyer nor his Colts bosses knew was that his high-water mark with the team peaked with the 1987 playoff run. Indianapolis did have that winning record in 1988, but he was fired during the 1991 season when the team started 0–5. After that season Meyer went into broadcasting for a few years before returning to the sidelines to coach first in the Canadian Football League and then in the short-lived XFL. Meyer's overall record as a head coach in the NFL was 54–50.

"Ron was fun," Colts owner Jim Irsay said. "He was way different than anyone we had before him." Meyer wasn't different enough, or he would have supervised more victories for the Colts.

"He won at Nevada, won at SMU, won at New England, and he won here," Irsay said. "Sometimes, though, success can be your worst enemy because of the expectations that come with that success. He has nothing to hang his head about."

DICKERSON BRINGS STAR POWER

When the Colts drafted Cornelius Bennett out of Alabama with their top selection in the 1987 NFL draft, they hoped to bolster the defense. But Bennett, the second overall player chosen, wanted a fatter contract than the Colts were willing to offer. Without playing a down, Bennett became an ex-Colt, moved in a three-team trade that netted the Colts all-pro running back Eric Dickerson, one of the hottest offensive forces in the game.

RONALD C. MODRA/SPORTS ILLUSTRATED/GETTY IMAGES

Bennett, who ended up back in Indianapolis after a successful career with the Buffalo Bills, was an unproven commodity at the time. Dickerson was a superstar. A salary dispute with his Los Angeles Rams got Dickerson shipped out, even after being Rookie of the Year and setting the all-time NFL single-season rushing record of 2,105 yards. For the Colts, acquiring a marquee name was huge.

The Colts had posted a 22–67 record between 1981 and 1986. They needed more juice. The novelty of having pro football was no longer enough for the fans, who grew annoyed—they wanted a winner in Indianapolis.

Robert Irsay was at the NFL owners' meetings and struck up a conversation with Georgia Frontiere, the Rams' owner. They must have lamented the challenges of signing big-name talent. Getting Dickerson's John Hancock on a contract was proving tiresome for Frontiere, and Irsay wasn't making much progress with Bennett. Irsay came away from the meeting thinking maybe Dickerson could be had in a deal.

He talked it over with his son Jim, the general manager, and Jim Irsay ran it past Meyer. Meyer had been Dickerson's college coach, and the duo shared a bond. When Jim Irsay asked if his coach thought it was worthwhile to take a shot at getting Dickerson, Meyer almost shouted, "I love it!"

Dickerson was going to be costly to sign, however, so the Colts determined that if someone else was willing to spend big for Bennett, they would let him go. Buffalo made the best offer. The Rams got high draft choices, the Bills got a future all-pro defensive player, and the Colts got the biggest-name player they had yet to introduce in Indianapolis.

It was the right time to come to Indianapolis. Meyer was new on the job, more of a rah-rah guy with a clearer offensive mindset. Plugging Dickerson in as the featured running back was a no-brainer. Even as he made the transition to a new team, he rushed for 1,011 yards with a 4.5 yards–per-carry average in 1986. But he was not a soloist in this band. Never as heralded but quite productive, Dickerson's backfield mate Albert Bentley turned in a fine year, averaging 4.4 yards per carry and gaining 631 yards.

RONALD C. MODRA/SPORTS IMAGERY/GETTY IMAGES

Eric Dickerson, center Ray Donaldson, and tackle Chris Hinton were selected for the 1989 Pro Bowl.

Mike Pagel was gone, and the Colts acquired Gary Hogeboom, a 6-foot-4, 200-pound thrower out of Central Michigan. Hogeboom was injured early, and once again it was Jack Trudeau, who had assumed the quarterback job the season before, inserted as the No. 1 guy. Hogeboom threw for nine touchdowns after recovering from his injury, but the 1987 bunch was not an overpowering Colts team. They were consistent, however, and not prone to streaks. After starting 0–2 the Colts finished 9–6 and reached the playoffs. They were one-and-done against the Cleveland Browns, but still, it was the playoffs. For the moment, that was enough. Things looked promising.

Meyer had an infectious, upbeat attitude. He was not a dour type like Kush. With Kush, half of the time you wondered if he was about to take a swing at you. Kush was all business, a military drill-sergeant type. Meyer got things done, but he came off as the kind of guy you might want to shoot the breeze with after hours.

Jim Irsay shared the same opinion. "Ron was fun," said Irsay. "He was flamboyant and had a lot of good qualities."

When the club was meticulously working through the details of the three-party Dickerson trade, Irsay said Meyer's mood stayed light, suggested they order pizza, drink some beer, and "rock and roll this thing"—which presumably meant they should hunker down until the deal got done.

It was shaping up for Meyer to have a long run in Indianapolis, and the Colts appeared to be a team on the rise. Unfortunately, things did

Head coach Ron Meyer had coached Eric Dickerson in college at Southern Methodist University, so he was thrilled to have another chance to watch him run for the Colts.

DON LARSON/GETTY IMAGES

MVP BOOKS COLLECTION

MVP BOOKS COLLECTION

not progress quite that smoothly. As is frequently the case when a team fails to meet expectations, the Colts were hampered by injuries, off-field issues, and trouble at the quarterback position.

Looking for stability and toward the future, the Colts drafted Chris Chandler out of the University of Washington in the third round. Hogeboom remained the front-runner for the quarterback job heading into the 1988 season, and he and Chandler split the assignment over the course of the season.

Chandler showed promise, and Hogeboom showed that he really was a No. 2 quarterback. Chandler would ultimately have a solid career, with two Pro Bowl appearances while playing for eight teams over 17 seasons—but he wasn't ready to push this team over the brink. The best the Colts could muster was a familiar 9–7 record, despite Dickerson's huge 1,659-yard performance. The team came up just shy of the playoffs.

For a team that had barely been treading water a year or two earlier, 9–7 wasn't half bad. Surely the Colts were on an upswing. The persistent Trudeau ended up as the starter once again in 1989, playing for most of the season and enjoying his best campaign—15 touchdown passes and 2,317 passing yards. Dickerson remained a rock in the backfield, gaining 1,311 yards. But the offense was short on big-scoring games, and the defense needed more help than it received.

Dickerson, center Ray Donaldson, and tackle Chris Hinton were selected for the Pro Bowl, but no defensive players were, reflecting the fact that the Colts were outscored 301–298 during the season and in each of the first three quarters in aggregate.

A three-game midseason swoon hurt the team's chances, but they were 8–7 going into the last weekend of the season. Coming off a 42–13 triumph over the Miami Dolphins, the Colts seemed to have momentum and motivation. They controlled their own destiny, knowing a victory would propel them into the playoffs. But destiny turned out to be depressing. In the season finale, the Colts were blasted by the Saints in New Orleans, losing 41–6. Again, no playoffs.

Quarterback Gary Hogeboom barks signals while guard Ben Utt and tackle Chris Hinton line up during a 30–10 loss to the Miami Dolphins in 1986. AL MESSERSCHMIDT/GETTY IMAGES

Despite their defensive deficiencies, the Colts would prioritize the quarterback position in the coming offseason, trading two valuable players to move into the No. 1 draft position. There, they intended to find their quarterback of the future.

ERIC DICKERSON

Prime-Time Runner

After you got past the thick goggles that shielded his eyes, making him appear like an alien who had just landed from outer space, Eric Dickerson displayed all of the other characteristics of the greatest running backs of all time. He was fast, he was strong, and he had good size.

Although more than a quarter of a century has passed since the Colts moved from Baltimore to Indianapolis, Dickerson is one of only a few of the team's Pro Football Hall of Famers to wear the uniform in the heartland.

Dickerson was born in Sealy, Texas, in 1960, and although he had pretty much made up his mind to play college football elsewhere, a plea from his grandmother to stay in Texas led him to Southern Methodist. The 6-foot-3, 220-pound back was a powerful running machine at SMU, gathering 4,450 yards rushing, scoring 48 touchdowns, and twice earning All-American honors.

The Los Angeles Rams made Dickerson their No. 1 pick in 1983, taking him second overall in the draft. The rookie of the year reached the Pro Bowl in his first season, one of six times he was selected for the all-star contest. He was an immediate sensation with 1,808 yards rushing and 18 touchdowns. Able to exploit defenses with speed and power, in his second season Dickerson rushed for an astonishing 2,105 yards, setting a new NFL record that still stands, and he averaged 5.6 yards per carry. There have been only six single NFL seasons where a running back broke the 2,000-yard mark.

The Rams seemed certain to feature Dickerson as the cornerstone of their offense for many years. However, the running back kept asking for more money, and arguments between player and front office escalated. Not even being a good locker room guy or making anti-drug public service announcements for the NFL could keep Dickerson a Ram. In a blockbuster, three-team trade that also involved the Buffalo Bills, Dickerson was sent to Indianapolis in 1987. The Colts parted with linebacker Cornelius Bennett and three high draft picks. The trade was appealing to Dickerson because it again linked him with his old college coach Ron Meyer.

Dickerson's appearance wearing the horseshoe was a good morale booster for fans, and it lifted the franchise, which improved from 3–13 in 1996 to 9–6 in 1997, although he had a slow start. Just a few days after the trade, Dickerson made his Colts debut and was held to 38 yards in 10 attempts. "I was a little nervous, but it went pretty good," said Dickerson, who was rushed into service

Eric Dickerson wards off two Patriots defenders while keeping his eyes downfield and planning his next move. AP PHOTO/ELISE AMENDOLA

without much practice. "I was surprised I got to play as much as I did. I felt like a rookie out there. I've got to learn a new system. I didn't know the plays, and I didn't want to mess up. I knew maybe two pass plays, maybe four running plays. I didn't want to be going the wrong way and bust a play."

Dickerson was a quick study, though, and rushed for 1,011 yards that season. The Colts won games they were used to losing and, as always, winning pays dividends. By the end of the season, Dickerson was expressing his pleasure at being in Indianapolis and his appreciation for the Colts giving him a $1.5 million–per-year contract.

"I know some people have raised their eyebrows and said, 'Hey, did we mortgage the future?'" Meyer said. "I think not. I see a back with tremendous longevity who's never been hurt, who is really in the youthfulness of his career."

In 1988, Dickerson proved just about as effective for the Colts as he had been for the Rams, rushing for 1,659 yards and becoming the first member of the franchise to lead the NFL in rushing since Alan Ameche in 1955. Dickerson's combination of skills and size, coupled with speed, meant he could run around people or over them, and he did some of each. "It's a rough sport, and you have to be mentally and physically prepared to play it," Dickerson said. "You'll be nervous. You have the jitters. Sometimes you're like, 'Damn, I don't feel like getting tackled all day, getting touched.' And then sometimes I just feel like running into somebody."

There is little doubt that Dickerson provided a big-time running option for the Colts. In consecutive years he rushed for 1,011, 1,659, and 1,311 yards before any problems popped up.

AL MESSERSCHMIDT/GETTY IMAGES

In 1989, Dickerson went over 10,000 yards rushing for his career, elite territory, and he reached the milestone faster, in 91 games, than any other running back. He also he set an NFL record of rushing for 1,000 or more yards for seven straight years, four times capturing the league's rushing crown.

When the Colts played the Rams back in Los Angeles, where Dickerson retained his permanent home, a 9,000-square-foot house in Malibu, the fans did not act as if they missed him. Many yelled at him. "Monopoly" game money, thrown to make the point that he was greedy for forcing the trade to Indianapolis over a debate for more cash, floated down from the sky. Dickerson offered verbal retaliation at the fans. "They're cheap," he said. "If they had thrown real money, I'd have picked it up."

Still effective when he was able, Dickerson had some injury problems in 1990. It was the first time in his career he was sidelined. Although his per-carry average was a solid 4.1, he toted the ball just 166 times for 677 yards.

Dickerson did worry about serious injury, and many times he ran out of bounds when he was sidestepping along the sidelines, admitting that he saw no point in plowing into tacklers when a play was doomed. "What are the out-of-bounds lines there for?" he said.

So talented that it didn't always look as if he was giving full effort, Dickerson seemed like a paradox. But the man couldn't change the way it looked when he ran. Perhaps for that reason he was never an unabashed fan favorite. Colts fans cheered his accomplishments but didn't appear to lavish unqualified love on him.

Dickerson even admitted publicly that he didn't care if he set the all-time NFL rushing record, seemingly within his reach, and then held by Walter Payton of the Chicago Bears. "The Payton record is no big deal to me," Dickerson said. "There's more to life than getting 16,000 yards." He was more concerned about walking away from the game with his health, and walking was the operative word. "People think it should be an honor

FOCUS ON SPORT/GETTY IMAGES

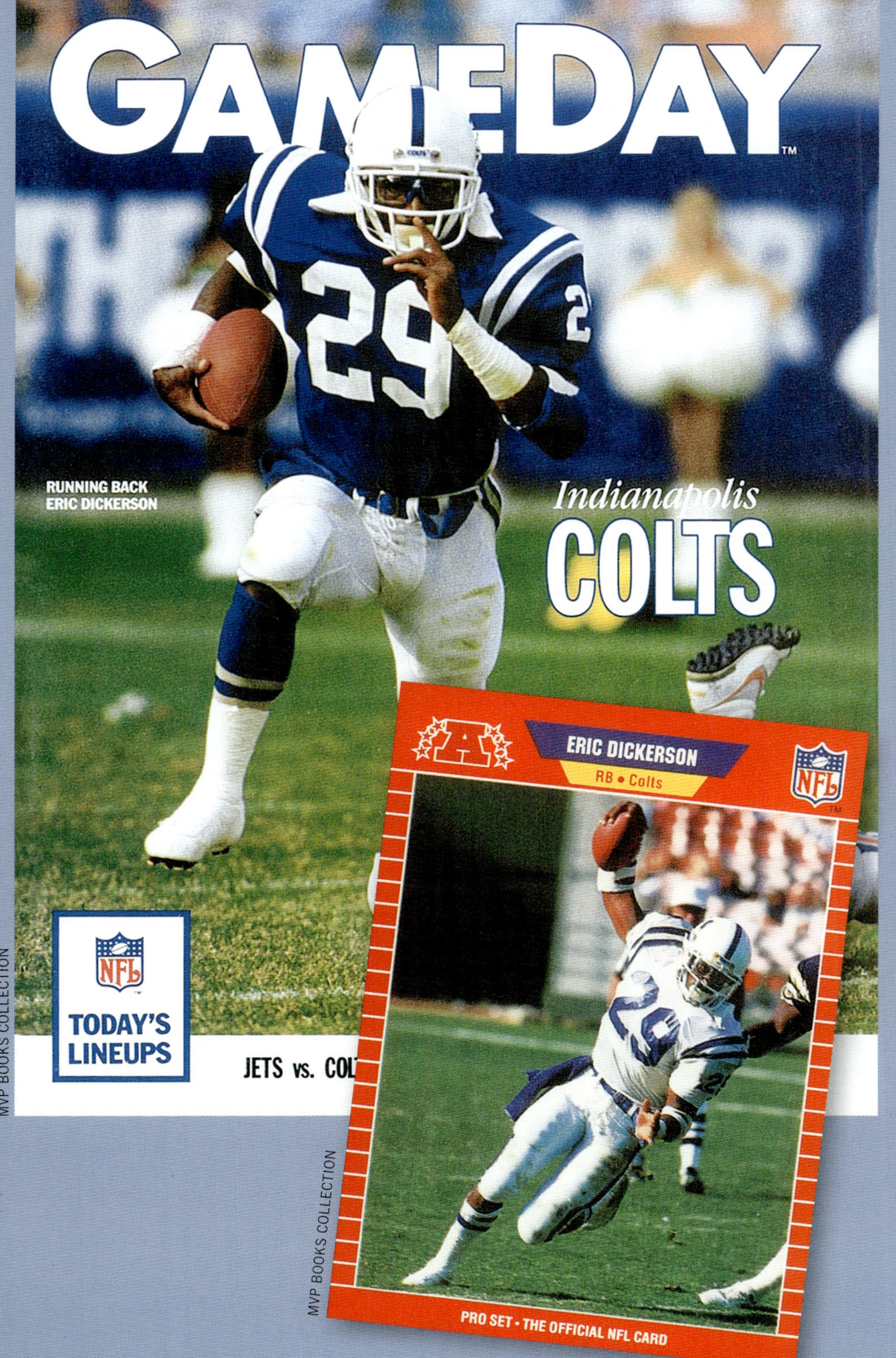

MVP BOOKS COLLECTION

MVP BOOKS COLLECTION

to run in the NFL. Hell, it's no honor. It's an honor to be alive, to have two legs that work, two eyes that work."

In an atrocious 1–15 1991 season, when injuries and off-field woes hindered the Colts, Dickerson struggled to play at full strength. He gained just 536 yards, and worse, his average of 3.2 was unacceptable. After a season like that, teams clean house to start fresh. It was nearing the time when Dickerson would depart from Indianapolis.

The running back who never got slowed up by injury during the first segment of his career began to get sidetracked with hamstring pulls and other injuries. He got into disputes with management and served suspensions twice during his final two seasons with the Colts. In the spring of 1992 Dickerson was traded to the Raiders for two draft picks.

Dickerson gained 729 yards for the Raiders and twice rushed for more than 100 yards. He ended up with 64 career 100-yard games and completed his career with a smattering of appearances in games for the Atlanta Falcons in 1993. Dickerson retired with 13,259 yards gained rushing and 90 touchdowns on the ground, and in 1999 he was voted into the Hall of Fame.

Dickerson served as a broadcaster on NFL telecasts after retirement and also worked for a TV station in Los Angeles. When he made a personal appearance in Indianapolis in 1996, Dickerson seemed relaxed and interacted with kids, signing autographs and acknowledging that he had many good times with the Colts.

"A lot of guys like to live in the past," he said, "but I don't. Football was a game that became a business, but I'll always love it."

ROHN STARK

His Boots Were Made for Yardage

When the Colts made Rohn Stark a second-round draft pick in the 1982 NFL draft, half the fans thought his name was Ron, and the other half of the fans wondered why they chose a punter so high. But Stark, who played his college ball at Florida State, was no ordinary punter. Stark stood 6-foot-3 and weighed 195 pounds. He was a two-time All-American for the Seminoles, but he was more athletic than most kickers. In track and field, Stark was a decathlete, one good enough to consider the U.S. Olympic trials as an option.

Growing up in Minnesota, Stark was an unlikely catch for FSU. When recruited he didn't know a thing about Tallahassee. "I had barely heard of Florida State," he said, "but I went down and I liked what I saw."

Rohn Stark shows off the extension and leg strength that helped make him a Colts draft pick. AL MESSERSCHMIDT/GETTY IMAGES

Florida State, and then the Colts, liked what they saw of Stark. He became an extraordinary punter, and three decades after making his Colts debut, his name still takes up considerable space in the Colts' media guide. For the longest time he was the undisputed best punter the Colts ever had.

COLTS
ROHN STARK
P

MVP BOOKS COLLECTION

When Stark came into the league, the Colts were still in Baltimore. He played 13 seasons with the Colts, most of them in Indianapolis. But Stark had a few odd trivia notes attached to his career. When he hung up his cleats in 1997, after 16 seasons in the league, he was the last former Baltimore Colt to retire from the NFL—and he's the only one who played for the Baltimore Colts and against the Baltimore Ravens.

A four-time Pro Bowl selection, Stark's best years were with the Colts, but he also played single seasons for the Pittsburgh Steelers (and made it to a Super Bowl with them), the Carolina Panthers, and the Seattle Seahawks.

Stark's powerful leg defined his NFL career and his stay with the Colts. For the Colts, Stark booted 985 times, a team record, with a high of 98 during the 1984 season, and four times he punted 10 times during a single game. Stark's punts accounted for 43,162 yards in a Colts uniform, and his career average with the team was 43.8 yards.

The best single-season average Stark recorded punting, also a team record, was 45.9 yards per kick in 1985. A huge amount of 111 of his punts during Stark's stay with the Colts went for touchbacks that opponents could not return. His career-long boot for the Colts was 72 yards on September 23, 1984, at Miami. He also had kicks of 69 yards and 68 yards twice for the Colts.

Almost the entire time Stark spent with the Colts the team fell short of fans' hopes and expectations. When he became a free agent, he signed with the Steelers. "I was an optimist," Stark said of his stay with the Colts. "I felt we were close every year." It was a chance to chase a ring that drove him to sign elsewhere. "When you play in one playoff game in 13 years," Stark said, "that doesn't inspire you to lengthen your career with a team."

INDY COLTS MAKE THEIR FIRST PLAYOFF

It took from 1984 until 1987 for the Colts of Indianapolis to be introduced to the playoffs. More precisely, the very last days of play in 1987, following a 9–6, labor-interrupted regular season under coach Ron Meyer.

The Colts started the season 0–2 but concluded with two victories to capture the AFC Eastern Division. That set up a first-round playoff game against the Cleveland Browns. This marked the Colts' first winning season and playoff berth in 10 years.

It might be said these were happy-to-be-there Colts, with an attitude of "Playoffs at last." It was not a team that had great faith it could march to the Super Bowl. Attendance for the playoff game was 78,586 at Cleveland's vast Municipal Stadium in a community used to gridiron success but which had been denied that for a while.

The Browns took a 7–0 lead in the AFC divisional contest when Ernest Byner scored on a 10-yard pass from Bernie Kosar. The Colts shrugged off the first strike and fought back in the first quarter. Jack Trudeau, the former Ohio State quarterback, was the signal-caller for the Colts, and he brought Indianapolis right back.

Trudeau, who fended off the challenge at the position from Gary Hogeboom, hit tight end Pat Beach for a two-yard touchdown, and Cary Blanchard kicked the extra point to make it 7–7. The same pattern followed in the second quarter. The Browns scored on a 39-yard touchdown pass, but the Colts rebounded with a 19-yard score on a throw from Trudeau to halfback Eric Dickerson. That made it 14–14 at halftime.

Whatever the Browns talked about in the locker room at intermission, however, paid off. Cleveland notched the only touchdown of the third quarter for a 21–14 lead but kept on scoring into the fourth period. The Browns led 31–14, and interceptions doomed the Colts' comeback, although they did get within 31–21. The clinching score in the 38–21 victory for the Browns came when Frank Minnifield picked off a Trudeau pass and ran it back 48 yards for a score.

The season was over, but general manager Jim Irsay, son of owner Bob, said the organization had to look at the playoff appearance as a steppingstone to better things. "When we got into the playoffs, everyone thought, 'Wow, great!'" he said. "If we didn't go any further, it was OK. Our goals now are a lot further down the road."

They were much further down the road than Irsay envisioned. Another comment Irsay made more or less haunted the team. "The history books are full of teams that were a flash in the pan, that made the playoffs one year and went right back down," he said. As it so happened, the Colts were one of those teams. Indianapolis finished 9–7 the next season but missed out on the playoffs and didn't make it back in until 1995.

Jack Trudeau's helmet goes flying as he is sacked by Al Baker in the fourth quarter of the Browns' 38–21 victory over the Colts in their 1987 AFC playoff game. AP PHOTO

THE JEFF GEORGE "ALMOST" YEARS

Jeff George was seen as a homebred savior when the Colts grabbed him with the No. 1 overall pick in the 1990 draft. It was apparent to Colts management that the team needed restructuring. By the 1990 season Chris Chandler was gone. Jack Trudeau was still around as a backup, but the rookie from the University of Illinois was the starter. George signed a rich contract, in essence receiving the keys to the car before passing driver's education, so there were bound to be some growing pains. "I honestly believe that I'm the guy to take this team to the Super Bowl," George said.

Jim Irsay, vice president and general manager (left), and Ron Meyer, head coach (right), present quarterback Jeff George with his new Indianapolis Colts jersey after George signed his 6-year, $15 million rookie contract—then the richest rookie contract in NFL history—at the Colts facility on April 20, 1990.
DON LARSON/NFL/GETTY IMAGES

Jeff George had raw skill and incredible arm strength but, much to the chagrin of fans in Indianapolis, never made the leap to become a great NFL quarterback. AL MESSERSCHMIDT/GETTY IMAGES

The team obviously shared that view, because George received a six-year, $15 million contract (including a $3.5 million signing bonus), and the Colts figured he could learn all that he needed to know on the field. There was tremendous pressure on the 22-year-old hometown Indiana kid, and although George's arm was mature, it was conceded that his head needed a little bit of work.

In high school, George was the national player of the year. In college, he excelled in the Big Ten. The price the Colts paid for George was a significant one. All-star tackle Chris Hinton and receiver Andre Rison were surrendered for the rights to the first overall draft pick. But the Colts felt it was worth it. After shuffling quarterbacks for years, they wanted a long-term solution.

By the end of the exhibition season in August, George was anointed the starter—and Jack Trudeau was the backup once again. "He's had excellent exposure thus far during the preseason," Ron Meyer said of George. "He just can't do much more than he's already done."

George made his debut September 9, and the Colts lost to Buffalo 26–10. He had his ups and downs throughout his first season, as most rookie quarterbacks do. George coped with a pulled abdominal muscle for a time, and between his injury and the occasional slump, Trudeau was called upon in relief from time to time.

Still, it was clear the Colts were now George's team. It seemed like a perfect match. He had attended Warren Central in Indianapolis and had thrown for more than 8,000 yards in high school. As Meyer put

"I honestly believe that I'm the guy to take this team to the Super Bowl."—Jeff George

Continuing the theme of highly touted prospects who fizzled out in the NFL, the Colts drafted defensive tackle Steve Emtman in 1992.

DON LARSON/GETTY IMAGES

MVP BOOKS COLLECTION

it, George had been playing quarterback most of his life, so the position wasn't new to him, only the level of competition. "This guy has lined up and played quarterback ever since he was old enough to say, 'Hut-hut,'" Meyer said. "I have the utmost confidence he will play very well."

At times George did, particularly in a 34–20 road victory over Cincinnati when he tossed three touchdown passes and did not throw an interception. But when Trudeau got hurt, the Colts did not quite trust George to negotiate the rest of the season on his own. They signed Joe Ferguson, the former Bills standout, to be a backup and mentor to the rookie. Ferguson, then 40, threw only eight passes in a Colts uniform, but he provided a veteran presence to aid George's learning curve.

What George had that no one can coach was a naturally powerful arm. He made throws that other quarterbacks didn't dare attempt, zipping line drives into tight coverage. What he didn't have yet was the experience to know when to make those throws and when to hold off. Yet as a rookie he threw 16 touchdown passes and just 13 interceptions. Most newcomers fare much worse.

There was considerable scrutiny, but George seemed able to handle it pretty well.

"This is every kid's dream," he said of playing in his hometown. He didn't want time on the bench to watch and learn. "I've never had the experience of not playing. That would be tough on me. I came out after my junior year instead of waiting because I felt I could play in the NFL."

There were critics who believed the Colts made a mistake in trading two established starters for the chance to get George in the draft. Among those critics was Eric Dickerson, who thought the team gave up too much to obtain the rookie.

Linebacker Quentin Coryatt pursues the ball during a 1994 game against the Tampa Bay Buccaneers. SCOTT HALLERAN/GETTY IMAGES

There were skeptics because of his high salary, too, and some questioned whether George could stand up to the rigors of the hard-charging NFL defenders who sought to break him in half. The early injury fueled questions about his "toughness," but George shrugged those views off.

"You're going to get your hits and take some big knocks," George said, "and that's just all part of it. I didn't think I had anything to prove. I think my play on the field has shown the people that I am for real, and I hope I'm going to be the player that they want me to be."

The Colts finished 7–9 in 1990 with George at the helm most of the time. It was a solid start for what seemed to be shaping up as an exciting George-Meyer era.

Yet that turned out to be the high point. George demonstrated improvement in his second full season behind center, passing for 2,910 yards and 292 completions but only 10 touchdowns. Of course, it was difficult to throw accurately when he was always on the run, and George was sacked 56 times. For the first time, George was booed in his hometown, although he tried to ignore it.

Fans grew more disenchanted, and George heard about it anytime he made an error. Then he compounded his faltering image problems with the occasional reckless comment. When he was asked why he was booed, George replied, "Because I'm good and I'm good looking." Only Muhammad Ali could have gotten away with a statement like that without inciting the masses.

Dickerson, the meal ticket out of the backfield, was injured and carried just 167 times for 536 yards. Almost impossibly, Indianapolis scored just 143 points in a 16-game season while allowing 381. Injuries, disgruntlement, and shortcomings at other positions all contributed to an unbearable 1–15 record in 1991. Only two of the losses

The Colts were outscored 381–143 in 1990.

were by less than a touchdown, while seven were by two touchdowns or more. The lone accidental victory was recorded in midseason when the Colts beat the New York Jets by a single point, 28–27. But by then Meyer was gone, fired by Irsay after an 0–5 start.

"We're embarrassed," said receiver Jessie Hester of the Colts' record. "We all have a bad taste in our mouths right now, and I hope we never forget the way we feel at this moment." It was a grim autumn in the heartland, particularly because the organization had begun the season feeling it was ripe for a playoff run.

When Irsay canned Meyer, who had just been given a contract extension, he turned to defensive coach Rick Venturi as an interim leader to finish out the season. Venturi coached the last 11 games, winning one, and neither he nor Irsay saw many signs of improvement. Injuries stockpiled, and the season spiraled downward.

The awful season was too much for Eric Dickerson, who continued to complain about the trade that had enabled the Colts to choose George. Dickerson's production had declined over the previous few seasons, and after the final game in 1991, Dickerson told anyone who would listen that he had played his last game for the Colts. He was right. That offseason, the Colts traded him to the Oakland Raiders for two draft picks.

One reward for being the worst team in the league—the only reward, really—is the No. 1 overall pick in the annual draft. The Colts decided that the best player for them was Steve Emtman, the gargantuan, aggressive, accomplished defensive end who had played for the University of Washington in the Pac-10. Emtman was so admired by award-givers during his last year at UW that he had to fight them off like offensive linemen. He won both the Outland Trophy and the Vince Lombardi

Rick Venturi was an unfortunate stopgap when the Colts fired head coach Ron Meyer in the middle of the 1991 season. DON LARSON/GETTY IMAGES

Award, which for a defensive lineman is a little bit like winning two Heismans. Emtman stood 6-foot-4 and was 293 pounds of muscle. Sculptors planning future trophies for big guys could have used his body as a model.

Although he received less fanfare, linebacker Quentin Coryatt was also selected in the first round by the Colts. Born in the Virgin Islands, Coryatt had been a star at Texas A&M. Bang, bang, rapid-fire, the Colts drafted the type of talent they felt was needed to repair their Swiss-cheese defense. Emtman was projected to be the franchise player of the defense, the flip side of the George coin.

There was less of a spotlight on Coryatt, who was a solid player from 1992 to 1998 before leaving as a free agent and signing with the Jacksonville Jaguars. But the spotlight was on Emtman from the start. He discovered quickly that he was expected to be a big-time player immediately.

The price for the rights to draft George with the first overall pick was steep—the Colts surrendered center Chris Hinton and receiver Andre Rison. (LEFT) AL MESSERSCHMIDT/GETTY IMAGES; (ABOVE) ALLSPORT/GETTY IMAGES

"I think the pressure is the hardest thing for me," Emtman said after his first exhibition game, upon realizing he was not going to be allowed to make mistakes like a regular rookie without half the planet noticing. "I try not to put pressure on. I just try to be myself and play the game."

Of course, up until then, being himself had meant disrupting offenses like a one-man wrecking crew.

Emtman's last Huskie team finished 12–0 during the same season the Colts finished 1–15. Emtman's friends hoped he wouldn't be selected by the Colts, a team the world saw as going nowhere fast.

"Everyone said a lot of bad things about the franchise," Emtman said of the cynics. "I haven't seen anything that upset me or made me unhappy. It looks to me that if there were bad things, everyone is headed in the right direction."

MARCHIBRODA TRIES AGAIN

Rarely do coaches get second chances in their careers, but the Colts' new coach for the 1992 season was a familiar face—Ted Marchibroda.

When the Colts brought Ted Marchibroda back for his second stint with the team, they probably didn't expect him to favor Jack Trudeau (opposite) over Jeff George. (ABOVE) AL MESSERSCHMIDT/GETTY IMAGES; (OPPOSITE) MITCHELL LAYTON/GETTY IMAGES

Marchibroda, a quarterback for the Pittsburgh Steelers and Chicago Cardinals in the 1950s, had coached the Colts between 1975 and 1979, when the team was still in Baltimore. At his welcome-back-to-the-Colts press conference in Indianapolis, Marchibroda mistakenly said he was glad to be back in Baltimore…oops.

His brain lock might have indicated he didn't know what city he was in, but Marchibroda assuredly knew what team he had signed on with. "It was great to return to the Colts," he said. "I have always wanted to come back since I was first head coach here. Here is tremendous pride in the Colts horseshoe, and I have always felt I was part of a great organization."

Marchibroda was old school but was not regarded as the same kind of disciplinarian as Frank Kush. His background indicated that he would be a good fit for tutoring Jeff George into prominence, but their personalities never meshed. Compared to the nightmare 1991 season, however, the initial pairing of Marchibroda and George and the rehabilitation of the team had the makings of a love fest.

There was considerable preseason talk of how the linking of Marchibroda and George was bound to pay big dividends, though the young quarterback was going to be asked to master a new format, the no-huddle offense.

"Jeff is adjusting very well," Marchibroda said. "He's grasping the offense, and he's showing that he can apply it. I know that Jeff is a football guy. He wants to be an outstanding quarterback in this league. He's absorbed everything that we said."

Well, maybe not everything. George threw seven touchdown passes and 15 interceptions that season, and good old Jack Trudeau once again saw his share of time under center. The Colts managed to recover from the ugly 1–15 season by posting a 9–7 record under Marchibroda in 1992. From a distance it looked miraculous, and the Colts finished the season on a five-game winning streak.

Trudeau always managed to insert himself into the equation. The Colts kept seeking out fresh contenders to be the No. 1 quarterback, but Trudeau kept getting his snaps. He didn't have the natural gifts of a gunslinging quarterback, though. Given ample opportunities to sink his claws into the starting job permanently, Trudeau repeatedly cemented his mediocrity.

With George in the picture and Marchibroda coming back as coach, the overall sense was that those two would become tighter than a high school couple on the dance floor. The unforeseen development was that George and Marchibroda didn't hit it off—but Trudeau and Marchibroda certainly did.

Marchibroda, said Trudeau, was "a fatherly kind of guy. I haven't seen anybody who's like him, really. He's somebody you can joke with a little bit, but he doesn't B.S. you."

Marchibroda demonstrated that he wasn't going to have unlimited patience with George. When the quarterback made enough mistakes in a given game, Marchibroda went to the bench, summoning Trudeau in relief.

George did not take this well. He mouthed off about the circumstances, and it seemed to create a permanent schism between player and coach. George was a no-show at the start of the next training camp, and it wasn't even clear why he wasn't present at first. He stayed away for 36 days and began lobbying for a trade.

As for Steve Emtman, his preseason prediction seemed validated in the team's 9–7 record, but if the team was headed in the right direction, it wasn't because of him. After signing a four-year, $9.1 million contract with the Colts, Emtman made it through only the first nine games of his rookie year before a torn ligament in his left knee sidelined him for the rest of the season.

After rehabbing and fighting his way back into playing shape, Emtman's second season ended in the fifth game when he tore a ligament in his right knee. Emtman spent more time in doctors' offices than he did on the field, and although he didn't give up, the Colts gave up on him. He eventually retired as a member of the Washington Redskins in 1997, never reaching his football potential.

The way the 1993 season went, it was unclear if Marchibroda had coached his last game for the Colts. They finished

The positive side of losing so many games is draft position, and the Colts had their fair share of coveted picks in the 1980s and 1990s. Bill Tobin and Jim Irsay made the most of their 1994 pick when they drafted Marshall Faulk, a future Hall of Famer from San Diego State.

(ABOVE) GETTY IMAGES; (LEFT) AL MESSERSCHMIDT/GETTY IMAGES

4–12, and once again the biggest problem was that the team couldn't find the end zone with a map and compass. There was no reliable featured running back, the Colts were out-scored 378–189, and despite a 57.5 completion percentage, George found the end zone just eight times. Reggie Langhorne was an unexpected bright spot, coming from little Elizabeth City State to catch 85 passes.

After the last down was played in that disappointing season, management adjourned to the front office for debates. What must be done to right the ship? The decision was made to jettison George. After four years with the team, he hadn't proven to be the leader the Colts had hoped for.

Distressed by the backsliding to 4–12 in 1993, Robert Irsay made some major moves to buttress the team's administration. This marked a change in philosophy. Young Jim Irsay, the owner's son, had been general manager for more than three years, but his father made the call to shake things up and import someone from outside the organization to focus on football matters only. Bill Tobin, who had known success with the Chicago Bears, was brought in as a vice president with de facto general manager powers, and his brother Vince, another ex-Bears figure, came along as defensive coordinator.

"I'm not dissatisfied with Jimmy at all," Robert Irsay said. "We made a mistake by not surrounding him with the type of talent that Bill Tobin brings. Tobin has a complete knowledge of the football business."

Marshall Faulk runs with the football during his first NFL game, on September 4, 1994, at the Hoosier Dome. JOE ROBBINS/GETTY IMAGES

"Who the hell is Mel Kiper anyway? . . . . [T]o my knowledge, he's never put on a jockstrap, and now he's an expert."—Colts Vice President Bill Tobin

Before the 1994 season began, George was exiled to the Atlanta Falcons, the same team with which the Colts made the unpopular deal to obtain his draft rights. This deal was not nearly as unpopular. Tobin made it clear that George made himself expendable by his behavior. "We had no assurance Jeff was going to show up this year," he said.

It was not clear if he meant physically for training camp or mentally on the field, but it was all the same to him. Tobin felt George had demonstrated his unreliability the year before when he missed more than a month of training camp. George had to go, and the Colts had to start over again.

Tobin had a good reputation for getting the most out of the annual player draft, and he immediately proved his savvy when he spent the Colts' first pick on Marshall Faulk, the future Hall of Fame running back. He also selected linebacker Trev Alberts of Nebraska with an additional first-round choice. Tobin passed on quarterback Trent Dilfer because he thought others would come through. That decision earned him ridicule from television draft guru Mel Kiper, who said moves like that were what caused the Colts to be "the laughingstock of the league."

The criticism infuriated Tobin, and he declared, "Who the hell is Mel Kiper anyway? . . . . [T]o my knowledge, he's never put on a jockstrap, and now he's an expert."

Trev Alberts, another 1994 draft pick, won the Dick Butkus award while playing for the University of Nebraska in 1993. JAMIE SQUIRE/ALLSPORT/GETTY IMAGES

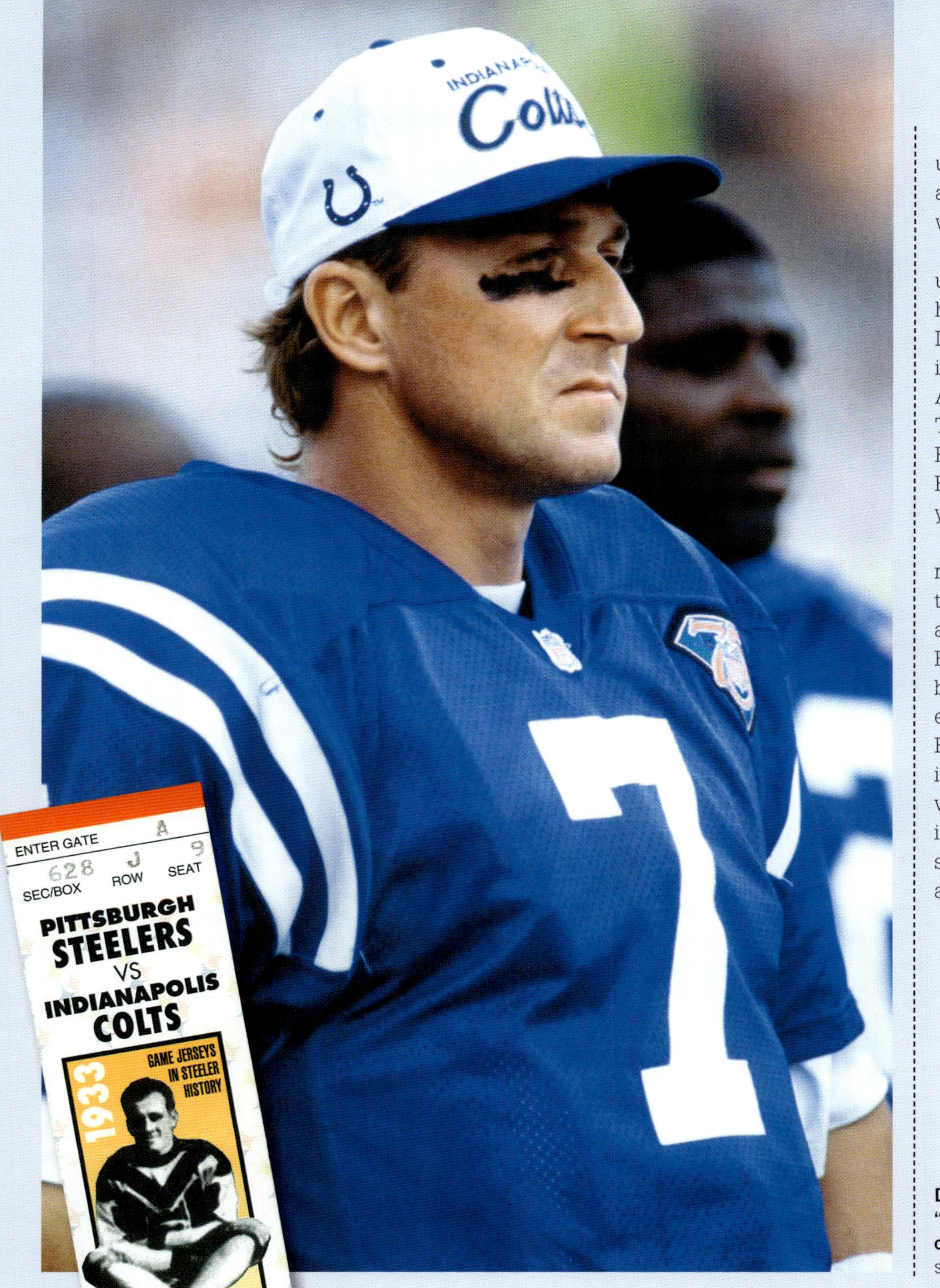

MVP BOOKS COLLECTION

Regardless of his choice of undergarments, Kiper is still considered an expert on the NFL draft, even if he was wrong about Tobin.

It was Marchibroda who was under the most pressure to succeed, and he did itso, in relative terms, by leading Indianapolis to an 8–8 record, a four-game improvement on the previous campaign. And he did without a marquee quarterback. The duties were split between Jim Harbaugh, acquired from the Chicago Bears, and Don Majkowski, whose best years were with the Green Bay Packers.

The "Majik Man" had an incredible rookie season for the Packers in 1989, throwing for 27 touchdowns, 4,318 yards, and 353 completions on his way to the Pro Bowl. Injured the next year, Majkowski bounced back, was injured yet again, and eventually replaced by a virtual unknown—Brett Favre. That was the end for Majkowski in Green Bay. Though Harbaugh had some verbal battles with coach Mike Ditka in Chicago, sharing the QB role went surprisingly well in Indianapolis in 1994—at least at first.

Don Majkowski couldn't summon the same "majik" in a Colts uniform that he'd pulled off earlier in his career in Green Bay.
SCOTT HALLERAN/ALLSPORT/GETTY IMAGES

JEFF GEORGE

Shoulda Coulda Woulda

When it came to pure talent, football people loved Jeff George. He could throw the ball so deep the fastest receivers couldn't outrun his arm. He was a rocket man in the pocket, and when the Colts acquired him with their No. 1 draft pick in 1990, they believed they had someone special.

In some ways, George had one of the most controversial, episodic, and inconsistent careers of any high-level quarterback. One minute he seemed on the verge of becoming a perpetual all-pro; the next minute coaches wanted to bench him. He was great sometimes, good often, and bad at inconvenient moments.

Originally from Indianapolis, where he threw for 8,100 yards at Warren Central High School, he was a one-year player at Purdue before transferring to the University of Illinois. George also had the chance with the Colts to capitalize on hometown goodwill. He never could quite do it.

In some ways the rockiness of George's 17-season journey through the NFL with eight teams was on display his rookie year with the Colts in the autumn of 1990. George looked very much like a rookie in his first exhibition game, heaving two interceptions. But coach Ron Meyer was committed to him.

The Colts traded up in the draft with the Atlanta Falcons to obtain the chance to pick George. They paid a big price, including receiver Andre Rison and tackle Chris Hinton, both Pro Bowl players, and two draft choices. George generated that type of buzz and notoriety by flinging a ball 81 yards in the air at the scouting combine.

"I think that's the one that made me the No. 1 pick," George said.

He had decided to leave Illinois after his junior year at a time when few players did, so the attention-getting heave gained him extra attention. There was considerable speculation that George would become the starter right from the outset of his rookie year, but the Colts did not announce that until closer to opening day. "Jeff George did not come here to sit on the bench," coach Ron Meyer said. "We did not make the trade to put him on the bench."

George started the first regular-season game of his career but took a hit so hard from Buffalo linebacker Cornelius Bennett that he could not finish the game. Then, before the end of September, a pulled muscle benched George for three-plus games. The 6-foot-4, 218-pound thrower was less upset than fans were and said he benefited from his time spent roaming the sidelines during games. It enhanced his quarterback education, he said. It might have made sense for the Colts not to toss George into the starting lineup immediately from the way he sounded. "I'm learning more each week," he said of that period on the bench. "Now I'm to the point where I'm recognizing the defenses and the disguising that goes along with that. And I feel like a veteran, really, when I'm out there because I'm making the proper checks and the proper reads."

After the team's 0–3 start and George's crisis, the Colts began to move and improve. The team finished 7–9, and George completed 54.2 percent of his passes for 16 touchdowns. He was sacked 37 times but threw three more TDs than interceptions.

Jeff George prepares to unleash a pass against the Raiders in 1991. DON LARSON/GETTY IMAGES

There was plenty of pressure on George stemming from the expensive nature of the trade, from being tossed in as the starter, and from performing under the shadow of a $15.5 million long-term contract. At the time it was the largest rookie contract in league history. "Jeff has done everything we had hoped for, and in some areas he has exceeded our expectations," said Jim Irsay, then the Colts' general manager.

George was pretty excited in those early days with the Colts, too. He had a nice fantasy going in his mind. "This is every kid's dream," he said. "The hometown boy leads his team to the Super Bowl." If only. The Colts were atrocious in 1991, and though they improved some in 1992 and 1993, George's time was up. There was not a fairy-tale ending to the Jeff George era in Indianapolis.

FAULK TO THE RESCUE

Almost from the first handoff he took in the pros, Marshall Faulk displayed his Hall of Fame destiny. The biggest reason for the Colts' spike in scoring in 1994—the offensive and defensive points were roughly equal—had little to do with who was playing quarterback and everything to do with the arrival of Faulk in the backfield. Faulk rushed for 1,282 yards and caught 52 passes as a rookie. Not that this should have been a major surprise after his spectacular career at San Diego State. In one game for the Aztecs, Faulk rushed for 386 yards and scored seven touchdowns.

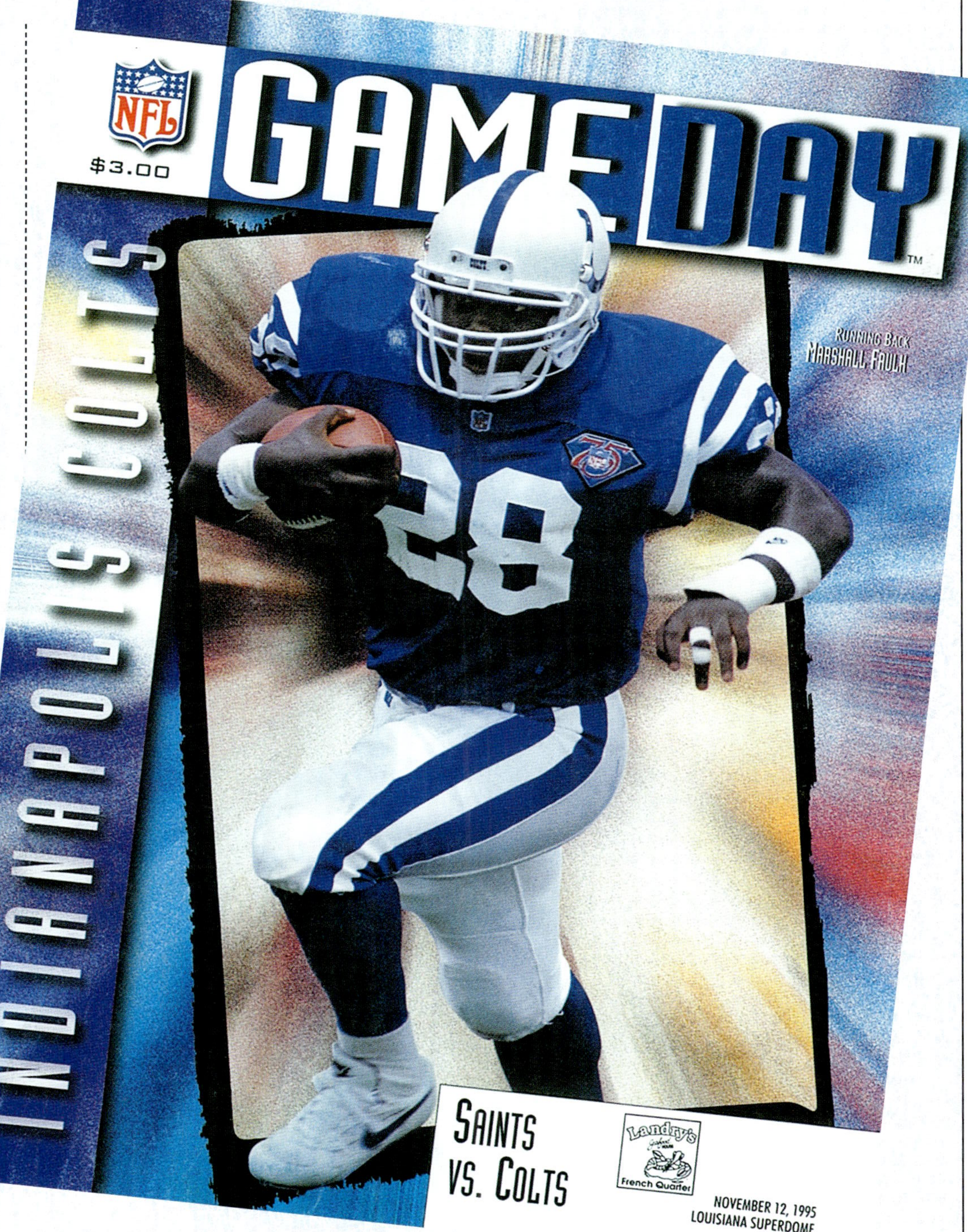

MVP BOOKS COLLECTION

At 5-foot-11 and 210 pounds, Faulk would be a seven-time Pro Bowl selection and was chosen for the Pro Football Hall of Fame in 2011. He rushed for 12,279 yards and scored 136 touchdowns in a career that lasted until 2006.

The Colts picked Faulk second overall in the 1994 draft to form the basis of a new running game and locked him up with a seven-year, $17.2 million contract, plus a $5.1 million signing bonus. It didn't matter how many millions Faulk earned. At the time that was the richest rookie contract ever, but he turned out to be a priceless acquisition, winning honors as Rookie of the Year.

About a month into Faulk's pro career he was gaining attention from media outlets such as *Pro Football Weekly*, which ran the following headline about the running back: "Colts' Faulk already earning rave reviews."

Faulk was a dominant player in college, and his mindset was to be the same kind of dominant player in the NFL. "At San Diego State," he said, "they put me on a pedestal, asked me to perform and pull them out of jams. I did that. At Indianapolis, I hope I can do the same for them."

Faulk told reporters that his determination came from following the example of his single mother who raised him and five siblings. She was his role model, he said. Almost immediately, Faulk demonstrated that he could be the same type of beacon for the Colts as he had been for San Diego State. Ted Marchibroda was certainly impressed right off the bat. "He is as good as I've seen," the Colts coach said. "I really think that the sky is the limit for Marshall."

Faulk turned out to be a workhorse back who had the speed to run outside, the vision to spot holes, and just enough power to

Marshall Faulk tries to stay inbounds as he is pushed by New York Jets cornerback Jerome Henderson during a 1998 game in Indianapolis. The first down set up a Colts field goal. AP PHOTO/CHUCK ROBINSON

Faulk out-runs Oakland Raiders defensive back Derrick Hoskins during a 1995 game in Oakland. AP PHOTO/AL GOLUB

fight his way past the first swarm of tacklers—not to mention the good hands necessary to catch passes coming out of the backfield. By word and action Faulk also made it clear that he liked getting the ball a lot. A team that didn't want to put the ball into Faulk's hands frequently would have been foolish.

"The first five or 10 carries are like a warm-up period," Faulk said. "After that, you're just getting into it."

After all was said and done, it was determined that he had accounted for 40 percent of the Colts' offense in his rookie season. The team went 8–8, and Faulk was modest when informed he had been chosen as the league's top rookie.

"It wasn't just me," Faulk said. "There were a lot of guys who did a lot of work. Eight-and-eight is not a season I'd like to be proud of, but it's a turnaround, a starting point."

It was that. The wins total was four games better than the 1993 season, and once again it looked as if the Colts had made the right move and could be playoff-bound soon. That fond wish soon came true as Indianapolis rallied at the end of the 1995 season to finish 9–7 and claim an American Football Conference wild card berth in the playoffs.

Defeating the New England Patriots 10–7 on the last day of the regular season clinched the playoff spot for the Colts. "It hasn't been easy getting into the playoffs," said Marchibroda, perhaps thinking of his need to juggle quarterbacks throughout the season. "Maybe it's so sweet because of the obstacles we've had to overcome to get here. We're on the right road now. [The team) knows how to win. They now know what it takes."

Faulk was hugely productive again with 1,078 yards rushing and 56 catches, but the emergence of Jim Harbaugh at quarterback gave the entire offense a major lift. And for the first time since 1988, the defense held opponents to fewer points than the offense collected.

Marshall Faulk was a seven-time Pro Bowl selection and was chosen for the Pro Football Hall of Fame in 2011. He rushed for 12,279 yards and scored 136 touchdowns in a career that lasted until 2006.

MARSHALL FAULK COULD DO IT ALL

Marshall Faulk was exactly what the Colts needed. When drafted second overall in the NFL in 1994, he became an instant star in Indianapolis, a transforming player who energized the offense by running and catching passes. From the moment he pulled on the horseshoe helmet he was The Man for the Colts, a throwback to the days of Lenny Moore, another great who could do anything coming out of the backfield.

The 5-foot-10, 210-pound Faulk, who grew up in New Orleans and then played in the sunshine at San Diego State, immediately sparked a previously moribund offense. He quickly proved capable of rushing for more than 1,000 yards on the ground and catching 50 passes per year. He was awarded the NFL's offensive rookie of the year award and was the Most Valuable Player in the Pro Bowl his first season. "He's bad. Bad to the bone," said Hall of Fame runner Tony Dorsett, upon watching Faulk.

The Pro Bowl showing opened a lot of eyes. Against the best in the league, Faulk rushed for 180 yards. The funny thing was a day before the game in an interview Faulk said, "I'm not here to showcase myself." He was indicating he had proven his ability already during the regular season. Then, sure enough, he went out and showcased himself.

Faulk did not grow up in luxury, indeed living in a housing project in a ghetto as a youth. He knew that had he not been noticed for his football ability, he might still be living in trying circumstances in the old neighborhood back in New Orleans. "I think about some of my friends who are still there," Faulk said, "and some of my friends who were killed there. I say to myself, 'I made it. I was one of the lucky ones to make it out.'"

And it did take some good fortune. As a youngster, Faulk was a neighborhood troublemaker, getting suspended from school on several occasions. But the guidance of Wayne Reese, his high school coach at George Washington Carver, steered him onto a better path. Reese told him that he could write a better ending for his life if he worked hard in school and that his athletic ability could earn him a college scholarship.

"Football changed my future," Faulk said. "It was something I really wanted to do. And in order to play football I had to go to school. Coach Reese taught me football, but he also taught me how to act. He straightened me out."

Although Faulk wasn't recruited as heavily as his ability might lead one to believe, he did have some choices. However, some of the schools would not commit to using him as a

Marshall Faulk cuts upfield during a game against the Baltimore Ravens in November 1998. SCOTT HALLERAN/ALLSPORT/GETTY IMAGES

Faulk had an incredible ability to change his speed and direction with little notice. The Hall of Famer was also a significant threat catching passes out of the backfield. DON LARSON/NFL/GETTY IMAGES

running back. Their vision was limited. The promise that he could stick with his favorite position was one reason he selected San Diego State. "I didn't know if I was going to be really good playing football," he said. "But I knew if I was going to play football . . . that I was going to play the position where I was happy, running back."

Faulk indulged a bit after he signed a multi-year, multi-million-dollar contract with the Colts, buying 11 cars (some for others) during his first two years in the pros. He was fearless on the field, enduring the bashings and bruisings that double-wide defensive linemen dished out, but off the field he enjoyed manicures.

If these choices seemed flashy, Faulk did not play that role in his sport. He was a joy to watch as he wiggled past tacklers, and he drew raves from his first weeks in the league on. He likely appreciated the honors that quickly began accruing, but he downplayed their value, saying they would mean more to him when his team began winning more.

Faulk seemed possessed of a preternatural calm. Whereas there are legends about some star athletes being so on edge before competition that they throw up, Faulk's reputation is of a man so cool that in the minutes before leaving the locker room he appeared on the verge of falling asleep. He relaxed and conserved energy for the explosions to come.

It didn't take long for teammates to realize they had been blessed with a special talent. Faulk said even in his rookie year linemen in the huddle were urging him to take charge, to make the big plays. They kept telling him they needed him to step up. The Colts had had an invisible running game for a while and certainly did need Faulk. Without Faulk, the Colts were 4–12 in 1993. With him in 1994, they improved to 8–8. Not that he was content with such a pedestrian record. "I watched the Colts on TV the year before, and each week they were getting blown out," he said. "This year we were . . . 8–8, but you can't be satisfied with that because a couple of plays and we're a better team."

At that point it seemed obvious Faulk was going to make the Colts a better team and that the franchise was focused on becoming a better team. For two years in a row after that, Indianapolis finished 9–7. That was a little bit better, and the Colts made the playoffs in both of those years.

Indianapolis coach Ted Marchibroda loved what Faulk brought to his team, and he could see all sorts of possibilities of how the young guy could lead the club. "He's as good as I've seen," Marchibroda said. "I really think the sky is the limit for Marshall." It was.

Unfortunately for the Colts, only part of Faulk's potential was realized in Indianapolis. After a calamitous 3–13 season in 1997, with Marchibroda gone and Lindy Infante in charge, Faulk was traded to the St. Louis Rams for two draft choices. As a centerpiece of an explosive offense, Faulk thrived in St. Louis, filling a starring role on a Super Bowl champion. He retired in 2006 and was elected to the Hall of Fame in 2011.

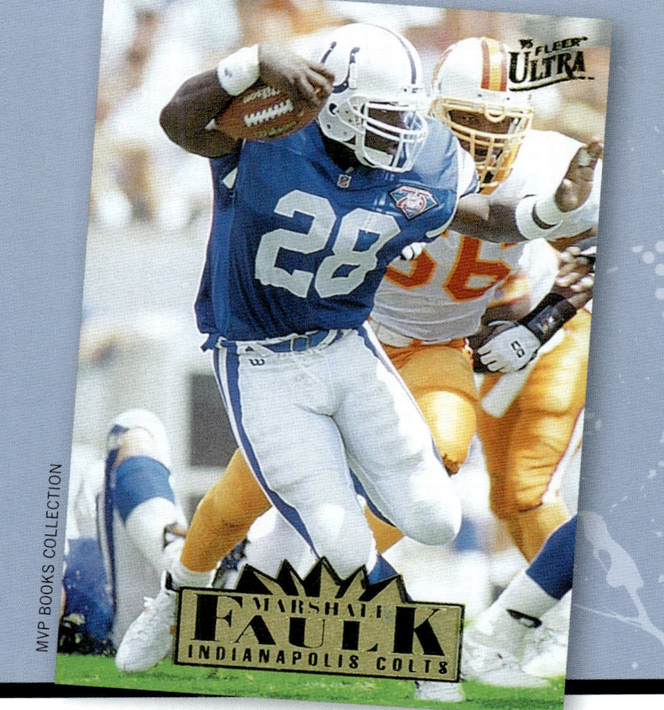

MVP BOOKS COLLECTION

HARBAUGH HAS THE LEADERSHIP TOUCH

The Colts had paid big money to Craig Erickson to become their starting quarterback in 1995, but when he went into a slump and Jim Harbaugh outplayed him, coach Ted Marchibroda had to go with the hot hand. Always a fiery leader, Jim Harbaugh had coveted an opportunity to play full time, and he lifted the Colts to their first truly exciting season since the move to Indianapolis. Harbaugh played a more efficient game that year, with a 63.7 percent pass-completion ratio and 17 touchdowns against only five interceptions.

Fans may have been happy just to see the Colts qualify for the playoffs, but neither Marchibroda nor the players had eaten their fill. Their stomachs hungered for more.

"I've said all along that the playoffs are a wide-open situation," Marchibroda said. "The toughest thing was getting there. Now that we are there, anything can happen."

Coaches utter that kind of phrase all of the time to boost their team's morale. But "anything" did happen as soon as the Colts made it to the postseason. When the Colts met the Chargers in San Diego on December 31, 1995, it was the franchise's first playoff game in seven years and only the club's second since 1977. When the Colts won 35–20, it was the team's first playoff win since 1971.

Most encouragingly, the Colts didn't wilt when Faulk went down with an injury. It would have been easy to become demoralized over the loss of the team's top offensive option. Instead, fullback Zach Crockett, 240 pounds of muscle, took over as the key ground gainer and totaled 147 yards.

"Some people think big guys can't run," Crockett said after the win. "I had to show them I could."

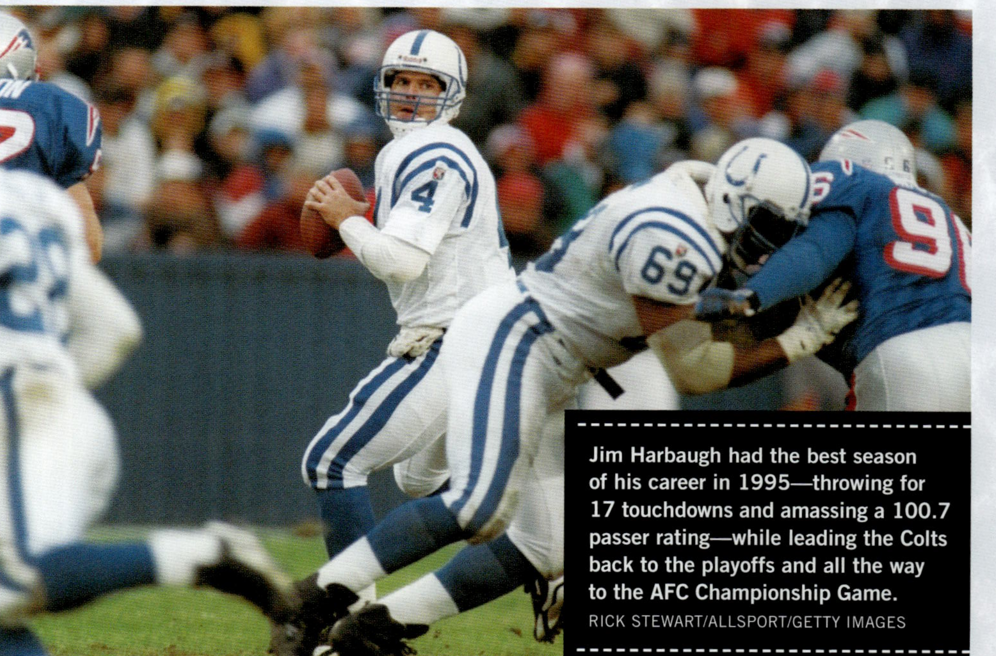

Jim Harbaugh had the best season of his career in 1995—throwing for 17 touchdowns and amassing a 100.7 passer rating—while leading the Colts back to the playoffs and all the way to the AFC Championship Game.
RICK STEWART/ALLSPORT/GETTY IMAGES

The underdogs of the playoffs became the fan darlings. One win wasn't enough. The Colts kept going, and a week later they stifled the favored Kansas City Chiefs before 77,594 fans at Arrowhead Stadium in a hard-fought 10–7 game. Jim Harbaugh was unflappable on offense, but this was the defense's finest hour, its biggest clutch performance in a long time—the Colts intercepted the Chiefs' Steve Bono three times.

Suddenly, the recently ridiculed "Dolts" were one game away from the Super Bowl. The road—and as a wild card team the Colts were on the road every week—passed through Pittsburgh, however. The Steelers have always been tough in the postseason, and virtually nobody thought the Colts would come out of Three Rivers Stadium with a pulse. Some Colts players' pulse rates were going like jackhammers before the kickoff, as they were literally in awe of the chance to play for the AFC Championship.

"I was in a daze for a while," said Colts linebacker Jeff Herrod. "That first series we went out there, and after the starting lineups and all of that I didn't know where I was. I never dreamed I would be in an AFC title game. It was overwhelming."

The result was oh so close. Pittsburgh led 20–16 in the closing minutes of the fourth quarter. A last chance came for Harbaugh, who had been nicknamed "Captain Comeback" for the manner in which he repeatedly led the Colts to come-from-behind victories during the season. The Colts got the ball one more time with the chance to pull off a miraculous win after the Steelers went ahead with a minute and a half remaining.

With little time on the clock and a great distance between them and the goal line, the Colts marched from their own 15-yard line to the Steelers' 29. There was time for one more play. Harbaugh took the hike with five seconds left, faded back, and threw a Hail Mary pass aimed at Aaron Bailey in the end zone. It fell incomplete.

"You can't come any closer than we did to making the Super Bowl," Harbaugh said.

He was right about that. The Colts' feel-good season had ended with one last gutsy, riveting charge.

"They had given us so much," Marchibroda said of his players' commitment. "They had no more. There's no question we got everything they had to give, maybe more. I can't think of one player who didn't play up to expectations."

Harbaugh certainly exceeded any expectations, bringing his team within a few inches of a dynamic upset. "Jim almost did it," Marchibroda said. "It was another Jim Harbaugh game." The trademark of a "Jim Harbaugh game" was playing with blood, sweat, and tears, from the opening kickoff until the final buzzer. Sometimes the result was pulling off a surprise win, but at the least it meant using every ounce of energy trying.

Harbaugh began the season as a bench-warmer, ended it as the NFL Comeback Player of the Year, and was chosen for the Pro Bowl in Hawaii. "More than I ever could have dreamed for," he said of the recognition.

The offseason was equally kind to Harbaugh, who signed a new, multi-million-dollar contract. Then, after meeting country singer Garth Brooks backstage at Madison Square Garden, Harbaugh was shocked when Brooks ripped off his shirt and displayed a Harbaugh jersey underneath. "One of the four or five best nights of my life," Harbaugh recounted.

The season included probably four or five of the best nights in the history of the Colts in Indianapolis, leading everyone—from Marchibroda to his players, to the front office, to the fans—to believe that the squad would be a big winner the next season. They all saw double-digit wins, another trip to the playoffs, and just maybe a Super Bowl in their future.

Running back Zack Crockett celebrates in the end zone after scoring a touchdown in the 1995 AFC Wild Card Game in San Diego. GETTY IMAGES

Blood, sweat, and tears were the trademarks of a Jim Harbaugh football game.

JIM HARBAUGH ALWAYS PLAYED WITH HEART

He was never going to make Colts fans forget Johnny Unitas or even Bert Jones, but Jim Harbaugh possessed the intangibles of a winner and the hard-nosed competitiveness of a football lifer. With the right supporting cast, he proved the Colts could be winners, too.

Jim Harbaugh grew up in a football family. His dad, Jack, was a coach, and his brother John became one, too. Harbaugh starred at the University of Michigan, where he was an All-American and held the NCAA Division I passing efficiency record for 12 years. He was a first-round draft pick of the Chicago Bears in 1987.

Harbaugh had up-and-down times with the Bears, including one year passing for 3,121 yards. But he and coach Mike Ditka had some sticky moments, and after seven seasons in Chicago, Harbaugh joined the Colts in 1994 for a $200,000 signing bonus and a $700,000 salary. Later, Ditka issued a glorious review of Harbaugh that might have surprised fans. "Jim Harbaugh personifies what an NFL player should be," Ditka said. "He's got more character, class, and heart than anybody can imagine."

Harbaugh was Indianapolis' field leader from 1994 to 1997, and his fire and outgoing personality provided an intense brand of leadership. He was a team guy first, with nimble feet and an ability to throw on the run. More than anything, he was a quarterback who could inspire teammates.

With Harbaugh at the controls, the Colts never seemed to be out of games, even if they trailed in the fourth quarter. Harbaugh earned the nickname "Captain Comeback" for his heroics during the 1995 season. The trend began on October 8, after the Colts trailed Miami 24–3 in the first half and appeared doomed. Harbaugh led Indianapolis on drive after drive, throwing one touchdown in the third period and two more in the fourth and leading the Colts to a 27–24 victory determined by an overtime field goal.

Just a week later Harbaugh guided the Colts to a fourth-quarter comeback in an 18–17 win over the San Francisco 49ers, a game also won by a field goal. In the last game of the regular season the Colts drove for the winning score in a 10–7 triumph over the New England Patriots. That game clinched a 9–7 record and sent the Colts into the playoffs. Harbaugh

Jim Harbaugh brought a toughness and competitive fire to the Colts offense, displaying a genuine sense of leadership. AL BELLO/ALLSPORT

Harbaugh throws downfield during the Colts' 25–24 victory over the Dallas Cowboys at Texas Stadium in 1996. BRIAN BAHR/GETTY IMAGES

engineered a playoff run that included victories over the San Diego Chargers and Kansas City Chiefs, plus a near-upset of the Pittsburgh Steelers.

The Steelers won 20–16 before Harbaugh ran out of magic, his final pass falling dead on an end zone Hail Mary from the 29-yard line. And Harbaugh hadn't even been the starting QB at the beginning of the season, trailing Craig Erickson on the depth chart. That was nothing new for Harbaugh, who had to scrape for everything he got after high school. He applied to many major football schools and remembered Notre Dame's form-letter rejection.

"When they started off, 'Dear Mike Harbaugh,'" Harbaugh said, "I knew it was all over."

Back-to-back 9–7 seasons in 1995 and 1996 made Colts fans believe they were just one small step away from being a playoff team. The Colts slapped its franchise player tag on Harbaugh and paid him $4 million for 1997. Fans may have thought Indianapolis was an inch from the playoffs, but preseason analysts disagreed. They didn't think the team would improve at all, which irked Harbaugh. "I hope our underdog era is finished," Harbaugh said, "because when people call us an underdog or Cinderella, that tells me they still think we're really not that good."

The football observers, not Harbaugh, were right about Indianapolis that year. The 1997 Colts finished 3–13. Harbaugh was sacked 41 times during the season but still hit 61.2 percent of his passes and threw only four interceptions while running the offense about two-thirds of the time. He also cemented his reputation as a quarterback who could scramble, rushing for 205 yards and averaging 5.7 yards per carry. Still, criticism of Harbaugh grew. "No matter who you are, you're going to hear it all in this league," the quarterback noted.

The 6-foot-3, 215-pound Harbaugh had a feisty outlook. He'd been taken for granted too often over the years and was in no mood to take guff from anyone on the field. During the 1997 season Harbaugh famously tangled with retired Buffalo Bills quarterback Jim Kelly. At the time the Hall of Famer was a broadcaster, and his on-air commentary labeled Harbaugh "a baby" for not playing through injuries more. Harbaugh, whom most considered a tough guy, was infuriated, and he and Kelly met to discuss the matter. The meeting ended with Harbaugh breaking a bone in his right hand when he punched Kelly in the head. Probably Harbaugh's biggest punishment stemming from the incident was being forced to sit down because of the hand injury.

Some quarterbacks make scouts drool and make fans "ooh" and "ahh" because of their picturesque form. Harbaugh was not as stylish and knew it. But he did have the savvy to make things happen. He understood that the marquee names in the NFL at his position looked as if they knew what they were doing more than he did because of superior form.

"I don't have the big arm like [Dan] Marino, [Troy] Aikman, or [Drew] Bledsoe," Harbaugh told a Chicago writer in 1995. "I don't have the ability to read coverages like a Steve Young. It's not how I envision what I want it to look like when I watch film. It looks kind of ugly. Half the time I'm scrambling or stumbling for a first down."

Still, Harbaugh got those first downs. Time was up for him in Indianapolis, however, after the 1997 disastrous finish, and he was traded to the Baltimore Ravens. In 2011, after a successful tenure at Stanford, he became head coach of the San Francisco 49ers.

MVP BOOKS COLLECTION

AT LAST

A Playoff Win for Indianapolis

Nothing quenches a fan's thirst like a playoff victory.

As thrilled as Indianapolis fans were to gain their very own National Football League franchise in 1984, and although they had a one-and-done appearance in the 1988 playoffs, by the mid-1990s those fans were definitely itching for another playoff team. That breakthrough finally occurred in 1995 when the Colts finished 9–7 under coach Ted Marchibroda and faced the San Diego Chargers in California. Many analysts felt the Colts were lucky to make the playoffs, and virtually no one picked them to defeat the Chargers. San Diego was only one year removed from a Super Bowl appearance. "We wouldn't mind at all being this year's Cinderella story," Marchibroda said.

Only 12 Colts on the 53-man roster had ever competed in a playoff game, so between their average winning record and lack of postseason experience, the glass slipper might well have been a good fit from the get-go.

1995 AFC WILD CARD GAME

INDIANAPOLIS COLTS 35 — **SAN DIEGO CHARGERS** 20

	1	2	3	4	Total
INDIANAPOLIS COLTS	0	14	7	14	35
SAN DIEGO CHARGERS	3	7	7	3	20

Before 61,182 fans on December 31, 1995, the Colts took on the hosts in the American Football Conference Wild Card Game. Beating the odds, Indianapolis upset San Diego 35–20, marking the club's first playoff win since 1971. Nearly a quarter of a century had passed since the Colts had put a W in the postseason victory column, and Indianapolis had suffered about as long as Baltimore had.

It was a season that began with the demotion of Jim Harbaugh at quarterback in favor of newcomer Craig Erickson, who was paid $2 million to take the Colts' controls. However, Erickson did not play particularly well, and each time Harbaugh got the call off the bench, he brought Indianapolis back. That year he earned the nickname "Captain Comeback."

Whenever Marchibroda inserted Harbaugh, he ordered him to "Let 'er rip." That became the team mantra, and Harbaugh had one of his finest seasons, completing 63.7 percent of his passes and being selected to play in the Pro Bowl. He was also named as Comeback Player of the Year and AFC Player of the Year.

The favored Chargers led 3–0 after the first quarter on a John Carney 54-yard field goal, but it was 14–10 Indianapolis at the half and 21–17 after three quarters. In crunch time, the fourth quarter, the Colts out-scored San Diego 14–3. Harbaugh threw two touchdown passes and the Colts received a shocking performance from rookie running back Zach Crockett. Subbing for the injured Marshall Faulk, Crockett rushed for 147 yards and two touchdowns. On a 33-yard score, Crockett compared the size of the hole his offensive line made to "the parting of the Red Sea. Once I got to the end zone, it was like a dream come true."

Rookie runner Zack Crockett made up for a quiet regular season when he led the Colts to their first playoff win since moving to Indianapolis.
AP PHOTO/LENNY IGNELZI

LINDY INFANTE

Offensive Guru

It was his offensive mind that made Lindy Infante attractive to the team's brain trust when it made him the new head coach of the Indianapolis Colts in 1996. It was his second chance at running an NFL team, and officials believed his tenure would be a success. Infante had been the boss of the Green Bay Packers from 1988 to 1991, and it hadn't gone that well. Overall, Green Bay was 24–40 during his four seasons in command. The Packers posted a 10–6 record under his watch in 1989, but he was fired after a 4–12 record in '91.

Infante made his reputation as offensive coordinator of the Cincinnati Bengals when the team won the AFC crown and played in Super Bowl XVI in 1982. That culminated Infante's long apprenticeship as an assistant coach at the high school, college, and pro levels. As a player he starred on the field for the University of Florida.

Before Infante got his break with the Packers, he was the head coach of the Jacksonville Bulls of the United States Football League, which went out of business after two years. The team was so-so on the field but attracted 46,000 fans per game, showing the world that the city deserved an NFL franchise. And Infante benefited from running his own professional program. "I firmly believe if I didn't have the head coaching experience in Jacksonville, I would have never been a head coach in the NFL," Infante said.

Infante, who had been offensive coordinator, succeeded Ted Marchibroda's second stint as coach of the Colts, and Indianapolis fared pretty well that season, finishing 9–7 with Jim Harbaugh at quarterback and Marshall Faulk in the backfield (although he was not healthy the whole year).

Regarded as something of an offensive genius, Infante installed a complex system. The Colts showed flashes, opening the season with four straight wins and putting together a three-game winning streak in the middle of the year. But they were inconsistent. The offense definitely worked better than the defense, with that side of the ball allowing more points than the offense scored. Infante was convinced that as soon as the Colts adapted to his methods they would succeed.

"I think it's like learning a new language," he said. "If you grew up in the English language and then were asked to learn Spanish, it would seem very complicated. But once you get the system of it, then it becomes easy to retain, easy to change, easy to manipulate, and easy to move forward with."

Lindy Infante's offensive genius wasn't enough to make him successful as a head coach in Indianapolis. AL MESSERSCHMIDT/GETTY IMAGES

For a season of growing pains, 9–7 wasn't bad. But, in retrospect, one Infante comment seems almost delusional: "I think our defense is the strong suit on our football team, and we work pretty hard in several areas to try and make their job easier," Infante said. Oops.

The Colts' hierarchy expected steady improvement, and that did not follow. The next year, 1997, the Colts finished 3–13. They still scored with great frequency but allowed even more points, 401, so nothing could save Infante. He was ousted and never again rose to the level of head coach in the NFL.

IRSAY THE ELDER TURNS OVER REINS TO IRSAY THE YOUNGER

There was one major exception to the upbeat mood at Colts headquarters following the high-achieving 1995 season. On November 29, 1995, owner Robert Irsay, 73 at the time, suffered a stroke that partially paralyzed and incapacitated him. A few months later, in April 1996, after showing limited improvement, the father passed responsibility for the team on to his son Jim, then 36.

The Irsays were the only prominent individuals close to the Colts that couldn't completely enjoy the playoff run. "It's been bittersweet," Jim Irsay said. "It's been a period of tremendous growth for me. With dad being incapacitated and incompetent, the machinery kicked into place for me to assume the leadership of the team. That was always his wishes."

Often in pro sports the difference of a few days can be the difference between night and day, proof that nothing ever stays the same with a team. In what seemed unfathomable to Colts fans most close to the team, a huge offseason change awaited after the 1995 joy ride.

On February 1, shortly after the end of the playoffs in early 1996, coach Ted Marchibroda's contract expired. "No-brainer, give him a new one," most thought. But negotiations didn't go smoothly. The Colts' administration offered a one-year, $600,000 contract. Marchibroda felt he deserved a two-year contract. He also believed he deserved a raise, because $600,000 was what he was paid while presiding over the magical Colts run of 1995.

"We're at ground zero," said Bill Tobin, director of football operations—not exactly what Marchibroda expected after the Colts' best season in a long time.

"Am I upset with the situation?" he asked. "Sure I am. Surprised and disappointed? Sure I am. We had the finest year they've ever had, my contract is up, and I'm supposed to go back to work for the same money? I don't understand that. This is not what I expected."

Jim Irsay has been the public voice of the Colts franchise since his father, Robert Irsay, handed him the reins in the spring of 1996. MICHAEL HICKEY/ NFL/GETTY IMAGES

Jim Irsay had been the Colts general manager in 1992 when he announced Ted Marchibroda's return to the sidelines as head coach of the team. In 1996, he and Bill Tobin let Marchibroda walk after the team's most successful season since their Super Bowl days. DON LARSON/NFL/GETTY IMAGES

If fans thought the two sides were posturing and that they would just sort things out quickly, they were mistaken. Soon enough, Marchibroda was out of work and replaced by new coach Lindy Infante. Talk about messing with success.

Although this was not a popular move, Bill Tobin had been proving he had some smarts otherwise. He was responsible for drafting Marshall Faulk, acquiring Jim Harbaugh, and for making several other sound draft picks. Tobin felt that too many hands took turns stirring the pot when he worked in Chicago, and he wanted clearly delineated lines of authority in Indianapolis.

"The scouts scout, coaches coach, and owners own," Tobin said. "If everybody does their job well, we'll celebrate at the Super Bowl."

That almost happened much more quickly than anyone expected. But failure to come to terms with Marchibroda hinted that Tobin merely wanted his own guys in place, to rise or fall with the people he selected. "Picking up Lindy Infante was probably the biggest and most important acquisition we made in the offseason," Tobin said of hiring the team's offensive coordinator for the 1995 season.

It turns out Mel Kiper had missed the mark. It was the personnel decision promoting Infante to head coach that he should have been critiquing, not the draft picks or counting on Harbaugh. But it took some time for that to become evident. The switch to Infante following Marchibroda's departure represented a nod to continuity. Infante had been offensive coordinator for the Colts,

Lindy Infante was a successful coordinator—but the Colts fielded awful defenses during his time as head coach. DOUG PENSINGER/GETTY IMAGES

and he could be expected to impart the same philosophy that had Indianapolis hot at the end of the 1995 season. But the circumstances of his elevation were a big surprise to him and the rest of the coaching staff, almost as surprising as it was to Marchibroda.

Infante and several coaches were watching TV in a hotel at the NFL scouting combine when the news of Marchibroda's departure broke. For a moment, Infante and the others wondered if a coach who was not with them was about to be named the successor and become their new boss.

"And kiddingly, I said, 'Who in hell isn't here?'" Infante recalled. Later that night when he got home there was a message from Bill Tobin asking to meet with him at the hotel in the morning. Infante wondered if he was about to be fired. When they met and talked football for hours, Infante said he was told he was the team's first choice to become the new head coach. It was an offer from left field for Infante, who thought he would be the Colts' offensive coordinator indefinitely and said he had been content with that.

"In my wildest dreams I never expected what happened to happen," he said.

Although the news that Marchibroda was gone and that Infante had been promoted was unsettling at first, supporters felt the Colts were headed in the right direction. The first-blush reaction to Infante was positive because the Colts began the 1996 season by going 5–1—no complaints. But things came unglued and the

> **"The scouts scout, coaches coach, and owners own. If everybody does their job well, we'll celebrate at the Super Bowl."**
> **—Colts Vice President Bill Tobin**

When the Colts drafted Marvin Harrison in 1996, they were getting a receiver who had the potential to become a superstar. But they needed someone who could throw him the ball.
ROBERT LABERGE/GETTY IMAGES

Colts suffered four straight losses, only one of them by seven points or less. All of a sudden the Colts were sitting at 5–5, and then no one was happy.

The major problem was the limitation of Faulk's maneuverability after he suffered a dislocated toe in the second game of the season. A little thing, it seemed, but it was a hurt that wouldn't heal. Then he injured a knee, too. Faulk, who had rushed for only 587 yards that season with a very-low 3.0 yards per carry average, regained his push-off strength near the end of the year, and the Colts began to motor again just in time.

It was a relief to Faulk that he could resemble his old self. "This is going from almost nothing to everything," he said in the closing weeks of the season. "At times I really felt this was never going to happen. I didn't think I would ever feel normal again."

A normal Faulk was very valuable. The Colts won three out of their last four regular-season games to sneak into the playoffs with a 9–7 record. Although Faulk had been slowed, more emphasis was placed on the offense. Harbaugh wasn't quite as sharp as he had been the year before, but a rookie receiver arrived in Indianapolis with a bang. Marvin Harrison, out of Syracuse, broke out with 64 catches.

Harrison was very anxious to turn pro and wanted to be an impact player right away. He didn't want to miss any training camp, so he signed a $5.8 million deal the day after camp opened. "No one wants to hold out and miss camp," Harrison said.

Just as he hoped, Harrison immediately turned heads in training camp and when the season began. He swiftly was on his way to becoming one of the top receivers in the league.

Harrison shined brightly in this turbulent season, and the team rallied in the stretch. Renewed and refreshed after a solid December, the Colts returned to the playoffs pretty much where they left off—

The 1997 Colts couldn't stop anyone—they surrendered 401 points on their way to a 3–13 record, the worst since 1991's 1–15 disaster.

Jim Irsay hired Bill Polian as his general manager after the Colts' disappointing 1996 season, and the two would find many reasons to laugh and celebrate during their time together in Indianapolis. AP PHOTO/MICHAEL CONROY

against the Pittsburgh Steelers. But rather than a nail-biter finish, this time they were swamped, going down 42–14.

The result simply proved the truth—the Colts were not as good as they had been the year before. They did not ride momentum out of their three-game playoff performance but were actually pretty much starting over under a new coach. With the raw materials the team had and with a second year under Infante, the team and its fans certainly expected to see things fall into place again.

That was the thinking, anyway, at the start of the 1997 season. Instead, the team fueled the bitterness inherent in the revived phrase "Same old Colts." It had seemed as if they were on their way to being considered one of the best teams in the league, but Indianapolis ultimately put itself into contention to be labeled the league's worst. If the franchise had taken one step forward during the preceding couple of seasons, it had now taken two giant steps backward.

Infante was the same creative offensive planner. Harbaugh still held the job much of the time (except for games lost to injury)

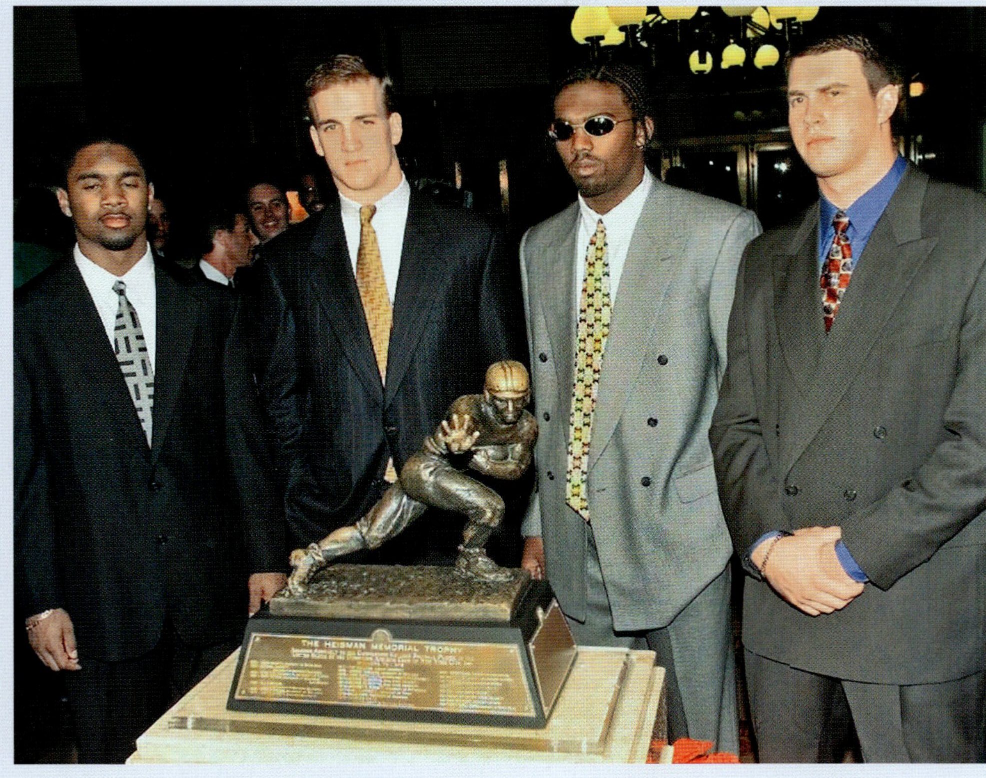

The 1997 Heisman Trophy candidates, from left to right: Michigan's Charles Woodson, Tennessee's Peyton Manning, Marshall's Randy Moss, and Washington State's Ryan Leaf. Although Heisman candidates don't always find success in the NFL, three of the four went on to excellent professional careers. The Colts would have their pick of the bunch in the 1997 draft.
AP PHOTO/ADAM NADEL

at quarterback. Faulk was back in gear, rushing for 1,054 yards and catching 47 passes, and Harrison, who grabbed 73 balls, took another step toward stardom.

So what was the problem? Defense. The Colts couldn't stop anyone. They surrendered 401 points, 88 more than the offense scored, and the team lost its first 10 games in a row. Groans could be heard all of the way across the Hoosier state. Going 0–10 to start the year was flat-out humiliating. The Colts did not fold, however, finishing out the year 3–3. The 3–13 record was the club's worst since the disastrous 1–15 mark in 1991 and was not something the administration had seen coming.

The season ended up being Infante's last year as Colts coach and his last year as an NFL head coach. "It's not a shock that it happened, but I was hoping it wouldn't," Infante said of his departure from Indianapolis.

Scrutinizing the big picture, Jim Irsay also decided that it was time for Bill Tobin to exit, too. Tobin was at his best on draft day, identifying new talent, but the Colts were not consistent enough during his tenure in charge of player personnel. Irsay installed Bill Polian, fresh off a stint as general manager of the Carolina Panthers, as the Colts' new team president.

The cupboard was not entirely bare of young talent, but there were holes to be patched, a coach to be hired, and a draft to prepare for. The rebuilding of the Colts would not take place overnight, but change beckoned. As the college football season played out, it was apparent that there were two potential franchise-changing quarterbacks that were going to be available in the 1998 NFL draft. Both Ryan Leaf of Washington State and Peyton Manning of the University of Tennessee seemed like can't-miss stars germinating at the most important position in the game.

As maneuvering for the draft played out, the Colts held the No. 1 choice. The big debate was which quarterback to take. It was felt that no team could go wrong with either player. Both young men were great talents and seemed destined for pro stardom. Leaf or Manning? Either one seemed like the type of quarterback who could lead a team for a decade. It was going to be a big decision, but not even Irsay and Polian could imagine just how huge a decision it would be. That single draft choice would completely shape the Indianapolis Colts for the next 15 years.

BIG TONY SIRAGUSA TALKED 'EM TO DEATH

At 6-foot-3 and 340 pounds, Tony Siragusa seemed as large as a dump truck. The way words flowed out of him, he was as loud as one, too.

A New Jersey guy who played for the University of Pittsburgh, Siragusa was ignored by NFL teams on draft day when he came out of school in 1989. But the Colts liked him enough to sign Siragusa as a free agent in 1990. He was just the right fit in the middle of 3–4 or 4–3 defensive lines.

Siragusa took his first paycheck of $1,000 to the bank, walked out with $1 bills and promptly brought it to a bar. Then he and his friends drank his wallet dry.

No one would ever suggest that Siragusa lacked a killer instinct. During a meeting at Pitt, coaches passed out the school fight song. Siragusa crushed the paper right there and said, "If I wanted to learn a school song, I would have gone to Notre Dame or Penn State. I want to kill people on the football field. That's why I came to Pitt."

Siragusa was one of the biggest players in the league during an NFL career that spanned 1990 to 2001. He spent his first seven seasons with the Colts and finished things off with the Baltimore Ravens, with whom he won a Super Bowl.

Frequently deployed to occupy two blockers on the offensive line at once, Siragusa wreaked havoc on opposing teams when he broke free. Of his 562 career tackles, 416 of them were solo. He also collected 22 sacks, had nine fumble recoveries, and recorded 28 deflections of quarterback passes.

Siragusa's nickname was "Goose," mostly because it sounded like Siragusa. But he also cultivated a madman image, perhaps to scare quarterbacks and halfbacks, perhaps because he was just a little offbeat. At one time or another, Siragusa owned a 16-foot boa constrictor, an alligator, and a tarantula. It was probably no coincidence that, like him, they could all terrorize when unleashed.

Siragusa joked around with the reporters but also delivered loud locker room lectures to teammates. "You hear about people with multiple personalities, and I guess I'm one of them," Siragusa said once, maybe before anyone could say it about him. "Sometimes I just want to go home and sit on the couch with my wife and hang out. Other times I want to get on my Harley and go and get crazy."

Given that eating was one of his hobbies, it is no surprise when Siragusa announced that he had gone into business selling "Goose's Baby Back Ribs." However, he also worked with family members to start a charity called the American Italian Association, designed to raise money for needy children.

Siragusa landed a role in the popular cable series *The Sopranos*, and he appeared in the movie *25th Hour*. After retiring from football in 2001, Siragusa became a sports broadcaster on NFL games, a job he still holds.

Before roaming the sidelines as an analyst for FOX, Tony Siragusa was a massive presence on the inside of the Colts defensive line.
GEORGE ROSE/GETTY IMAGES

INDIANAPOLIS COLTS RECORDS, 1984–1997

1984	4–12
1985	5–11
1986	3–13
1987	9–6*
1988	9–7
1989	8–8
1990	7–9
1991	1–15
1992	9–7
1993	4–12
1994	8–8
1995	9–7
1996	9–7
1997	3–13

*Strike-shortened season

The Peyton Manning era was an incredible one for fans of the Indianapolis Colts. RICK STEWART/GETTY IMAGES

MVP BOOKS COLLECTION

Part III

1998-2012

As it is in most professional sports, the team that plays the worst gets a shot at the next year's top draft pick, and in 1997 the Colts were that team—the worst in the NFL. With that top pick the Colts chose Peyton Manning, the All-American quarterback out of Tennessee. Rarely has a draft choice made such a difference in the history of a single football franchise. The selection of a player destined to go down in history as one of the best ever at his position, who has been one of the most durable players in the history of the league, uplifted the Colts from lousy team to perennial playoff team.

Manning was a day-one starter in 1998, earning rookie of the year honors along the way. He became the public face of the franchise, the rock of the offense, and the star-caliber, all-pro player who carried the team to routine 10-win seasons and two Super Bowls, including one Super Bowl championship.

Astutely using the player draft and making sharp trades, the Colts did not waste Manning's talents but rather ensured, by the addition of other top talent, that he could shine. Receivers such as Marvin Harrison, Reggie Wayne, and Dallas Clark lined up to catch his passes. Running back Edgerrin James provided the necessary balance out of the backfield. First-rate leader Jeff Saturday not only snapped the ball from center, but he also was a clubhouse leader. On defense, the Colts added stalwarts such as Dwight Freeney and Robert Mathis as complementary defensive ends. The wise hiring of Tony Dungy as head coach provided the steady bench leadership to guide these stars to greatness.

The Peyton Manning era in Indianapolis technically ran through the 2011 season, but a serious neck injury that required several surgeries cost him the entire season. Until then, Manning had played brilliant and injury-free football, right through the 2010 season. But the Manning era came to an end in March of 2012 when the team had to choose between paying a not-quite-healed Manning a $28 million bonus, or releasing him.

In a tearful press conference owner Jim Irsay and his biggest star ended their partnership, each wondering how the other party would fare in their new lives.

THE PEYTON MANNING ERA

Most of the time in the National Football League you have to be bad to get good. The Colts are living proof of the impact a top draft choice can make.

Flanked by Jim Irsay and NFL Commissioner Paul Tagliabue, Peyton Manning shows off his brand new No. 18 jersey. AP PHOTO/ADAM NADEL

Manning watches from the sideline with head coach Jim Mora and longtime offensive coordinator Tom Moore. AP PHOTO/KEVIN RIVOLI

Of course, like most things in life, there are no sure things in the NFL draft. But choosing Peyton Manning with the No. 1 pick in 1998 was as close to a lock as the Colts could come. Provided he stayed healthy, the Colts thought Manning could be a star for years, the first building block in the renovation of the team.

Going with his gut feeling and relying on a little bit of investigative work, owner Jim Irsay, in consultation with newly hired general manager Bill Polian, authorized NFL commissioner Paul Tagliabue to utter the famous words, "With the first pick of the draft, the Indianapolis Colts select quarterback, University of Tennessee, Peyton Manning."

This was neither a draft-day surprise nor a draft-day disappointment to fans who study the potential draft picks like stock portfolio investments. Philadelphia Eagles fans were once foolish enough to boo the choice of Donovan McNabb as their future quarterback. Colts fans were smarter than that. Their only demand of Colts management was to sign Manning and get him to training camp in time so the rebuilding could commence.

Irsay may have learned on the job, the beneficiary of a front office job at the ripe age of 23 with the team under his father's ownership, but he had educated himself well. He made the final calls on Colts personnel, but one thing he learned was that he could not make all of the necessary decisions alone. He made sure to surround himself with solid football people.

Almost as quickly as sunrise on the day after the final gun of the 1997 season, Irsay announced the hiring of a new front office guru. Bill Polian had served as general manager of the Buffalo Bills between 1986 and 1993. Magical things happened on Polian's watch in upstate New York. He hired Marv Levy as coach and brought in players who became the foundation of multiple Super Bowl teams.

By 1993 the Bills had appeared in three straight Super Bowls. They couldn't win one of those, but their record was the envy of the American Football Conference. Yet Polian was fired by owner Ralph Wilson. Polian and team treasurer Jeff Littmann could not get along, and Polian lost the power struggle and was shown the door. Next, Polian supervised the quick ascension of the expansion Carolina Panthers

The Colts bested Ryan Leaf's Chargers in their first head-to-head meeting with the quarterback they passed up for Peyton Manning.
VINCENT LAFORET/GETTY IMAGES

between 1994 and 1996. Carolina recorded the rather amazing feat of reaching the NFC Championship Game in only its second year of existence.

Then Irsay came calling and dangled the dual titles of GM and team president. About 15 minutes after the 1997 season ended, Polian changed addresses. In consultation with Irsay the Colts quickly dispatched coach Lindy Infante and replaced him with Jim Mora. Mora had a much better NFL résumé from his days leading the New Orleans Saints. In New Orleans, Mora was expected to turn around a perennially bad team, but in 1997 he was doing television commentary. Polian figured the team-builder side of Mora could do the job in Indy, and he fetched him from the sidelines.

So the Colts had a new general manager, a new coach, and a new quarterback. Put them all together, and in 1998 they had the same old 3–13 record. It was an inauspicious start for the trio. But as Manning gained seasoning his rookie year, Polian plumbed the waiver wire and brought in fresh faces. Mora sought to shape a new attitude. And by the group's second year together, the Colts of 1999 turned in a remarkable 13–3 year, although they only lasted one game in the playoffs. The tough 19–16 loss to the Tennessee Titans felt a little bit better when the Titans went all of the way to the Super Bowl.

JIM IRSAY ORCHESTRATES THE SHOW

Jim Irsay may get as much pleasure out of rock 'n' roll as he does out of football. If he had his druthers, he might have a hard time choosing between induction to the Rock and Roll Hall of Fame in Cleveland or the Pro Football Hall of Fame in Canton, Ohio.

Making music is Irsay's passionate hobby, but trying to make and keep the Colts winners is his professional responsibility. The son of Robert Irsay, Jim Irsay inherited ownership of the Colts after his father's death in 1997. Jim Irsay was 12 when his father gained control of the Colts, still located in Baltimore, and he was 23 when he became general manager. He was 37 when he became the sole owner of the Colts, and it has been his society to rule for more than 15 years. The entire Peyton Manning era that includes Indianapolis' two trips to the Super Bowl, one win and one loss, has played out on his watch, and the buck stops with him when it comes to selecting a new coach or pulling the trigger on an expensive contract.

Irsay, who attended Southern Methodist University, not only plays the guitar, but also he has indulged in the purchase of rare guitars owned by favorite music stars such as Elvis Presley, the Beatles' George Harrison, and the Grateful Dead's Jerry Garcia. He also spent more than $2 million to gain possession of the original manuscript of *On the Road*, the iconic book written by Jack Kerouac.

However, it has cost Irsay considerably more to put together a powerful football team featuring Peyton Manning and others who earn multi-million-dollar contracts. Irsay has a reputation of being a fan-friendly owner determined to provide a winning team. He is also a frequent Twitter user, and used that medium to make it clear to fans that, regardless of the price tag, he was not going to let all-pro Manning get away. Throughout negotiations he was reassuring to fans. "Everybody wants a Peyton," Irsay said. "If you have a chance to get him, [you] take him and keep him."

From his guitar collection to his Twitter feed, Jim Irsay is not the typical NFL owner. AP PHOTO/AJ MAST

The owner probably reveled as much as the fans did in the Colts winning their first Super Bowl since relocating from Baltimore to Indianapolis. "It's unbelievable to be world champions," Irsay said after the Colts defeated the Chicago Bears 29–17 in the 2007 Super Bowl. "We fought through so much adversity. We've been after it for a good part of this decade, and we got it done tonight here in Florida. We are going to celebrate, me and my family."

When Irsay was presented with the Lombardi Trophy, emblematic of the Colts' success, he thanked God, his whole organizational team, and coach Tony Dungy. "I am so proud of my men," Irsay said.

Peyton Manning audibles during a 2010 game against the Oakland Raiders. AP PHOTO/KEVIN TERRELL

PEYTON MANNING

Groomed for Greatness

He was born to be a quarterback. The son of all-pro Archie Manning, who single-handedly made the New Orleans Saints feel good, Peyton Manning was a student of the game from a young age. As soon as he was old enough to comprehend them, Peyton was listening to his father's game tapes dating back to the days he starred at the University of Mississippi.

Other youngsters liked silly things, but young Peyton was all business. He dreamed of becoming a quarterback just like Dad, and in the end he excelled beyond his or his father's wildest dreams. A superstar growing up in Saints territory, Manning was hotly pursued by colleges all over the country.

From the time he was tiny it was presumed that Peyton Manning would follow his father to Ole Miss to become the next great thing. Archie and his wife Olivia, who met on the campus and shared idyllic times in Oxford, wanted him to follow that path, especially after older brother Cooper, a wide receiver, chose that college. In the end, though, Peyton was swayed by the entreaties of the University of Tennessee and became a Volunteer instead of a Rebel. Allegiances are firm in Southeastern Conference territory, dating back generations, and Peyton was portrayed as a traitor by too-serious football fans. His father, long a hero to the multitudes of the Magnolia State, was unjustly vilified. Archie refused to influence his son and let him make his own choice.

As a player addicted to film study, Peyton Manning outworked and out-studied all competitors for the quarterback job at Tennessee, and he was in charge of the offense by the end of his freshman season. His ownership of the most critical position on the field was never threatened over the remainder of his time at UT.

Although there was a clamoring for Manning to turn pro after his junior year, he chose to stay at Tennessee for four seasons. Some thought the tune "Rocky Top" must have driven him crazy, but Manning felt he had unfinished business. He hoped to lead Tennessee to a national title and win the Heisman Trophy. Neither happened, but Manning still garnered many honors. By the end of his final year with the Volunteers, it was apparent that either he or Washington State's Ryan Leaf was going to be the top pick in the NFL draft the next spring—a pick the Colts had earned as the league's worst team in 1997.

No football fan could have predicted the divergent paths the year's two top college quarterbacks' careers would take. The Colts selected Manning, who became one of the greatest players in NFL history. Leaf started slow, and then things got worse. He had off-field troubles and was out of the game within a couple of years, frequently labeled the greatest draft bust of all time. Owner Jim Irsay looked like Albert Einstein for choosing Manning.

The Colts needed Manning, and Manning wanted to get started with the business of playing pro football as soon as possible. Neither side wanted a prolonged contract hassle. Manning was in a position to command big bucks, and the Colts didn't hesitant to pay him. His rookie contract called for a maximum of $48 million, provided he met all types of incentives. It may have provided some observers a chuckle when Manning's first purchase with his first paycheck was a $200 pair of cowboy boots.

There was no bench-warming for Manning. He was the starter from game one and was likely one of the most poised rookie quarterbacks ever to take a snap—but even Manning had a learning curve. Although he completed 326 passes for 3,739 yards and 26 touchdowns, he had one rookie typical weakness: he threw 28 interceptions. Ouch. The Colts were still a work in progress, duplicating the previous season's 3–13 record—but there was hope for the horseshoe.

Those who risked their reputations in the front office by selecting Manning were pretty darned happy with the new guy. Bill Polian, president and general manager of the Colts when Manning was on the big board, made sure the 6-foot-5, 230-pounder with the golden arm landed in Indianapolis. But not even he expected Manning to be so good so fast. "The improvement is phenomenal," Polian said. "I've never seen improvement like this from a rookie in all my years."

Polian had barely seen the tip of the iceberg. When it came to football, Manning was a workaholic. He wanted to be the best, and he was willing to put in the time and effort to do so. The guy spent more time in the dark than a coal miner. He was watching game film while other players were reclining on the beach. He was also a demon for offseason workouts, and Manning wasn't shy about calling up receivers and asking them to meet him for some individual throwing time. It was all about building rapport and developing rhythm with his guys so things would fall into place at crunch time the next fall.

Manning looks downfield during a 2009 game against the Jets at Lucas Oil Stadium. ANDY LYONS/GETTY IMAGES

The meticulous preparation paid off, and Manning built a strong bond with his receivers. He continued to improve each year, recording one of the most amazing seasons ever by a quarterback in 2004 when he threw for 336 completions, 4,557 yards, and a new league-record 49 touchdowns against only 10 interceptions. Three Manning receivers caught at least 10 touchdown passes apiece.

Season after season, Manning's statistics were astonishing. He threw 31 touchdown passes in 2006, 31 in 2007, 27 in 2008, 33 in 2009, and 33 in 2010. By the end of the 2010 season Manning had thrown for 54,828 yards, 11 times totaling more than 4,000 yards passing in a single season. His career pass completion percentage stood at 64.9 percent.

Manning's hard work also came with accolades: an 11-time Pro Bowl selection, Manning is the only four-time recipient of the NFL's Most Valuable Player award. Brett Favre won three such awards, and the only other quarterbacks to earn even two are Joe Montana, Steve Young, Kurt Warner, and Johnny Unitas.

(LEFT) MVP BOOKS COLLECTION; (ABOVE) STEPHEN DUNN/GETTY IMAGES

"Just being with those names makes it more special," Manning said, "and I am very humbled to be on that list."

Despite being sidelined by neck surgery in 2011, Manning had also been a durable player for the Colts, making 227 consecutive starts, including playoff games, between 1998 and 2010. That put him second on the all-time list behind Brett Favre, though Manning holds the record for most consecutive starts at the beginning of a career, because Favre first had been a backup for the Atlanta Falcons. Although Favre owns most of the meaningful statistical records for quarterbacks, Manning has been gaining fast in recent seasons. Depending on the longevity of his career, he seems likely to break them all. After the 2010 season Manning had career totals of 54,828 yards passing and 399 touchdown passes. Only Favre and Dan Marino have thrown for more yardage in the NFL. The situation is similar with touchdown passes. Favre holds the NFL record with 508, and Marino has 420.

Manning's fame has spread far beyond the boundaries of pro football. Generally considered to be a fairly bland yes-sir, no-sir guy who doesn't joke around, Manning began to change his image when he started making humorous commercials for MasterCard. He received favorable reviews for minute-long snippets where he often poked fun at himself. Then he hosted *Saturday Night Live* and was the centerpiece of a hilarious skit with him playing a devilish Manning making fun of his own public service commercials. Sportswriters wanted to know if Manning was going to be appearing in movies. "I'm still waiting for Hollywood to call me," he said.

Everyone else called, though. Manning was linked to many worthy causes, from children's hospitals to his own Peyback Foundation. That outlet donated nearly $4 million to charitable causes in its first 10 years. Manning, through the foundation, has sponsored annual football games at the Colts' home stadiums for local high schools, given out scholarships, purchased Colts game tickets for disadvantaged young people, distributed grants to dozens of community organizations, and funded the Peyton Manning Children's Hospital at St. Vincent in Indianapolis. The list of Manning's charitable good works is as long as his NFL statistical record.

But Manning continued to debunk his "Mr. Perfect" image in commercials and on other fronts, proving he was just a regular guy. He teamed up with his dad, Archie, and younger brother, Eli, who was just beginning to emerge as a pro star with the New York Giants. They made commercials for ESPN that produced chuckles. On *Saturday Night Live*, in the opening monologue, Manning spoofed the fact that his mother had failed to play pro football. "She never made it to the NFL," Manning lamented.

"Got cut by the Dolphins. Tried Canada for a bit. She's a real disappointment for all of us."

Those types of lighthearted appearances and roles transformed Manning's image for good. So he wasn't just a drone who sat in the dark studying film all of the time. Hey, the guy had a sense of humor.

The Colts rolled on, winning 12 games per year under Manning's leadership and completely controlling the AFC South Division. Finally, with Manning at the controls, Indianapolis won the Super Bowl after the 2006 season. Topping the Chicago Bears seemed to be inevitable after the Colts qualified for the big game. They had waited years for the opportunity, and Manning seemed unlikely to fall short. Neither he nor the Colts did.

Holding off the Bears 29–17 was the crowning achievement of Manning's career. By night's end he was wearing instantly produced Super Bowl Champs gear and clutching the Lombardi Trophy in his right hand. He smiled big and shared the moment on the field with his coach, Tony Dungy, and his teammates. But Manning didn't go wild performing a jig or turning cartwheels. He seemed more reflective than giddy about the moment he had always craved. "It was an emotional game, and I think everyone is really drained right now," he said. "We put a lot of hard work and effort into this." But don't be fooled by his seemingly subdued attitude, Manning said. He planned to party and celebrate long into the night with his teammates.

Manning didn't relax after the Colts' Super Bowl victory. He thought Indianapolis could become a regular in the big game. Things didn't exactly play out that way, but not because of anything Manning failed to do. As the years passed, it became clear that Manning had become one of the greatest football players in the history of the NFL.

Indianapolis made its second visit to the Super Bowl under Manning's guidance after the 2009 season but lost to the New Orleans Saints 31–17. The Colts began the season 14–0 and were making a run at an undefeated campaign for a time.

In May 2011, Manning underwent what was portrayed as minor neck surgery. No one imagined that this critical moment could lead to the end of Manning's stay in Indianpolis. It was his second such operation in two years, but it was months before training camp was scheduled to start. He figured to be at full strength in time to play. However, even the league's labor dispute could not provide Manning enough time to heal properly, and a Manning watch began. Would he play before the end of training camp? Would he be ready for the season opener? Would he come back after missing the first games of his pro career? As time passed, the Colts shrouded Manning's condition in secrecy, and he barely spoke at all about it. But the team did not place their star quarterback on the season-ending injured reserve list.

It was not until the day of the Colts' 14th game of the season that team vice chairman Bill Polian announced that although Manning was showing signs of progress in limited workouts, he would not play a down for the Colts in 2011. He had not regained arm strength and was not in shape to suit up as the curtain fell on a dismal season where his teammates had inexplicably fallen apart with their leader sidelined.

The Colts finished a horrible 2-14, and a determined Jim Irsay began revamping the front office and roster immediately. Heads rolled, and a pricey deadline loomed large: Manning was due

MVP BOOKS COLLECTION

a $28 million bonus on March 8, 2012. The day before the deadline, Manning and Irsay conducted a press conference that broke Manning's career-long ties to the team. It was a tough business decision to jettison Manning, but Irsay could not let sentiment rule his team.

Manning's farewell press conference was an exercise in grace. He was grateful for all of the good years and expressed no bitterness at being exiled from his team."I sure have loved playing football for the Indianapolis Colts," Manning said. "This town and team mean so much to me. It truly has been an honor to play in Indianapolis. I do love it here. I will leave the Colts with nothing but good thoughts and gratitude."

One of the most brilliant players in NFL history, a player who had been identified exclusively with the Colts for 14 years, was on the free agent market. He entertained interests from many teams, visited with a few, and signed with the Denver Broncos for the 2012 season. He would be wearing a new uniform the next time Colts fans saw him play.

EDGERRIN JAMES BECOMES

Sporting dreadlocks and flashing a gold tooth when he smiled, fans in the heartland did not know quite what to make of running back Edgerrin James when he was drafted from the University of Miami in 1999. But he proved to be a critical addition to the offense that season, rushing for 1,553 yards and winning the rookie of the year award.

Unlike the applause that rippled across the heartland when the Colts nabbed Peyton Manning in the draft, Indianapolis fans were not as satisfied with the choice of James. They didn't know enough about his talent, and they didn't like his seemingly threatening look. Some fans reportedly threw items at their television screens when James was announced as the Colts' next great running back.

Bill Polian actually teased Colts interns that day by saying, "You guys have to draw straws to see who starts my car tonight." It never got quite as dire as car bombs, but the front office wasn't forgiven until James showed his stuff on the field. Actually, the front office should have been showered with praise. James was better than advertised right away.

After James rushed for 112 yards in the season opener, sportswriters were kind enough to ask James what he thought of his home fans reacting so negatively when he was picked. He handled the hand-grenade question well. "Fans are going to have their opinions," James said. "The good side is, once you make some plays and help the team win, you see people turn around and say, 'Man, I was dead wrong about you.'"

It took only a couple of 60-minute performances for James to make fans think that way.

Perhaps James was impervious to criticism because he took the hard way to the pros. He grew up in Immolake, Florida, where migrant labor flourished during harvest time. His mother worked in a cafeteria, his parents never married, and his family needed food stamps to survive for part of the year. Few believed he would someday become an National Football League star.

"All my life has been about proving myself," James said. "I've been through so much that what I'm going through now is nothing. You get so accustomed to hearing bad things said about you. People used to say I'd never make it in college because of where I come from, and I've proved them wrong."

Well, James made it at Miami, and he made it big with the Colts, though not before a 21-day holdout that netted him a $49 million contract. If the Colts hadn't believed in James, they wouldn't have chosen him ahead of Texas' Ricky Williams, the Heisman Trophy winner who played the same position.

"A lot of people talked about our reasoning," said Indianapolis owner Jim Irsay. "It's because he's the best football player. We think he's going to fit with Peyton, and those guys are going to be a lot like Emmitt Smith and Troy Aikman. That combination is something that we think is special."

A quarterback's best friend is a solid rushing attack, which is exactly what Edgerrin James brought to Peyton Manning's offense. JEFF KOWALSKY/AFP/GETTY IMAGES

MANNING'S SIDEKICK

It didn't take long for Irsay's intuition and savvy to be proven correct. James did produce more than Williams, and he and Manning made for a lethal duo in the backfield, doing nearly as well as that old Dallas Cowboys twosome.

All of a sudden the Colts had star quality at the skill positions. Manning was an all-star quarterback. James was an all-star running back. And Marvin Harrison, who caught 115 passes in 1999, was an all-star wide receiver. Still, football teams are not built in a day, and the Colts regressed slightly in 2000, posting a 10–6 record. That mark would have looked like something at the end of a rainbow just a few years earlier, but these Colts had higher, loftier goals.

Manning, who took over as the quarterback in training camp right out of the University of Tennessee, not only started every game in 2000, but he also took every snap and threw 571 passes. Somehow his arm didn't fall off. The Colts had begun using a no-huddle, hurry-up offense that didn't give defenses enough time to make adjustments with fresh personnel.

Manning herded his team to the line of scrimmage and then watched defenders scurry around and wonder what he was going to call. If it looked as if they guessed right and lined up in a formation that seemed likely to stuff a play, Manning shouted out an audible. Manning's finger movements and hand jive became such a trademark that it almost seemed as if he were using American Sign Language.

Some observers made fun of Manning's gestures, but nobody could say much because he made things work. "Laugh all you want," he seemed to be saying, "but as long as we're chewing up yards for first downs and scoring touchdowns, we don't care."

James signs footballs for some lucky Colts fans.
JONATHAN DANIEL/ALLSPORT/GETTY IMAGES

MVP BOOKS COLLECTION

With Peyton Manning, Edgerrin James, and Marvin Harrison, the Colts had legitimate stars at the three major skill positions.

EDGERRIN JAMES FOOLED EVERYONE

The guy with the unusual first name had the look to match, with dreadlocks and gold teeth. But on the field he had the style that combined speed and power to make him one of the finest running backs in Colts team history.

Edgerrin James played his college ball at the University of Miami, and he was Indianapolis' No. 1 draft pick in 1999. With the passing game already working on eight cylinders, James represented the missing link in the Colts' offense. The team needed a complementary big back to balance the passing-running offense, and he was the man.

Initially, Colts fans were not so sure if James was going to fill the need at running back. They were clamoring for Indianapolis to take Ricky Williams, the Heisman Trophy winner, and when the team drafted James, some people acted as if he was an unwelcome consolation prize. James proved them wrong by outperforming Williams.

"The way I work, I'm going to show what I'm capable of doing," James said. "I won't let the team down in any fashion." He did not, and those who questioned the Colts' choice during James' training camp holdout soon found themselves backpedaling. After a brief cameo at the end of the exhibition season, James burst into the league with an NFL-best 1,553 yards. He caught 62 passes for another 586 yards, and scored 17 touchdowns for 102 points. You can't just replace a Hall of Famer, but James certainly lessened the pain felt by the loss of Marshall Faulk.

James followed up his rookie year with a similar, if not better, second year. He rushed for 1,709 yards and caught 63 passes while scoring 18 touchdowns. Throwing in a two-point conversion, he accounted for 110 points, nearly as many as a kicker.

The tremendous showings were noticed around the league, and James reached the Pro Bowl in his first two seasons. "It's nice," James said at the end of his second year. "I'm two-for-two [as a Pro Bowl choice] and hopefully I can keep it going. I guess we've got a lot of respect from around the league, from fans, from everybody." At the peak of their time spent together,

When fans questioned the decision to draft James, he answered by leading the league in rushing in his rookie season. AL MESSERSCHMIDT/GETTY IMAGES

MVP BOOKS COLLECTION

James rushes upfield during a 2002 game against the Redskins in Washington.
AL MESSERSCHMIDT/NFL PHOTOS/GETTY IMAGES

quarterback Peyton Manning, receiver Marvin Harrison, and James were the Colts' Three Musketeers on offense; the three were frequently selected as all-stars. James made the Pro Bowl four times for the Colts, and his combination of power and speed made him a very challenging foe for tacklers to bring down.

In 2001 James suffered the type of setback that has ruined many a career. He tore a ligament in his left knee and sat out the last chunk of the season. He totaled just 662 yards rushing with 24 catches before he went down. The Colts tumbled down, too, interrupting their improvement with a 6–10 record as they tried to adapt to life without James. This was not the best stretch of James' professional life. He stayed home in Miami to rehab rather than hanging around the Colts' facilities, which earned him some criticism, and he missed minicamps. His 2002 season had its moments when he rushed for 989 yards, though his per-carry average dropped. That was Tony Dungy's first year as coach, and the Colts rebounded to a 10–6 record.

In 2003, James and the Colts got better. He was back to his usual self, rushing for 1,259 yards and catching 51 passes as Indianapolis finished 12–4. Until that season, James had clung tenaciously to his preferred hairstyle—dreadlocks. When tacklers began pulling his hair, he re-evaluated. A game against the Cleveland Browns convinced him to make the change. "That made me rethink," James said. "I gave in right there. I can't go through that all year. It was best for me to go ahead and chop it off."

Unlike the biblically renowned Samson, who lost his strength when his hair was sheared off, James' loss of his long locks was more psychological than physical. He was still nearly unstoppable, turning in that excellent season in 2003 and rushing for 1,548 yards in 2004, while again being a major threat out of the backfield with 51 grabs. For a player with reconstructive knee surgery, James did not appear to have lost a step, and in the culminating season of his Colts career, he darted for 1,506 yards in 2005 as Indianapolis put together a 14–2 record.

James became an unrestricted free agent after that season, and his original plan was to stay with the Colts and win a Super Bowl with Manning, Harrison, and the rest of his teammates. "This is a cool place to play," James said, "but one thing about it, I'm not married to a team. If a team wants to keep you, they find a way to keep you."

And if a player wants to stay, he finds a way to stay. Instead, James completed his career with short stints on the rosters of the Arizona Cardinals and Seattle Seahawks. James ended up leaving the Colts the year before they won the Super Bowl.

MR. DUNGY TAKES OVER

Despite the Colts' prolific offense, their defense pretty much imploded in Jim Mora's third year, giving up 486 points in the 2001 season, including an amazing 200 points in the second quarter alone. The Colts finished an unhappy 6–10, and changes had to be made. Mora was fired, and in the biggest surprise of the offseason, Tony Dungy was unexpectedly available. After Tampa Bay let Dungy get away, Jim Irsay swooped down like an eagle hovering over a lake and plucked his favorite fish out of the water.

Tony Dungy brought a consistency and leadership to the Colts locker room that the team hadn't seen in many years. TOM PIDGEON/GETTY IMAGES

"I was always taught that you become a champion by doing the little things very well, not by being a magician."—Tony Dungy

Dungy had worked wonders with previously underachieving defenses in both Tampa Bay and Minnesota, and it was clear that the Colts believed he could fix their glaring deficiencies on that side of the ball. Irsay signed Dungy to a five-year, $13 million deal, but Dungy made it clear he felt there was no magic wand that was going to protect Indianapolis' end zone.

"I was always taught that you become a champion by doing the little things very well," Dungy said, "not by being a magician."

Colts fans didn't care whether Dungy studied tricks performed by David Copperfield or hired tag-team sumo wrestlers to keep opposing offenses out of the end zone, as long as the Colts stopped surrendering so many points.

Tony Dungy's marching orders were pretty clear when he was brought aboard for that 2002 season. No talk of rebuilding—just get us to the playoffs. Dungy quickly did just that, leading the Colts to a 10–6 record. The defense was a startling 173 points better, employing 7 of the same 11 men Mora had. That was a neat trick. Of course, one of the newcomers was the impressive defensive end Dwight Freeney.

"It's not what you do; it's how you do it," Dungy said. "You have to get guys to play hard, down in and down out. It's attitude, and you've got to have good players."

Peyton Manning again was the only Colt to throw a pass all year, this time tossing 591 of them for 4,200 yards and 27 touchdowns. His completion percentage was 66.3 percent. Given his pedigree as the son of a former NFL quarterback and the way he had groomed himself for the task of becoming one, Manning was sometimes viewed as a kind of royalty, a prince in waiting for stardom.

But that did not stem from anything he said. Manning didn't worry about how many hours it took each day to formulate a game plan, to improve his own knowledge of the game and his ability. Dungy, and later coach Jim Caldwell, always said that it was great for a team when the hardest worker was the best player. Manning was as blue collar on the field as any teammate, paying with his sweat as much as anyone else to make all gears turn smoothly on Sundays. Organized practices might have ended in time for dinner, but Manning stayed at the practice complex until 9 p.m. on many nights.

"You bust your butt all week for a three-hour game," he said. "When you

MVP BOOKS COLLECTION

Dungy made an immediate impact on the Colts' defense. Here, Dwight Freeney and Idrees Bashir sandwich Eagles quarterback Donovan McNabb, forcing a fumble during a 2002 game. EZRA SHAW/GETTY IMAGES

lose, that's why it makes you sick, because you feel like you've wasted your time. When you win it makes you really feel special, because you've worked for it."

That attitude rubbed off on other players who were not as talented as Manning. With him as an example, they probably worked harder than initially planned. Unfortunately, the team's 2002 return to the playoffs was pretty ugly—the Colts lost to the New York Jets 41–0.

Dungy had been pretty successful with the Buccaneers, taking Tampa Bay to four playoff appearances in six years. "A Super Bowl win with the Bucs would have been wonderful," Dungy reflected after his firing. "I could have used that platform in a tremendous way. But I think my getting fired had an even greater impact. It's easy to be gracious when you're getting carried off the field in celebration. It's more difficult when you're asked to pack up your desk and your pass-code doesn't work anymore.

"I think people look more closely at our actions when the emotions are raw and our guard is down. That's when our true character shows and we find out if our faith is real."

Dungy certainly departed from his job in Tampa with his faith unshaken, and there didn't seem to be any doubters out there, either. He was still solidifying his reputation as a top-tier NFL coach, though. He had laid the foundation in Florida, but his status rose with his triumphs in Indianapolis.

From that first playoff loss going forward, the Colts matured into one of the NFL's elite teams. Dungy came to town to win, to complete the job he started in Tampa Bay and lead a team to a Super Bowl championship.

Bill Polian and Tony Dungy were the backbone of a strong Colts leadership team, overseeing seven straight seasons of at least 10 wins during their time together. AP PHOTO/MICHAEL CONROY

TONY DUNGY

Man for the Moment

When Tony Dungy was hired as the Indianapolis Colts' new coach after being let go by the Tampa Bay Buccaneers in 2002, it was seen as a good match. By the time he stepped down as the Colts' coach in 2008, he was being begged to stay. Dungy had become a national figure and was considered the nearly perfect team leader. He was more than a mere football coach; Tony Dungy was a cultural symbol of what a modern dad and caring man should be. Indeed, the Colts and Dungy were very, very good for one another—both the team and the coach were more popular when they broke up than when they met, becoming stars of the NFL.

Dungy led the Indianapolis Colts to their lone Super Bowl championship to date, in command when the Colts defeated the Chicago Bears in 2007, a triumph that made him the first African American coach to win a Super Bowl title. Between time served at Tampa Bay and in Indianapolis, Dungy became the first coach to lead NFL teams to the playoffs in 10 straight seasons.

At 6 feet and 188 pounds, Dungy was not the biggest football player coming out of the University of Minnesota in 1976. He went undrafted, but he signed as a free agent with the Pittsburgh Steelers. Dungy played three seasons in the league as a defensive back, two with the Steelers and one with the San Francisco 49ers, and was a practice squad member for the New York Giants before he retired to begin his coaching career.

Coach Dungy roams the sideline during a 2007 preseason game against the Bengals. JOE ROBBINS/GETTY IMAGES

Dungy was originally a quarterback and was stunned when he was not drafted by an NFL team to play that position. He flirted with the idea of playing for the Montreal Alouettes in Canada under Marv Levy, where he could have challenged for the quarterback job. Instead, while knowing it was iffy he would make the NFL, he signed that free-agent deal with Pittsburgh.

With the Steelers, Dungy achieved a rare and unlikely feat. A combination of unusual circumstances saw Dungy called upon to play quarterback in the same game he had already played as a defensive back. Dungy intercepted a pass on defense that day and threw an interception as quarterback.

Dungy was a member of the 1978 Pittsburgh Steelers' Super Bowl title team and led the team with six interceptions. "It was one of those miracle years," Dungy wrote later in his best-selling autobiography, *Quiet Strength*. "I was healthy, and it seemed like every time I took the field, the ball was headed my way."

After retirement, Dungy remained in the sport, first as an assistant coach with the Steelers, where he rose to defensive coordinator, then with the Kansas City Chiefs and the Minnesota Vikings before he became head coach of Tampa Bay in 1996. That was the big jump he had been waiting for, and Dungy was the Bucs' head man through the 2001 season. "Head coach of the Tampa Bay Buccaneers," Dungy said, "I couldn't believe I'd actually gotten the job. I was especially humbled when I thought about all the times I had fallen short and all the African American coaches who had gone before me but had never gotten this chance."

Dungy won 11 games with Tampa Bay in 1999 and made four playoff appearances in six seasons. The Bucs lost in the first round every time, and that likely cost Dungy his job. His mark with Tampa Bay was 54–42, but there was impatience in the front office. The Bucs wanted to win immediately. Dungy was fired following a nine-win season and a first-round playoff loss but didn't stay unemployed long. Colts owner Jim Irsay wanted Dungy in Indianapolis as fast as he could slam the car door. "You're the only person I want for this job," Irsay said.

One of Dungy's trademarks as a defensive coordinator had been the cover-2 defense, and he brought it to Indianapolis in his suitcase. Essentially a zone defense with players having responsibility for areas and two safeties playing deep to take away the long-ball threat, it's a defense that has been emulated by many in the NFL. "I've always said if you can count to three, you can play in this defense," Dungy said, which might have been something of an exaggeration. "If you can count to three fast, you can play it well."

Dungy blossomed in Indianapolis, as did the Colts under his firm hand and soft voice. Dungy was not a screamer on the sidelines. He came across as wise, instructing without raising his voice. He sought to make a very good team into a great one.

The new coach preached trust to his players and told them if they bought into his program they were going to win. Win the Colts did, starting in 2002 with 10 victories, then following with seasons of 12, 12, 14, 12, 13, and 12 wins. In Dungy's second season the Colts reached the AFC Championship Game, and in early 2007 the Colts upended the Bears to win the Super Bowl.

During his tenure with the Colts, Dungy became a national personality, as much for his off-the-field endeavors as his coaching success. He was active in community causes, urging single dads to be involved in their children's upbringing. He became a very active speaker for the Fellowship of Christian Athletes, as well as Athletes in Action, always quite vociferous about his strong religious beliefs. One community program he began was called Mentors for Life, designed to help young people. He also worked extensively with Big Brothers Big Sisters in Indianapolis. All the while, the Colts kept winning.

Viewed as a beacon of common sense for many, Dungy and his family were struck by tragedy when his 18-year-old son Jamie committed suicide near the end of the 2005 football season. The stunning development in a caring family caused Dungy to take a brief leave of absence from his team and was the subject of national attention.

When the phone rang at 1:45 a.m. three days before Christmas, Dungy knew it could not be good news, and his first thought was that he hoped one of his players was not in trouble. "It wasn't until days later, when I was standing over Jamie's casket and preparing for the visitation," Dungy says in his book, "that it really started to sink in and become real: I'm never going to see him again."

About 1,500 people attended Jamie Dungy's funeral, and Dungy gave a eulogy. As part of his comments he said, "Parents, hug your kids each chance you get. Tell them you love them each chance you get. You don't know when it's going to be the last time."

Dungy had been very generous with his time and energy helping others in need, so there was an outpouring of sentiment

Dungy addresses the media the morning after winning Super Bowl XLI. ELIOT J. SCHECHTER/GETTY IMAGES

to support his family after his son's death, with cards and letters streaming into the Colts' offices.

Colts players reacted strongly to the death of Dungy's son. "Players were surprised and upset emotionally about it," said quarterback Peyton Manning. "Everybody said a team prayer for coach Dungy and his family." Dungy returned from his break to coach the Colts in the playoffs.

Dungy helmed the Colts through 2008, winning the Super Bowl victory and making repeated trips to the playoffs. Upon retirement, Dungy surprised many when he emerged as a talented and popular studio football analyst with some of the most incisive commentary on the air. Dungy had always been a quiet man who seemed to avoid controversial statements, so it was a change of pace for him.

Despite his background as a defensive coach, Dungy developed an excellent relationship with quarterback Peyton Manning. STEPHEN DUNN/GETTY IMAGES

POSTSEASON SUDDENLY

The Colts' 2003 achievements made it clear that they now played with the big boys of the National Football League. They finished 12–4 and won two playoff games, but then they came up against the New England Patriots' buzz saw. In what would become an annual ritual, the Colts were a punching bag for Bill Belichik's team as it muscled its way to the Super Bowl.

In 2004, the Colts were a pretty remarkable group of players. Their offensive circus was so potent they needed three rings and big top to display it properly. It was surprising they finished only 12–4, because Indianapolis scored 522 points. Peyton Manning set a record that season with 49 touchdown passes, and Edgerrin James rushed for 1,548 yards. Marvin Harrison caught 86 passes for 1,113 yards, and that wasn't even a team best—Reggie Wayne grabbed 77 balls for 1,210 yards. For good measure, third receiver Brandon Stokely caught 68 passes for another 1,077 yards. Stokely had been acquired as a free agent in 2003 but had been hurt for most of the year. He made a bang the next year while deferring to Harrison as the No. 1 option. "He's the main weapon in this offense," Stokely said. "He opens things up for the rest of us." No matter who got open, Stokely knew that Manning would find him.

The Colts had a wealth of talent at the skill positions, and that included the placekicker role. Mike Vanderjagt, who was born in

Manning and Dungy had a unique relationship in which the quarterback was given almost unprecedented freedom over play selection at the line of scrimmage. RICK STEWART/GETTY IMAGES

AN ANNUAL DEAL

"The sad thing is, he's a good kicker. He's a good kicker, but he's an idiot." —Peyton Manning on Mike Vanderjagt

Ontario, Canada, and proved his accuracy in the Canadian Football League, hit 86.5 percent of his career field goal attempts. Though Vanderjagt's foot won a lot of games for the Colts, it ended up in his mouth on one infamous occasion.

Following the 41–0 playoff loss to the Jets in 2002, Vanderjagt foolishly criticized coach Tony Dungy and Manning on a Canadian cable TV show. Neither took the commentary well, but Dungy was

MVP BOOKS COLLECTION

Mike Vanderjagt was impressively accurate during his career with the Colts—but all it took was one ill-advised comment to change public perception of the kicker. ANDY LYONS/GETTY IMAGES

calmer than Manning. The quarterback shared his thoughts at the Pro Bowl, calling Vanderjagt an "idiot kicker who got liquored up and ran his mouth off." Manning continued, "The sad thing is, he's a good kicker. He's a good kicker, but he's an idiot." Things were smoothed over sufficiently for Vanderjagt to remain a Colt through 2005.

For all the varied firepower, a Super Bowl appearance continued to elude the Indianapolis Colts. They clobbered the Denver Broncos by a score of 49–24 in the first round of the 2004 playoffs, but the Patriots would again end their season, grounding the Colts' high-flying offense with a dominant 20–3 divisional round victory.

Peyton Manning set a record in 2004 with 49 touchdown passes.

MARVIN HARRISON DID HIS TALKING ON FIELD

The talent was obvious, and Marvin Harrison was eager to make it big. It didn't take very long for the Colts to realize that their 1996 No. 1 draft pick was going to be something extraordinary. It took a little while for Harrison to get used to the pace of the pro game and adjust to the offense, but he led the team in receiving that year with 64 catches.

Harrison and quarterback Jim Harbaugh connected with one another just fine. And then things got better, especially after Peyton Manning arrived on the scene.

As the duo grew and played together, it became obvious that Harrison and Manning had a unique telepathy. Harrison used his 4.4 speed (though he had been timed in the 4.3 range in track) to run precise routes and get open, and Manning would have the ball in his hands the second he turned around. Their timing and synchronization was a beautiful thing to see, and they were remarkably productive for the Colts' offense as the team advanced from borderline playoff contender to perpetual playoff threat.

Harrison came out of Syracuse University and played his entire career in Indianapolis. He was a fixture in the city, but he made his impact with his actions, not his mouth. He was not a chatty guy but one who showed his stuff with his hands and feet. He was like that from the beginning and maintained that approach for the duration of his career.

After a first-rate training camp, Harrison earned a starting wide receiver position as a rookie. Not that coach Lindy Infante was surprised. When Bill Tobin made Harrison the team's top draft pick, Infante said, "That meant he had all the athletic skills, plus the mentality, plus the personality. He's a bright young man. He came in and learned this offense very quickly."

In the first preseason game of his NFL career, Harrison caught six passes for 85 yards—in one half—and his 25-yard touchdown catch on a Harbaugh pass propelled the Colts to a 20–13 victory over the Arizona Cardinals. Until he was heavily targeted in the second half, he was more focused on rookie basics. "Me being a young guy," he said, "I was just going with the flow. I wasn't worried about catching or running. I just wanted to execute my assignments."

Soon enough the execution came naturally, without having to think about it too much, as Harrison eased into the

Marvin Harrison catches a fourth-quarter touchdown pass in a win against the Miami Dolphins in 2006. GREGORY SHAMUS/GETTY IMAGES

role of go-to receiver. One guy he impressed was Harbaugh. "It's always great to be associated with greatness," Harbaugh said.

During that first season Harrison was the subject of a personality profile in the *Game Day* program that revealed the following: his favorite singer was Anita Baker, his favorite athlete was Mike Tyson, he really liked the movies *Scarface* and *The Fugitive*, and he rooted for the Philadelphia 76ers. He also noted that the best advice he ever got from a coach was, "Play every play as if it was your last." That's sound advice for a player in any sport.

Harrison got started with a bang that lifted his confidence as he entered the 1997 season, his second. One year in a pro system was a big help in that transition from college. "Last year I didn't even put my abilities to work," Harrison said. "I was just trying to learn the system, do the correct things on the field." He did the right thing most of the time, and it showed in his production. Although Harrison caught 73 passes his second year, the Colts had a lot more problems and finished 3–13. The downswing caught Infante in the backlash, and he was replaced by Jim Mora. Harbaugh was replaced as well, by rookie and No. 1 overall NFL pick Manning. It was the beginning of a beautiful friendship between Manning and Harrison.

DIAMOND IMAGES/GETTY IMAGES

MVP BOOKS COLLECTION

Manning was a thrower from the start, but he was a rookie quarterback in a veteran's league, and it took some time for him to adapt. He threw a lot of interceptions, the team had flaws, and he had to dump the ball off frequently. Harrison's catch total hit just 59, but from then on he and Manning made incredible music together. Harrison recognized that the duo could be special as a tandem. "When Peyton got here I saw a quarterback who works as hard as I do," Harrison said. "I thought, 'This could be something.'" It was.

"We always seem to be on the same page," Harrison said. In 1999, Harrison caught 115 passes. In 2000, he caught 102. In 2001, he caught 109. In 2002, he caught an astonishing 143 passes. It was a mind-boggling run. The 143 catches in 2002 is the NFL single-season mark, 20 more than any other receiver has caught in a year. And over the next four seasons Harrison caught between 82 and 96 balls per year. Harrison was lightning fast and he was strong, though he was only 6 feet and about 180 pounds, very light for all the blows he took during his 13-year career.

Manning said that Harrison's attributes as a receiver went well beyond physical skills. He saw the field, he understood dynamics of plays unfolding, and he had a tremendous memory for situations he had been through in the past. "Some guys need to see things on a grease board," Manning said. "I like when you can see it in your mind. And that's what Marvin does, too. He visualizes. He sees things in his mind so well."

Harrison was an eight-time Pro Bowl selection who caught 1,102 passes in his career, third on the all-time NFL list. His catches gained 14,580 yards, and he scored 128 touchdowns, the most in a single season being 15 twice. There is no doubt that Harrison will be elected to the Pro Football Hall of Fame in Canton, Ohio, when he becomes eligible.

THESE GUYS CAN CATCH

Marvin Harrison was in place with the Colts before Peyton Manning arrived, but he was the type of big-play receiver needed to mesh with a big-play quarterback.

Management never rested in its efforts to surround Manning with significant talent. Harrison was not big, but he was fast and a quick study of the professional game. He was already on his way to stardom by the time Manning was drafted, and Harrison had a phenomenal career for Indianapolis. Ultimately, during the 2011 season, he was inducted into the Colts' Ring of Honor, with his name displayed on the front of a balcony at Lucas Oil Stadium. The tribute took place during halftime of a Colts game in November of that season.

As was typical of him in his playing days, Harrison did not say very much when handed a microphone to address the 63,000-plus fans in the stands. He offered a brief thank you and said it was an honor to be honored. Harrison always had a

Reggie Wayne hauls in a pass that Peyton Manning dropped right over his shoulder, beyond the outstretched hand of a Tennessee Titans defensive back.
AP PHOTO/AARON M. SPRECHER

Tight end Dallas Clark stretches for a fourth-quarter pass that helped secure a 27–22 victory for the Colts over the Dolphins in 2006.
AP PHOTO/DARRON CUMMINGS

reputation for reticence. As bold as he was in his routes, he rarely had much to say to sportswriters, and teammates joked that he could go an entire practice without saying a word to them, either.

One of the Colts' key additions in 2001 was No. 1 draft pick Reggie Wayne. Wayne proved to be the perfect complement to Harrison, giving Manning two all-star receivers to choose from.

Wayne would have been a No. 1 target on most teams, but Harrison and Manning had a special rapport. It took Wayne three years to get his first 1,000-yard season, but he ended up sticking around Indianapolis for years after Harrison retired. "Reggie is a playmaker now," Manning said of Wayne. "You have to look for a guy like him on third downs. You feel good. You trust him. He's going to be in the right spot and make the catch."

Indianapolis kept filling in the blanks in the lineup with top-notch draft picks. In 2003 the Colts tabbed tight end Dallas Clark out of Iowa with their first-round selection. Clark, who is 6-foot-3 and weighs 252 pounds, stood out early in his career. He caught 29 passes as a rookie. Year-over-year, almost without fail, his totals increased. Yet no one was prepared for Clark's 2009 campaign when he became such a regular target for Manning. Performing like another wide receiver, Clark caught 100 passes for 1,106 yards that season. That made him the leading tight end receiver in the NFL and a selection to the Pro Bowl for the first time.

The emergence of Clark, adding to the popular selections at wide receiver, gave opponents one more thing to worry about in trying to hold down Manning and the Colts' explosive offense—as if the Colts weren't formidable enough.

RIVALRY

Colts vs. Patriots

During the 2000s, when the Indianapolis Colts emerged as one of the best teams in the National Football League, their path to the Super Bowl was frequently blocked by the New England Patriots, who rolled to three Super Bowl titles. The rivalry grew more intense with each passing season, and comparisons between New England star quarterback Tom Brady and the Colts' Peyton Manning became regular fodder for fans, sports talk radio shows, and newspaper columnists.

Although neither player talked about it, others busily measured Manning against Brady. Manning usually got the nod on stats—usually, but not always—but Brady had a much larger jewelry collection. Manning had his astonishing 2004 season when he threw for a record 49 touchdown passes, but darned if Brady didn't break that mark by throwing for 50 in 2007.

With both teams perennially contending in the AFC, it figured that they would bump heads in high-stakes games on numerous occasions. Between 2001 and 2011, the Colts and Patriots claimed six AFC titles. The Patriots led the all-time rivalry 46–29 as of the end of the 2011 season. They even had the edge on Indianapolis soil, winning 20 to the Colts' 17 contests in the Hoosier state.

Pats quarterback Tom Brady made the first start of his NFL career on September 30, 2001, downing the Colts 44–13. The present rivalry was born. Indianapolis came into the game 2–0, but Manning did not have a good day, throwing three interceptions.

A memorable game that felt like a playoff battle was a November 30, 2003, regular-season contest in Indianapolis. Both teams were 9–2 coming in. Although Manning threw four touchdown passes, Brady pulled out the win with a touchdown pass to Deion Branch, sealing the win for the Patriots 38–34.

On January 18, 2004, the Patriots won the AFC crown with a 24–14 victory over the Colts. Adam Vinatieri, who became the most famous placekicker in Patriots history, kicked five field goals that day. Later that calendar year, to start the regular season, the Patriots beat Indianapolis 27–24, after trailing 17–13 at the half.

On January 16, 2005, New England won the AFC Divisional Game 20–3 over the Colts. Of all things, the Patriots won with the ground game, as Corey Dillon rushed for 142 yards—and with defense, as linebacker Teddy Bruschi recovered two Colts fumbles. After that demoralizing defeat, the Colts-Patriots matches turned, with Indianapolis gaining the upper hand for the next several years.

"It's been a great rivalry for a lot of reasons," Brady said. "We've played a lot of meaningful games against them." Indeed, rare is the season when the road to the Super Bowl, or at least deep into the playoffs, does not pit the Colts against the Patriots.

"There's been a lot of great days over the years," said Colts coach Jim Caldwell in 2010. That year a *Sports Illustrated* writer proclaimed the Brady-Manning showdowns within the rivalry to be "the greatest QB rivalry in the NFL. Ever."

As an illustration of Colts fans' anti-Patriots fervor, they became New York Giants fans by proxy when the city of Indianapolis hosted the 2012 Super Bowl, which featured the Patriots and G-Men in a rematch of Super Bowl XLII. Fans voiced their opinions with a chorus of "boos" during media sessions, at the Super Bowl Village, and at the NFL Experience. It helped that the Giants were led by Peyton Manning's younger brother, Eli—but Colts fans didn't need any extra incentive to root against the Patriots.

The Colts and the Patriots prepare to clash at the line of scrimmage. AP PHOTO/WINSLOW TOWNSON

STAYING THE COURSE

Whether the bitter defeat made the Colts angry, more determined, or more experienced, it did not seem to affect the team the next season. The Colts of 2006 were as good as usual, finishing 12–4. The first win came in the so-called Manning Bowl, when Indianapolis bested the New York Giants 26–21 in a game that pitted Peyton against his younger brother, Eli.

It was a good game for fans and a better game for Colts fans. Adam Vinatieri, the newly acquired kicker who had previously played for the nemesis Patriots, connected on four field goals. Young Eli, the less experienced Manning, played quite well, throwing for 247 yards and two touchdowns, but older brother Peyton was the winner and could afford to be gracious with his post-game comments. When asked if he spoke to his brother as they left the field, Manning said he did.

"I told him I was proud of the way he competed," Peyton Manning said. "I enjoyed watching him play in person." That was a rare occurrence, given their age difference and the nature of playing on different teams in different cities concurrently. But family feelings aside, it was better to be on the winning team.

The best teams find a way to win when they are not playing at their best, and in the third week of the regular season, the Colts had one of those days. They beat the Jacksonville Jaguars 21–14, pulling it out despite Jacksonville controlling the ball for twice as long. "We did a great job of hanging in there," said defensive end Dwight Freeney.

Indianapolis' fourth straight win to start the season was even tougher to salt away. The Colts beat the New York Jets 31–28 after trailing in the fourth quarter. New York was boosted by a 103-yard kickoff return from Justin Miller, but Manning engineered a late score. "We've got some veteran players who know how to make big plays at crunch time," Dungy said.

The games kept getting closer and closer, but Indianapolis continued to prevail. The Colts moved to 5–0 when they edged the Tennessee Titans 14–13. A Reggie Wayne diving catch provided a crucial first down, and he caught the winning touchdown pass soon after.

At that point in the season, defensive back Cato June was correct in describing the Colts as "a team that's going to find a way to win." However, there was no question that the Colts were relieved to squeak by the Titans after being favored by almost 19 points. Thinking back to other close games in his life when his team was heavily favored, Wayne said, "It's like we used to say when we were in college. 'Those guys are on scholarship, too.'"

Peyton Manning was the major reason the Colts could win the close ones. Manning never got flustered, always showed leadership, and had the talent to parade the Colts down the field when a ticking clock required urgency and precision. Manning was precise all day long when the Colts topped the Denver Broncos 34–31. Manning led a fourth-quarter rally and completed 32 out of 39 pass attempts for 345 yards on the day, connecting with Wayne for three of his touchdowns. "You

The Manning brothers wish each other well after an early-season matchup between the Colts and the Giants in 2006. RON ANTONELLI/NY DAILY NEWS ARCHIVE VIA GETTY IMAGES

After Edgerrin James posted back-to-back 1,500-yard seasons in 2004 and 2005, some were surprised the Colts let him walk away in free agency—but rookie rushing back Joseph Addai was a pleasant surprise in 2006. MICHAEL HICKEY/NFL/GETTY IMAGES

can't overemphasize how good he is," Tony Dungy said of his quarterback.

The Colts never seemed to have a blowout. Every game was tense. Moving to 8–0 at the expense of the New England Patriots was very satisfying, and the Colts overcame the Patriots with defense more than any other facet of the game. Their five forced turnovers helped the Colts to a 27–20 win.

"We just tried to be 11 guys ball-hawking," said defensive end Robert Mathis after the victory that left the Colts the only unbeaten team in the NFL. "We had them in a chase position most of the night," Manning said. "That was part of the plan, and it worked out well for us."

The Colts won their first nine games—No. 9 was another one-pointer, 17–16, over Buffalo. Although the mark has been bettered since, the triumph was a milestone. It was the first time since the NFL's founding in 1920 that a team started 9–0 two years in a row. Indianapolis had survived close game after close game before losing to the Dallas Cowboys 21–14, on a day when the Colts committed four turnovers. "Today we couldn't dodge a bullet," Dungy said. "You play a good team and you make a mistake, and it's going to cost you."

Still, by then the Colts were running away with their division once again. Indianapolis rebounded from the Dallas loss neatly, exploding for a 45–21 win over the Philadelphia Eagles. This game was a coming-out party for rookie running back Joseph Addai. After Edgerrin James left for the Arizona Cardinals as a free agent, the 5-foot-11, 214-pound Addai, who starred at Louisiana State, was his heir. Addai ran for 171 yards and averaged a healthy 7.1 yards per carry. When the game ended, Addai gathered his offensive linemen for a group hug in the end zone. "I wanted to share the moment with them and congratulate them on doing such a good job," he said.

Center Jeff Saturday, the Plymouth Rock in the middle of the Colts' line, appreciated the gesture and said the way Addai performed was good for everyone. "Joseph ran great," Saturday said. "It's obviously fun when you can run the ball like we did tonight."

During the regular season the Colts had only one true clunker of a game, a 44–17 loss to Jacksonville. But as they wrapped up the 12–4 year, the Colts had already proved they could win with regularity during the regular season.

Jeff Saturday (63) and the Colts offensive line paved the way for Addai's breakout game against the Eagles in 2006. DREW HALLOWELL/GETTY IMAGES

The 2005 and 2006 Colts were the first team in the history of the NFL to begin consecutive seasons with 9–0 records.

JEFF SATURDAY
At the Center of the Action

You can't overstate the importance of having an excellent center, particularly in a complicated system like the one run by the Colts. Jeff Saturday was an ideal fit with Peyton Manning. DILIP VISHWANAT/GETTY IMAGES

For a time some years ago there was a series of commercials about E. F. Hutton & Co., a one-time stock brokerage house. The premise was, "When E. F. Hutton talks, people listen." Well, the same is true for Jeff Saturday, the star center for the Indianapolis Colts. For 13 years Saturday was the team's voice of reason and the sturdiest pillar on the offensive line.

The 6-foot-2, 295-pound blocker finished his 13th season with the Colts in 2011 and might also be described as Peyton Manning's main bodyguard. Saturday is not just the guy who hikes the ball to the star quarterback when he calls for it; he is one of his chief protectors.

A five-time Pro Bowler, Saturday is one of the most prominent faces of the Indianapolis franchise, unusual in that linemen are often anonymous. Saturday, however, is very active in community affairs, lending his time, efforts, and cooperation to innumerable charitable efforts.

Working with the NFL Players Association, Saturday also played a pivotal role during the summer of 2011 in negotiations for the NFL's collective bargaining agreement, the passing of which averted a long-term labor impasse that could have jeopardized the season. Instead, the players and owners inked a 10-year agreement. As one of the key bargainers, Saturday graciously and enthusiastically embraced New England Patriots' owner Robert Kraft when the deal was cemented. Kraft's wife had recently passed away, yet the owner remained committed to reaching an agreement with the players. Saturday called Kraft "a man who helped us save football." Their warm hug at the end of tense negotiations was a highly visible sign of peace that football fans sought.

With the Colts' line in flux, it would have been better if training camp had begun on time. But as he had been for some time (though more so in 2011 because new talent was being blended in), Saturday served as the voice and leader of the offensive line. "You will see how these young guys are progressing," Saturday predicted during the exhibition season. But he was raring to play for real. "I'm looking forward to being able to hit some other people and make it count."

It was much more fun being on the field, even for practice, than it was sitting in long meetings trying to hammer out a labor pact. "I went to all of those meetings so I could come to these," Saturday said. "I can tell you I would much rather be out on the field playing ball." That was easy for Saturday to say at the time, but what he didn't see coming was the most trying year of his career. The Colts started poorly and seemed to get worse. When things hit a low point, Saturday took charge in a closed-door, players-only meeting—just as he had as a player rep—forcefully imparting the message that things had to change.

Saturday's exact wording was not revealed, but the Colts listened closely and said he gave them an earful. Once again, it was Jeff Saturday the leader talking, and Jeff Saturday the player snapping the ball.

MVP BOOKS COLLECTION

THESE GUYS CAN HIT

The biggest stars of the Colts' defense during their finest years were defensive ends Dwight Freeney, drafted from Syracuse in 2002, and the less heralded Robert Mathis out of Alabama A&M in 2003. Freeney became one of the greatest pass rushers in NFL history, surpassing 100 career sacks in 2011. A little bit of a late bloomer, Mathis also paid dividends for a long time.

Dwight Freeney is a big and strong defensive end, but his position is about more than wrestling blockers with brute strength. Freeney is no weakling at 6-foot-1 and 268 pounds, but he's even faster than he is powerful. His quickness and slippery moves are what transform him into a heat-seeking missile aimed at quarterbacks.

Freeney was for years the Colts' sackmeister, the man on the defense who strikes fear into the hearts of opposing offensive players. He is the guy counted on to disrupt foes, throw them off of their game plans, and make quarterbacks so nervous they can't concentrate on what they're doing. He jukes and fakes and can run around blockers so fast they get caught up in his backwash as he swims past, or they try to grab and clutch him and get called for holding. Freeney makes offensive linemen look bad when they can't keep him out of their backfield.

"He's almost like a tornado," said former teammate David Thornton, "spinning around everywhere nonstop, tearing up everything in sight." Freeney has reduced his pass rushing to a science based on his study of linemen's tendencies. "I can tell you if a guy is leaning forward a little," Freeney said, "chances are the bull-rush is probably not going to be a great rush this week. I'll go with more speed-rush, get him leaning forward to drive and missing me. A guy who likes to sit back, I'm going to get into him a little bit stronger and do power moves like the bull-rush."

With an arsenal including a mean bull rush and a speedy spin move, Dwight Freeney makes it his business to get to the quarterback.
(TOP) JOE ROBBINS/GETTY IMAGES; (BOTTOM) MVP BOOKS COLLECTION

The Colts knew exactly what they were getting when they selected Freeney. In a game against Virginia Tech in college, Freeney recorded 4 1/2 sacks on Michael Vick. A two-year starter for the Orangeman, Freeney recorded 17 sacks in his senior year. The Big East was glad to see him go.

Freeney was on a Hall of Fame pace from the beginning of his pro career, destroying quarterbacks and anyone else who got into his way. Sometimes Freeney occupies two linemen at once, allowing a teammate to break in for a tackle. Former Colts coach Tony Dungy said that's part of Freeney's value. "He has an impact on the play and the blocking schemes whether he touches the ball or not, just being out there," Dungy said.

A six-time Pro Bowl player, Freeney notched 16 sacks during the 2004 season to lead the NFL, and he has more than 100 career sacks. Freeney's attributes—an ability to run the 40-yard dash in 4.48 seconds, remarkable for a defensive lineman, and a vertical leap of 40 inches—are what make him so difficult to cope with for linemen. Freeney repeatedly proved his worth to the Colts, who rewarded him with a six-year, $72 million deal in 2007. "Anytime you have a guy like that, he can be a real difference maker in the ballgame," said Colts quarterback Peyton Manning.

Mathis grew up in Atlanta and attended a historically black, off-the-beaten-path college that didn't play a high-profile schedule that garnered national TV exposure. But as soon as the 6-foot-2, 245-pound Mathis got his chance in the pros, he made his mark.

A high school guidance counselor asked Mathis what he planned to do with his life. He said, "I'm going to play in the NFL." The counselor was skeptical. When he asked Mathis what his Plan B was, Mathis replied, "Don't have one. I'm going to play in the NFL." That singular determination is one of his defining characteristics.

One reason to doubt Mathis at the time was his size. As a senior in high school, he was 5-foot-10 and admits that his listed weight of 195 pounds was exaggerated. Absolutely no one recruited Mathis for college play. He didn't even get form-letter feelers. The Alabama A&M coach discovered Mathis while watching game film and offered his last scholarship to a player who looked fast and hustled.

A lot of time spent in the weight room and in front of open refrigerator doors aided Mathis' growth during college. He became a home-wrecker on defense who wreaked havoc on quarterbacks and anyone else who dared to carry the ball near him. He recorded 20 sacks and forced 10 fumbles in his senior year alone.

Still, there was no indication that any pro team even knew he existed. Mathis put together his own highlight film and sent it to NFL teams. On draft day, the Colts grabbed him. That gave Mathis a chance, and he spent three years doing damage on special teams before he became a starter—and a star—in 2006.

"His effort is unbelievable," Freeney said of his defensive end partner.

By the 2011 season, Mathis was a three-time Pro Bowl selection. He had traveled far by doing the same type of stuff he did in college. He had compiled four 10-sack seasons and had answered that old guidance counselor. "Coming from where I came from, you don't think stuff like this happens to people like me," Mathis said.

Robert Mathis makes his presence felt on the opposite side of the Colts defensive line from Freeney.
(TOP) MICHAEL HICKEY/GETTY IMAGES; (BOTTOM) MVP BOOKS COLLECTION

TIME TO WIN IT ALL

By 2006 it was not enough for the Colts to merely qualify for the playoffs. It was not idle thinking to believe this team could finally win a Super Bowl for Indianapolis, and the team felt incomplete without that Lombardi Trophy.

Adam Vinatieri kicks one of his five field goals against the Ravens—his leg was the lone source of scoring for the Colts in their 15–6 victory.
CHRIS MCGRATH/GETTY IMAGES

As the Colts learned, the most important thing is to win the first playoff game, given the single elimination nature of the NFL playoffs. Everyone knows: you lose, you go home. The Colts were matched up with the Kansas City Chiefs in the AFC Wild Card Game, and Indianapolis prevailed 23–8.

At various times during the season, the Colts' defense had been maligned for being the weak point of the team, but not in this game. Indianapolis held the Chiefs to 44 yards rushing and 126 total offensive yards in a shut-down performance. "Our defense did a great job," Reggie Wayne said. "I guess they wanted to shut up a lot of critics."

After the previous season's opening-round loss to the Steelers, a playoff win was critical to the franchise's morale, belief in itself, and the organization's commitment to the way it did business.

The second round of the playoffs loomed as more challenging. The Baltimore Ravens were renowned for their defense, and the Colts rode a high-scoring offense. The game seemed like a collision between an immovable object and an unstoppable force. Indeed, it was a game played out in the trenches. Peyton Manning was held in check with only 170 yards gained through the air and two interceptions. But the Colts' defense was again fabulous, forcing four turnovers. The Ravens hardly sustained movement of the ball.

Indianapolis was robbed of its usual big-play offense, but the Colts did just enough to bring Adam Vinatieri, a legend for

The Colts defense came up huge on the road against Baltimore in the 2007 playoffs. Here, Antoine Bethea hauls in an interception.
DOUG PENSINGER/GETTY IMAGES

his success with the Patriots, into field-goal range. He once again distinguished himself against the Ravens, making five field goals to provide all of the Colts' points in a 15–6 win.

"You just feel like he [Vinatieri] is going to make everything when he goes out there," Dungy said. "In games like this, it's necessary." Thanks to one of the most prominent sports heroes from the state of North Dakota, the Colts moved on to the AFC Championship Game against—wouldn't you know it—the Patriots, Vinatieri's old team.

The prize for the winner of the Colts-Patriots game was a trip to the Super Bowl. The Patriots had seasoning on their side. The Colts had hunger on theirs. Down 21–3 at one point, Manning rallied his guys—but things were still looking iffy in the closing minutes of the fourth period. New England led 34–31 and had Indianapolis pinned on its own 20-yard line with 2:17 to play. Was there enough time to go 80 yards? "There was no doubt in anybody's mind that we were going to take the ball down and score," recalled Dungy.

Dallas Clark taps his toes to complete a crucial reception during the AFC Championship Game. DOUG BENC/GETTY IMAGES

Bryan Fletcher was an unlikely hero in the Colts' triumph over the New England Patriots in the AFC Championship Game. ROB TRINGALI/ SPORTSCHROME/GETTY IMAGES

Perhaps Dungy should have issued an all-points bulletin to the people of Indianapolis, who were biting their nails down to the cuticles. A couple of minutes later, after a seven-play drive, the Colts got the touchdown they coveted, a three-yard run by Addai. Wayne made two key catches, but lesser-known Bryan Fletcher's 32-yard play was the flashiest of the journey downfield. "Those are dreams you have as a kid," Manning said of reaching his first Super Bowl game.

"I'm really happy for Peyton," coach Tony Dungy said. "He was very, very calm. He had to bring us from behind three or four times. It was fitting."

Indianapolis won its biggest game to that point at home in the RCA Dome, with 57,433 of their own fans cheering the result and roaring as confetti fell from the ceiling.

At last, more than two decades after the Colts slipped away from Baltimore, Indianapolis had a Super Bowl entrant. One of the biggest heroes of the Patriots game was tight end Dallas Clark, who caught six passes for 137 yards. "I've never been prouder," said Dungy, who was taking a team to the Super Bowl for the first time.

The victory over the Patriots sent the Colts to Miami, where they would meet the Chicago Bears in Super Bowl XLI on February 4, 2007. The Bears had not won the Super Bowl since coach Mike Ditka's Monsters of the Midway dominated the 1985 season. One of the main story lines of the present-day confrontation, however, was Bears coach Lovie Smith. Smith was a former assistant to Dungy in Tampa, and the game would mark the first time two African American head coaches faced off in the Super Bowl. Both men recognized the

AP PHOTO/JEFF ROBERSON

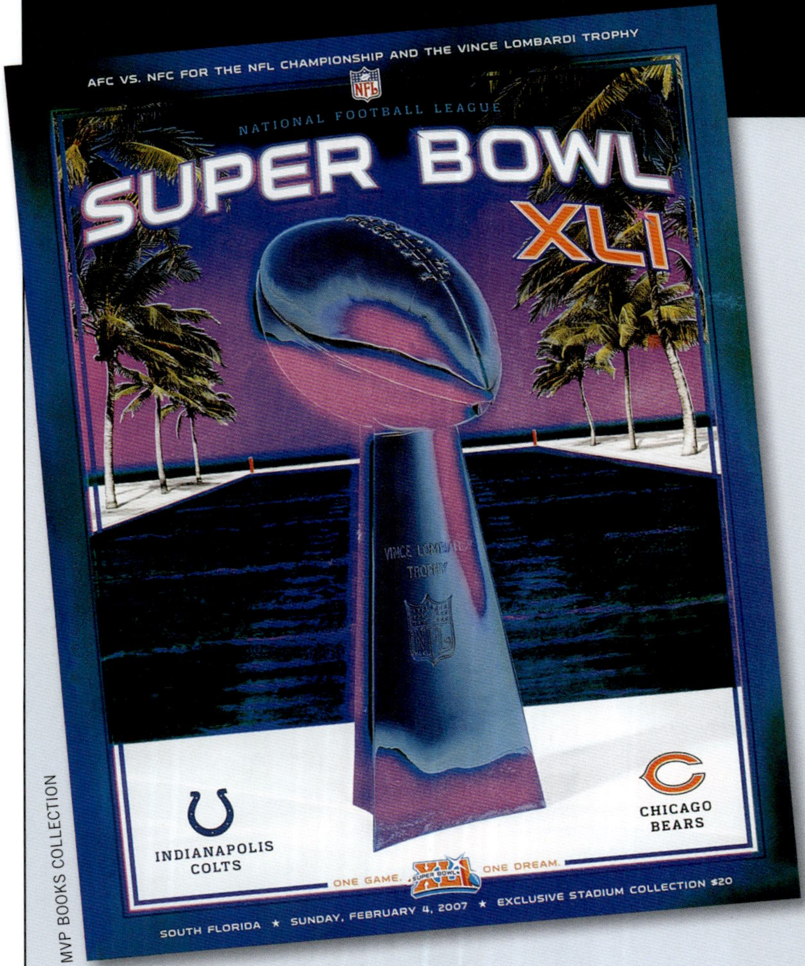

MVP BOOKS COLLECTION

significance of the moment—not many years earlier it had taken a full-fledged lobbying campaign for black coaches to even be interviewed for the NFL's top jobs. Regardless of which team won, it would be the first time any African American coach had led a team to the Super Bowl title. It turned out to be Dungy making that history, though his team immediately fell behind the Smith's Bears.

Chicago's Devin Hester was in the process of establishing himself as perhaps the greatest kick and punt-return man in NFL history. Pre-game speculation centered on whether the Colts should even kick to him, but they did just that on the opening kickoff. Sure enough, the speedster flew down the field, delivering a shocking early blow to the Colts with a 92-yard romp for a touchdown. The game was only seconds old, and Indianapolis trailed 7–0.

Indianapolis did not get rattled, though—at least not visibly. "We've been in those situations before," said Colts receiver Marvin Harrison, who watched the play unfold from the sideline. "When we're down, we never panic. We just know we have to go out there and move the football, and that's what we did."

To illustrate that they were not set back too much, the Colts retaliated before the end of the first quarter with an 80-yard TD drive that culminated in a 53-yard pass from Manning to Wayne. The Bears scored again before the period ended, but the second quarter belonged to the Colts. Vinatieri kicked a 29-yard field goal, and Dominic Rhodes scored on a one-yard run to give Indianapolis a 16–14 halftime lead.

"We talked a lot at halftime about how we just had to keep our poise and continue to play to have a chance in the fourth quarter," Dungy said.

All of the scoring anyone could muster in the third quarter was field goals. Vinatieri kicked two, and the Bears' Robbie Gould kicked one. So it was 22–17 Indianapolis as the fourth quarter began, hardly a comfortable lead for the Colts. Back and forth the offenses went, contained by the defenses. A big play could be a difference maker for either side. The Bears trailed by less than a touchdown, and the Colts wanted to add pad their margin.

The breakthrough came on a surprising play, but neither offense provided it. Colts defensive back Kelvin Hayden picked off a Rex Grossman pass and returned it 56 yards for a touchdown. There was no catching the Colts after that.

Indianapolis banked a 29–17 victory, the first Super Bowl crown for the club since it relocated from Baltimore, a milestone in franchise history. The final gun triggered a celebration in the stands, on the field, and back home in Indianapolis. "Now it's time to party," announced safety Bob Sanders, who intercepted a pass as well. "Now we can just let loose and enjoy it."

It was a crowning moment for many Colts who had played together for years. Some of them had been through the leanest times. Some of them had experienced only good seasons that ended with near-misses and disappointment. Not this time around.

Harrison was one of those who predated the success and contributed mightily to making the Colts a success. "We've done whatever we've had to do

Reggie Wayne races toward the end zone for a long touchdown in Super Bowl XLI.
MICHAEL ZAGARIS/GETTY IMAGES

to win football games," he said of that marvelous season. "This team just does what it has to to win. I just know we're world champs right now."

Those previous close-call defeats were wearisome in the offseason, and it was a relief— and nearly disorienting—for players to conclude a season with a win. Unless you capture the Super Bowl, a playoff team always goes out with a loss. "It was a long time coming for us," said defensive end Dwight Freeney. "I'm still amazed. We're the world champs. We knew we could do it."

No one in the lineup earned the moment more than tackle Tarik Glenn, the 1997 No. 1 draft pick out of California who labored through the difficult years before management acquired all of the talent that surrounded him. He couldn't help but muse about the peculiarities inherent in every NFL season. This championship felt as if it was a year late. Only a season earlier, the Colts had everything going for them and were knocked out in the first round of the playoffs. This year, when things did not go as smoothly and they lost four times, they ended up winning it all. "Last year, it was like the perfect season," Glenn said of 2005. "We had the perfect scenario. We had all the first-round byes, the best record in the NFL, and it didn't work out. We took the long route this year, and we learned how to fight.

"When we got down early in this game—on the first play of the game—we knew we had the ability to fight back regardless of what the score looked like. That's why this team has a fighting heart, and that's why we won the game."

The Colts defense played a significant role in their Super Bowl XLI victory, getting key interceptions from both Bob Sanders and Kelvin Hayden. (ABOVE) BRIAN BAHR/GETTY IMAGES; (LEFT) JED JACOBSOHN/GETTY IMAGES

Manning directs his offense during Super Bowl XLI, faced with the challenge of beating Chicago's stellar duo of linebackers, Brian Urlacher and Lance Briggs. NICK LAHAM/GETTY IMAGES

Tony Dungy hoists the Lombardi Trophy to the delight of Colts fans gathered for a rally at Lucas Oil Stadium. TASOS KATOPODIS/GETTY IMAGES

THE SUPER BOWL DREAM COMES TRUE

The Super Bowl at last. The Baltimore Colts had been in their share of title games, but it took a long time for the Indianapolis Colts to make it to the most watched sporting event in the United States. Indianapolis will always remember February 2007 fondly.

For years Indianapolis had played well enough to get into the playoffs. For years they had played well enough to win playoff games. But they had not sustained that success well enough to reach the Super Bowl, until the 2006 season when they finished 12–4.

In the year that Joseph Addai replaced Edgerrin James in the backfield with his own 1,000-yard season, and in a year when Peyton Manning put together a 31-touchdown-pass, 9-interception season with 4,397 yards gained, everything came together.

AFC champs and undefeated at home in the regular season, the Colts won three playoff games to reach their first Super Bowl. Indianapolis toppled Kansas City 23–8, edged the Baltimore Ravens on the road 15–6, survived a 38–34 shootout with the New England Patriots, and found itself as one of the last two teams standing for a showdown in Miami with the NFC Chicago Bears.

Although the Bears had not been as consistent as the Colts in recent years, it had been a long time coming for that franchise to get back to the big game as well. If Manning had become the king of offensive football, Chicago's middle

SUPER BOWL XLI

INDIANAPOLIS COLTS 29 — **CHICAGO BEARS** 17

	1	2	3	4	Total
INDIANAPOLIS COLTS	6	10	6	7	29
CHICAGO BEARS	14	0	3	0	17

Reggie Wayne runs in the rain for a 53-yard touchdown reception during the Colts' Super Bowl XLI victory over the Chicago Bears. DONALD MIRALLE/NFL/GETTY IMAGES

linebacker Brian Urlacher had emerged as the premier defensive player in the league. And he had never played in a Super Bowl. In one of his early press conferences, Urlacher joked about how much space Manning's biography took up in the team media guide. "Only 18 pages, that's it, huh?" Urlacher said. "He's great. He will be, numbers-wise, the best of all time when he's finished playing. It's a big challenge for our defense."

In the history of the Super Bowl, the team that gets ahead early has often stayed ahead, so it was the goal of both clubs to get on the scoreboard first and to contain the opposition. The Bears featured one of the greatest return men of all time in Devin Hester, who electrified fans and shocked the Colts by returning the opening kickoff 92 yards for a touchdown. Robbie Gould booted the extra point, and Chicago led 7–0 after just 14 seconds of play.

This was not what the Colts wanted. Because it was raining, it seemed as if the weather might be an obstacle to Manning and the passing game. There were some iffy moments gripping the ball, but the moisture did not turn out to be a major factor. "Obviously, it didn't look great after the opening kickoff," Manning said, "but kind of like we've done all playoffs, no panic whatsoever. Everybody stayed calm."

The Colts bounced back when Manning fired a 53-yard strike to Reggie Wayne for a score. But the Bears, with Rex Grossman calling the signals, scored again within two minutes and came out of the first period with a 14–6 lead.

Indianapolis owned the second quarter, collecting 10 points for a

MVP BOOKS COLLECTION

Colts fans celebrate their Super Bowl XLI victory in Indianapolis.

TASOS KATOPODIS/GETTY IMAGES

16–14 halftime lead, and Adam Vinatieri notched field goals of 24 and 20 yards in the third quarter for a 22–14 lead before Gould nailed a 44-yarder. So the Colts led 22–17 heading into the fourth quarter. It was better to be ahead than behind, but it was certainly not a safe lead.

Defenses were in control during the fourth period. The Bears could not rally, and Manning could not extend the lead. The game-breaker finally came on an unexpected play. Colts defensive back Kelvin Hayden, who grew up a Bears fan in Chicago, plucked a Grossman pass out of the air and ran it back 56 yards for a touchdown. Hayden's first career interception represented the final points of the day and provided the Colts with an adequate cushion. "I was just glad that I had the fundamentals, and I am glad just to make the play," said Hayden, who said he was on guard against receiver Mushin Muhammad's route from film preparedness. "I am blessed that I did not step out of bounds, as it was a big part of the game, and now we are Super Bowl champions. Come tomorrow I am back to being a Bears fan."

Maybe so. But at that moment Hayden was definitely more popular in Indianapolis than he was in Chicago.

The Colts had been viewed as an offensive steamroller for some time, but defense played a huge role in the Super Bowl and in the playoffs, and Manning noted it. "We truly got here as a team," Manning said. "I'm proud to be a part of them. I wanted to be on a team that won the Super Bowl. To me that's what it's been about. In years past when our team's come up short, it's been disappointing. Somehow we found a way to have learned from some of those losses and we've been a better team because of it."

NOTHING EVER STAYS THE SAME

After they finished the regular season 13–3 in 2007, it appeared that the Colts had every chance to return to the Super Bowl and win two in a row. They definitely seemed to have the credentials to pull off that rarity.

Bob Sanders delivers one of his signature blows to Titans wide receiver Drew Bennett in 2005. Bennett eventually lost control of the ball, and Sanders came up with the interception.
AP PHOTO/JOHN RUSSELL

Joseph Addai had been a 1,000-yard rusher as a rookie, and he repeated that feat in his sophomore season. Peyton Manning was in top form with 31 touchdown passes against 14 interceptions. Marvin Harrison wasn't quite done, but Wayne was now Manning's top target with 104 catches for 1,510 yards and 10 touchdowns. Dallas Clark scored 11 TDs. The defense allowed only 262 points for the season.

Although Dwight Freeney and Robert Mathis were playmakers on the outside of the defensive line, the spirit of the defense was safety Bob Sanders. Standing only 5-foot-8, he played much bigger than his size. He roamed the field terrorizing offenses. "Bob's the best open-field tackler in football," Clark said.

The only problem was that Sanders could not stay healthy. Nicknamed "The Hitman" because he hit so hard, Sanders was such an impact player in 2007 he was named the league's top defensive performer. "I think this year I really played like I wanted to play," Sanders said. "I give a lot of credit to my teammates, who helped me stay consistent in practice and in games."

Once again the Colts had home-field advantage for a playoff game, but any talk of a dynasty was spiked quickly when the San Diego Chargers rolled into Indianapolis and flew home with a 28–24 upset win.

MVP BOOKS COLLECTION

Just like that, the season was over after a single playoff game. And Sanders was hurt yet again versus San Diego, suffering a shoulder injury that required surgery.

By then Sanders had missed as many games because of injury as he had played in (24 each). Although he was a tremendous asset when healthy, he got paid millions of dollars for not playing, too. Sanders went from a stress fracture in his right foot to two shoulder injuries to a knee injury to a torn bicep. He missed 12 to 15 games in some seasons, not to mention minicamps and other offseason workouts. Eventually, the hard-hitting safety parted ways with the Colts in February 2011. There was no way the team could continue to risk counting on him and paying him if he couldn't suit up. When he was released, Sanders had played only nine games in the preceding three years. "I always will consider myself a Colt," Sanders said at the time. Not long after, he officially became a San Diego Charger.

> **"I always will consider myself a Colt."—Bob Sanders**

A year after the hurtful playoff loss to San Diego, an instant replay occurred. In 2008, the Colts ran up a 12–4 record and lost once again to the Chargers in the first round of the playoffs. It was 23–17 loss, this time in overtime.

Despite a 13–3 regular season in 2007, Manning wasn't able to lead the Colts to a playoff victory over the San Diego Chargers. STREETER LECKA/GETTY IMAGES

MVP BOOKS COLLECTION

BOB SANDERS

Refused to Play Small

In some ways Bob Sanders might have been the best defensive player in Indianapolis Colts history. Then again, he just might have been the most frustrating player in Indianapolis Colts history.

When he was healthy, Sanders was a demon on defense, a phenomenal player who could single-handedly disrupt the opposing team. "His presence makes us better," said Colts linebacker Gary Brackett. "He's a game-changer." The only problem was that he was rarely healthy. Sanders kept getting injured and missing entire seasons or all but a few games in a season. Those circumstances ruined his potential value and stifled his talent, which was considerable.

Sanders joined the Colts in 2004 after a college career at Iowa. Although he is only 5-foot-8, Sanders is remarkably powerful at 206 pounds. Nicknamed "The Hitman" for his hard tackling, Sanders was the NFL Defensive Player of the Year in 2007 and a cornerstone of the Colts' defense during their Super Bowl championship run. Coach Tony Dungy said Sanders was so good that the defensive back should be called "The Eraser" for his ability to wipe out his teammates' mistakes.

Sanders said the main reason for his success in nailing ball-carriers is something he learned in pee wee football. Coaches taught tacklers to stay low to the ground for leverage. "It helps me now being explosive in short areas," Sanders said, "because it's a combination of power, speed, and quickness. You've got to bring it all together."

When Sanders was on his game, he uplifted the entire Colts defense and was named to two Pro Bowl teams. But ankle and knee injuries and a torn biceps interrupted his playing time and efficiency. To illustrate how dominant Sanders was at his best, at one point when he seemed to be shutting down offenses at will, a series of jokes ran on the Internet about his prowess. Some of them went like this: "Superman wears Bob Sanders underwear," or "When Bob Sanders executes a pushup, he does not push himself up; he pushes the earth down."

Bob Sanders was an exciting force on the back end of the Colts secondary before injuries derailed his career. JOE ROBBINS/GETTY IMAGES

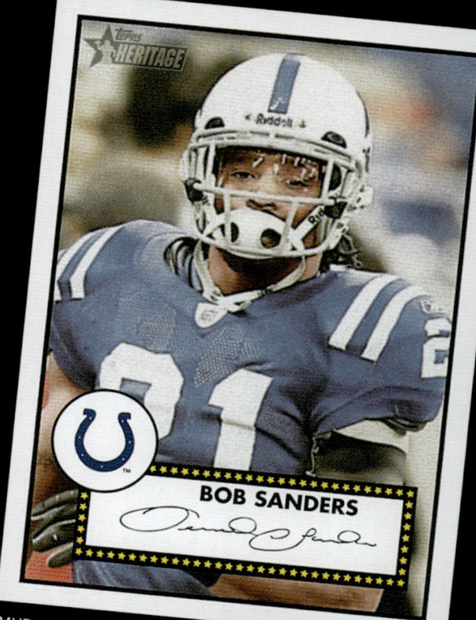

MVP BOOKS COLLECTION

One thing Sanders never did in a Colts uniform was take plays off. Maybe he just hit too hard for his own good, although he said that was a personal trademark from the time he began playing football as a youth. "As a kid, I would play until I passed out," he said in a rather alarming statement. "I would run to the store. I would run to my friend's house. My mom would tell me to slow down, but I couldn't. I didn't know how. That's just me."

As a pro he ran to glory, but it seemed as if he ran into too many brick walls. Eventually, Sanders parted ways with the Colts and signed a one-year contract with the San Diego Chargers in 2011. He did not last through the end of September before another knee injury put him on the season-ending injured reserve list for the fourth straight year.

LUCAS OIL STADIUM

A Modern Football Palace

As part of Indianapolis' continuing focus on sports in its downtown area, the Colts became tenants of the spectacular new $720 million Lucas Oil Stadium beginning in 2008. Lucas Oil seats more than 64,000 people for football, replacing the RCA Dome (which had originally been named the Hoosier Dome). The Dome served as the Colts' first Indianapolis home from 1984 to 2007 and cost about a one-tenth as much as Lucas Oil to construct. It was built on spec, on the theory that Indianapolis would more easily attract a NFL team if the city had already built a modern stadium. The strategy worked.

In 2008, the RCA Dome, which held just over 60,000 for football, was imploded at a cost of $3.5 million. The prime downtown real estate space it occupied is now used for other purposes.

Lucas Oil Stadium—which can be expanded to a 70,000-seat capacity for special events such as the 2012 Super Bowl—did not skimp on frills, with 137 luxury suites inside the 1.8-million-square-foot structure. The stadium's retractable roof can open or close in about nine minutes but must remain closed if thunderstorms are nearby or the temperature dips below 40 degrees.

MVP BOOKS COLLECTION

August 24, 2008: The Colts' first preseason game in Lucas Oil Stadium.
AP PHOTO/TOM STRICKLAND

Ribbon-cutting for the distinctive retro-looking brick building featured Governor Mitch Daniels and Indianapolis Mayor Greg Ballard on August 16, 2008. The first football games played in the stadium actually involved Indiana high school football teams, and the nation was introduced to Lucas Oil through an NBC *Sunday Night Football* broadcast in 2008, when the Colts met the Chicago Bears.

One reviewer praised the stadium enthusiastically, noting, "The amazing thing about Lucas Oil Stadium is that it manages to feel immense and intimate at the same time." Used as a selling point for Indianapolis to attract more events, Lucas Oil Stadium hosted NCAA basketball regional play and a Final Four in 2010, in addition to the inaugural Big Ten football championship in 2011.

"The stadium is one of the brightest gems in Indy's crown," wrote a commentator for a web site focused on vacations. The writer also ratcheted up the stadium's own "fan-friendly" description to "over-the-top-opulent."

Tourists tour it, and other events are scheduled there during the 350 or so days the team does not need the building. But above all else, Lucas Oil Stadium is the home of the Indianapolis Colts.

COACH-IN-WAITING CALDWELL

At the end of the 2008 season, Tony Dungy stepped down from his position as coach. At age 53, Dungy wanted to pursue other things in life, and right-hand man Jim Caldwell was promoted to head coach.

Caldwell had been on the Colts' staff for seven years before assuming the top job for the 2009 season. Caldwell had an extensive background as a college assistant coach, including time spent at Penn State, Louisville, and Colorado. As a player Caldwell had been a defensive back for Iowa.

Unlike most new coaches who take over teams that are reeling from losses where the preceding coach was fired, Caldwell stepped into a sweet position, with a playoff-caliber team lead by stars such as Manning, Wayne, Freeney, Mathis, and center Jeff Saturday.

Quiet by inclination and stoic by habit, Caldwell displayed no fieriness in public. He rarely changed expression on the sideline or at press conferences and practically never joked around. What he did do was make the transition from Dungy's administration to his a smooth one. The Colts won their first 14 games in a row in 2009, finished 14–2 in the regular season, and looked sharp when the playoffs opened.

The Colts were awarded a first-round playoff bye and hosted the Baltimore Ravens at Lucas Oil Stadium in their first game. Although defense was not as much of an overall asset as it had been over the preceding few years, it was the dominating factor in this 20–3 win. Manning had just been named Most Valuable Player of the NFL for a record fourth time, and the Colts had an extra week of practice to prepare. It showed.

"I thought we had good preparation coming into this game, thought we came out sharp and kind of set the tempo from the get-go," Manning said.

Indianapolis' defense created four turnovers and held the Ravens' leading rusher Ray Rice to 67 yards on the ground.

"It was a heck of a performance," Caldwell said. "Our defense did a tremendous job."

In his first season as head coach of the Colts, Jim Caldwell picked up where Tony Dungy had left off, posting a 14–2 record.
AP PHOTO/GAIL BURTON

MVP BOOKS COLLECTION

TAKES OVER FOR SUPER RUN

Robert Mathis tackles Ravens running back Ray Rice, part of a dominant defensive performance by the Colts in the AFC Divisional Playoffs. ANDY LYONS/GETTY IMAGES

The next round pitted Indianapolis against the New York Jets. New coach Rex Ryan had been a blustering figure much of the year. His bold pronouncements and trash-talking amused Jets fans and irritated other coaches and opponents. The Jets kept up the routine in the week leading up to their match with the Colts, but they didn't play up to the level of their chatter. Before the playoffs began Ryan announced that the Jets should be favorites to win the Super Bowl despite their 9–7 record. They promptly beat Cincinnati and San Diego for the right to play the Colts in the AFC Championship Game.

Indianapolis won 30–17 with Manning throwing for 377 yards and three touchdowns. The TD passes were caught by Austin Collie, Pierre Garçon (he caught 11 passes for 151 yards), and Dallas Clark. The Jets did lead by as much as 11 points, 17–6, in the first half, but the Colts took the lead in the third quarter, held it, and extended it.

"I thought we just kept our mouths shut and went to work this week," Manning said in an obvious reference to what the Jets might not have done.

Caldwell became the fifth rookie coach to take a team to the Super Bowl, and he praised Manning for the way he handled the pre-game buildup and the pressure of the game itself. "Peyton had just an outstanding game," Caldwell said. "He's one of those guys who can adjust to different situations. A real champion."

The Colts were on their way to another Super Bowl, back to Miami to play the New Orleans Saints. The Colts always had good luck when Super Bowls were scheduled for Miami, but this time they could not conquer the spirited Saints in that club's first-ever Super Bowl game. The Saints prevailed in a 31–17 contest.

Coach Sean Payton had all of the answers, and Drew Brees flashed the leadership he had demonstrated all season as the beloved franchise uplifted the mood of downtrodden New Orleans, still suffering the violent effects of Hurricane Katrina.

"This is pretty important to everyone, and they remind us daily how important it is to them," Payton said before the Super Bowl.

Brees, the Saints quarterback and patron saint of the team, won the game Most Valuable Player award and became the darling of all Louisiana. "This is incredible," he said. "I mean, are you kidding? Are you kidding me?"

The game actually started pretty well for the Colts. They led 10–0 in the first quarter and were within striking distance in the fourth quarter, trailing only 24–17 and holding the ball. Then

Receiver Austin Collie grabs a pass during the AFC Championship Game against the New York Jets. JOE ROBBINS/GETTY IMAGES

Dallas Clark and Pierre Garçon celebrate a touchdown during their 30–17 victory over the Jets, a win that sent the Colts to Super Bowl XLIV.
MARK CORNELISON/LEXINGTON HERALD-LEADER/MCT VIA GETTY IMAGES

MVP BOOKS COLLECTION

Saints defensive back Tracy Porter out-flanked Reggie Wayne, intercepting a Manning pass and running the ball back 74 yards for the clinching touchdown.

Manning completed 31 passes for 333 yards and a touchdown, but it wasn't enough this time. Manning thought his team had made several big plays but acknowledged that the Saints made more. As much as the Saints wanted to revel in their victory, it seemed as if the Colts wanted to cleanse their memories immediately, almost pretending as if the loss had not occurred.

"I lost my last college game, too," said receiver Pierre Garçon, "and you never want to dwell on it. But it happens. You take it and use it as motivation to come back again next year."

That seemed to be the common theme in the Indianapolis locker room. The players had come so close to claiming the Super Bowl title but couldn't get that last win of the season. They made it sound as if the discouraging defeat would provide them with extra desire in the 2010 season. Indeed, Caldwell said as much: "We're going to take our disappointment and let it fuel us a bit."

The Super Bowl is almost always the highest-rated television show of the year, though historically high ratings have been more difficult to come by since the airwaves were diffused by cable channels. Yet this Super Bowl lured in viewers by the millions, with an estimated 106 million watching the game at any given time and 151.6 million people tuned in to it at some point during the action. The Nielsen Co. declared that this Super Bowl game was the most-watched television program of all time, superseding the old title holder. The former record-holder was the final episode of *M*A*S*H* in 1983.

Indianapolis' popularity, the presence of the high-profile Manning, coupled with the underdog surprise New Orleans and its inspiring back story seemed to account for the increased viewership. Even NFL Commissioner Roger Goodell declared the championship was "clearly more than a game. I keep thinking of the word 'magical,'" he said. "When you think about the relationship between the Saints and the Gulf Coast and the city of New Orleans, it was more than just a football game and more than just a football team. The hopes, the dreams, and the struggles of that community were all reflected in that football team. It was a great night for the people in New Orleans and the Gulf Coast region."

Not such a great night for Colts players, though. Echoing his teammates and coach, Wayne suggested that the tough loss would be a boon to the next season's chances to come back and pick off another Super Bowl win. "I'd rather win than lose," Wayne said, "but I think once we get this feeling out of the way, we'll be determined to come back and get another shot at it."

Manning throws downfield during the Colts' loss to the Saints in Super Bowl XLIV. TERRY GILLIAM/MCT VIA GETTY IMAGES

Manning and Caldwell are focused in the moments before kickoff at Super Bowl XLIV. ANDY LYONS/GETTY IMAGES

JIM CALDWELL

Brings His Own Coaching Style

Jim Caldwell succeeded Tony Dungy as head coach of the Colts but was fired after the disastrous 2011 season. AP PHOTO/PHELAN M. EBENHACK

Tony Dungy was a tough act to follow. It's never easy to be the guy in the job after a legendary or famous coach decides it's time to go. But Jim Caldwell was the coach-in-waiting after assisting Dungy, and he got the chance to run the Indianapolis Colts by himself in 2009.

A naturally quiet man, Caldwell was an Indianapolis assistant for seven years before he was promoted. Caldwell, a college defensive back at Iowa, was 44 when he took the reins.

Dungy left the first-time coach with an impressive team. For most of Caldwell's first season it appeared as if the Colts might go undefeated, winning their first 14 games in a row and clinching a playoff spot so early that the team was engulfed in an unusual debate. Should Caldwell keep relying on his starters, or should he rest them in preparation for a playoff run?

The temptation to chase a perfect 16–0 season was there, but Caldwell chose to play backups and the Colts lost their last two games of the regular season. The goal, he said, was winning the Super Bowl, not worrying about the most wins during the regular season. The Colts had a first-round bye but then bested the Baltimore Ravens and New York Jets to reach the Super Bowl against the New Orleans Saints. The Saints, however, seemed to be a team of destiny. Playing at home in a city recovering from a hurricane, they brought a party like Mardi Gras to their community with a 31–17 win.

"I'm moving on. I'm looking ahead," Caldwell said not long after the loss, indicating he does not dwell on things. "That's not my nature. It doesn't keep me up at night. It gnawed at me for a while, and now I'm beyond it. Gotta look forward." Such a reaction seemed in accordance with the man's general demeanor. Caldwell is soft-spoken and displays little emotion, whether on the sidelines or at press conferences. Sometimes observers wish he would show more fire.

In Caldwell's second season, the Colts were ravaged by injuries, but they regrouped after stumbling to a 6–6 start, winning their final four regular-season games and reaching the playoffs for an NFL record ninth straight year. That was an encouraging finish, and the Colts looked ahead to 2011 with the belief that a healthy team could continue its dominance of the AFC South Division. Peyton Manning had neck surgery after the season and seemed certain to be ready to go. No one imagined a second or third surgery would be required or that the starting quarterback would miss the entire season—but that's exactly what happened.

By mid-November of the 2011 season, the Colts were 0–10. When Caldwell was asked if he could have envisioned such a scenario back in September, he said, "I haven't had nightmares like that in a long time."

As the Colts continued to struggle, the question was whether the nightmare would get worse for Caldwell—would he be dismissed from his position after three seasons? After the Colts concluded their 2011 season with a 2–14 record, that question was answered. Owner Jim Irsay fired Caldwell and he joined the Baltimore Ravens as quarterback coach.

SECOND TIME AROUND AT THE SUPER BOWL

Playing before 74,059 fans in Miami, the Colts were the favorites to win Super Bowl XLIV, which would have been their second Super Bowl title since 2007. They began the 2009 season 14–0, creating talk of becoming a rare team to complete a regular season undefeated. New coach Jim Caldwell's decision to give ample rest to many of his starters after the team clinched the best record in the AFC was controversial, especially when the Colts lost their last two games before the playoffs.

But as Caldwell and other team officials noted, no one was going to remember the record if the team won the Super Bowl. The big prize at the end of the season was the most important thing.

The Colts out-scored opponents in every quarter during the fall of 2009 as they accumulated 416 points and held foes to 307. They were a well-balanced outfit, and quarterback Peyton Manning was his usual terrific self with 33 touchdown passes and 4,500 yards gained through the air.

A playoff bye and victories over the Ravens and Jets had advanced the Colts to Miami for the ultimate game. It was the fourth time in franchise history, counting Baltimore and Indianapolis, that the Colts had reached the Super Bowl. Coincidentally, all four were played in Miami. Things began just the way Caldwell hoped they would, with the Colts moving out to a 10–0 first-quarter lead on drives of 53 and 96 yards. The long drive made Indianapolis appear unstoppable. New Orleans inched back into contention with two field goals in the second period, but still trailed 10–6 at the half.

The second half belonged to the Saints, however. Quarterback Drew Brees, who had emerged as a community leader during New Orleans' troubled times, was experiencing the best football season of his life, and he carried the Saints to a decisive lead with 10 points in the third quarter and 15 in the fourth. New Orleans' defense deflected all Colts comeback tries. The crucial play came in the fourth quarter when Tracy Porter intercepted Manning to put the game out of reach.

For the Saints, the Super Bowl was more than a championship game; it was a cause. New Orleans had never won a Super Bowl, and the city had been ravaged by Hurricane Katrina, a vicious storm that had burst levees, wreaked havoc along the Gulf Coast, killed many, and disrupted the lives of millions in 2005. The Superdome, the Saints' home field, had been at ground zero of the storm. The dome was not only severely damaged, but it also had become an emergency shelter for the city's desperate residents.

SUPER BOWL XLIV

NEW ORLEANS SAINTS 29 — **INDIANAPOLIS COLTS** 17

	1	2	3	4	Total
NEW ORLEANS SAINTS	0	6	10	15	31
INDIANAPOLIS COLTS	10	0	7	0	17

The city of New Orleans was still very much in the healing process when the Saints produced the best season in team history, and the victory in Super Bowl XLIV spread joy to their battered city. Some said the Saints had fate on their side. The Colts had Manning on their side, which had always been enough to inspire confidence. All autumn it seemed to be the Colts' year, but on the first Sunday in February, the magic belonged to the Saints.

After the defeat, the Colts seemed a little bit dazed. They had trouble believing that their dream season ended with another team hoisting the Lombardi Trophy. Manning had resurrected the Colts' offense so many times when it stagnated. He sparked comebacks when the team needed them most and energized big offensive explosions to put many games out of sight. But in the final game of the season, the Colts just couldn't overcome the Saints' smoothness. "We played well in our first playoff game, played well

Peyton Manning settles under center during Super Bowl XLIV. AP PHOTO/DAVID DRAPKIN

two weeks ago, and at times made some plays against the Saints," he said. "We just didn't play well enough to win."

Although Manning is a popular player and the Colts are a pretty popular team around the country, it was fair to say that those rooting for the underdog cheered for the Saints and their devastated community that time around, almost as if the city deserved a sports consolation prize in exchange for all the suffering it had endured.

During his MVP season, Brees had become an icon in New Orleans. He brought pleasure to a place that needed a distraction and had given considerable unrequited love to the Saints for years. Brees was asked if he felt more than the usual pressure to provide a title to New Orleans. "People have asked me so many times, 'Do you look at it as a burden or extra pressure? Do you feel like you're carrying the weight of the city on your team's shoulders?'" Brees said. "I said, 'No, not at all.' We look at it as a responsibility. Our city, our fans, gave us strength, and we owe this to them."

The Saints went marching in, and the Colts were left looking forward to next year.

INJURIES GALORE CANNOT HALT COLTS

The Colts began the 2010 season with the same expectations they held during the preceding decade, with a firm belief they could reach the Super Bowl. No one can foretell the future with assurance, and the future in sports is iffier than most. The 2010 campaign became a very difficult challenge for the Colts. Injury after injury sidelined key players. The Colts suffered so many injuries it was as if an epidemic ran through the locker room—though with sprains, strains, and breaks instead of the flu.

With Dallas Clark among the many injured Colts in 2010, tight end Jacob Tamme became a target for Peyton Manning. JED JACOBSOHN/GETTY IMAGES

The head count each week was like a checkers game, with Caldwell moving pieces here and there, upgrading backups to starting positions, using third-stringers for key roles, and getting some players back to health, only to see others go down. It was a bizarre sequence of events that rarely allowed the team to compete at full strength.

Offensive linemen were particularly hard hit, and when running back Joseph Addai went down, the Colts' running game was severely affected. Dallas Clark went out for the year and backup tight end Brody Eldridge was hurt, too. The partnership between Peyton Manning and Reggie Wayne was never better connected and never needed more. Wayne caught 111 passes for 1,355 yards, and at times the link between Manning and Wayne seemed to be the only offensive option.

Manning spread his throws out as much as possible when Wayne was covered. Garçon figured into more plays, catching 67 passes, and newcomer tight end Jacob Tamme came through with 67 catches as well. Austin Collie played terrific ball until he was knocked out of the lineup by two concussions that ended his season. Rookie Blair White had his moments, catching 36 passes, but the split-second timing Manning had with his top guys was missing.

Manning was as good as ever, most of the time. He threw an astounding 679 passes and completed 450 of them for 4,700 yards and 33 touchdowns. Receivers with whom he wasn't as familiar ran some incorrect routes and contributed to his 17 interceptions, but overall Manning completed passes to 15 different receivers during the course of the season. By mid-November the Colts were relying on defense as much as anything the offense could generate.

Manning confers with another of his young and inexperienced receivers, Blair White. JOE ROBBINS/GETTY IMAGES

Indianapolis raised its record to 6–3 with a 23–17 victory over the Cincinnati Bengals on a day when Manning did not throw a touchdown pass and gained just 185 yards through the air. Donald Brown, who replaced Addai in the starting lineup, rushed for just 50 yards. So this win warranted a big thank-you to the defense, which forced Cincinnati into five turnovers. The Colts accumulated three interceptions off of Carson Palmer, gathered in two fumbles, and scored three sacks. Colts defensive tackle Antonio Johnson, a 310-pound truck, made sure he took good care of the fumble he recovered. "You just grab it and try to hold on," he said. "It was a great day for the defense."

But those great days did not come along every week. Just as the Colts felt they might have accomplished something with that win, they dropped three games in a row to New England, San Diego, and the Dallas Cowboys. The Cowboys loss, 38–35 in overtime, hurt more than the others because the Colts felt they should have won. Their record had dropped to 6–6, not exactly the mark of a playoff contender.

The game against the Cowboys was one of the worst of Manning's career. He threw four interceptions, and two of them were run back for touchdowns. Manning was used to throwing touchdowns for the Colts, not the other guys. "I don't make excuses," Manning said. "I need to make better reads. I've just got to play better."

The result demonstrated what a thin margin the Colts had. With so many important players out of the lineup, those who were playing had to play well for the team to have a chance at victory. "It does wear on you," Jim Caldwell said of the injury list.

The AFC South Division was not particularly strong. No team was running away with the title as the Colts struggled. There were four games remaining, and the Colts had only one way into the playoffs. They had to win the division because they knew their record wouldn't be good enough to earn a wild card spot. "We've got to win out," veteran linebacker Gary Brackett said. "That's the bottom line. I think we have to win out."

In the recent decade, four-game winning streaks had been almost routine for the Colts. The next week Indianapolis edged division rival Tennessee 30–28 on the road. One down. The Colts followed up by toppling Jacksonville 34–24 at home and Oakland on the road 31–26. Going into the final regular-season game, Indianapolis knew that a second defeat of the Titans would clinch its playoff berth.

The Jaguars unexpectedly helped out the Colts as well, their loss providing another way into the playoffs, even if the Colts were to lose to Tennessee. It was in part an Adam Vinatieri day. He came out kicking and he finished the game kicking, his toe giving the Colts a 23–20 win for their 10th triumph of the season.

"There's no question this was a game we wanted to win," Manning said. Neither Manning nor his teammates wanted a back-door entrance to the playoffs. They wanted to go in strong, believing they could keep their late-season momentum going. The Colts were beginning to look like the Colts that the rest of the league knew, and they wanted to leave prospective opponents worried.

Even running back Addai was healthy enough to play again, though 17 other players were on the season-ending injured reserve list by the last game. "It's been a bumpy road," Addai said. "We were able to come together and help each other."

Reggie Wayne was still Manning's go-to target in 2010. Here, he catches one of his 111 balls on the year—for a touchdown against the rival Patriots. ROB TRINGALI/SPORTSCHROME/GETTY IMAGES

"A lot of people said we were finished," said tackle Charlie Johnson. "I can't say enough about this team. We got our goal accomplished today."

Coming from so far down, it was a remarkable achievement to win 10 games, win the division, and extend the season. The Colts even got a home game in the opening round of the playoffs, another opportunity to entertain the New York Jets.

The Colts were still spread thin, but their winning streak left other teams wondering what to make of them. Could the Colts keep it going? Could they win games in the playoffs, too? There was no reason for Indianapolis to believe it couldn't. The Colts had already proved a lot of people wrong, so what was one more week and one more win?

Indianapolis had 65,332 fans making noise on its behalf at Lucas Oil Stadium, but the 11–5 Jets didn't seem particularly bothered by that. Employing their own stingy defense, the Jets squeezed the spark out of the Colts' offense many times and methodically went about scoring. Slowly—but methodically. The one monster drive the Jets put together took longer than Moses

The Colts went head-to-head with the New York Jets in the 2010 AFC Championship Game, but the fans' "all in" attitude wasn't enough to will Indianapolis to victory. ANDY LYONS/GETTY IMAGES

Pierre Garçon runs past the Jets' Antonio Cromartie for a 57-yard touchdown in the AFC Championship Game. ANDY LYONS/GETTY IMAGES

wandering in the desert, or so it seemed. Starting on their own 13-yard line, New York marched 87 yards on a dizzying, 9-minute-and-54-second trip to the end zone.

The clock-eating drive gave New York a 14–13 lead. But one of the things that made Manning's fame over the years was his ability to lead his team to fourth-quarter comeback victories. The Colts got the ball on their own 20-yard line as time was running out, but Manning fired quick passes to move the Colts down the field and set up Vinatieri for a potential go-ahead field goal. Based on his past Super Bowl performances for the Patriots, Vinatieri had earned a reputation as perhaps the best clutch kicker in NFL history.

The Colts lined up, the snap was made, and Vinatieri was as true as ever, booting the ball cleanly 50 yards between the uprights. The Colts led 16–14, and Vinatieri had apparently added to his legend with another playoff game–winning kick.

Despite the raucous Lucas celebration, there was only one problem. The game was not over. About a minute remained. The Colts did a lousy job covering the ensuing kickoff, handing the ball to Jets quarterback Mark Sanchez on his own 47 yard line. He pulled a Manning. Using the clock, Sanchez steered New York into field-goal position. Less than 60 seconds later Sanchez turned over the Jets' hopes to unheralded kicker Nick Folk, who was far less seasoned or accomplished than Vinatieri. It didn't matter. On this occasion, he was just as accurate. Folk kicked a 32-yarder as time ran out, and the Jets ended the Colts' season with a 17–16 thud.

"Our guys fought hard all year long," Caldwell said when it was over. "We just ran out of time."

"We didn't want it to end like this," said Colts safety Antoine Bethea. "It's going to take a long time to get over it."

LABOR CRISIS AND MANNING DOWN

After the 2010 season the Colts had a lot of healing to do—both psychically and mentally. They all felt the next season had to be better than the last. Injured players had months to recover, and all were expected to regain their strength. Peyton Manning announced he was going to have neck surgery in May, a seemingly minor maintenance procedure that would easily allow him enough recovery time to be ready for training camp in August.

Much to the surprise of the Colts, their fans, and the entire NFL community, Manning's operation turned into a much larger pain in the neck than anticipated. Complications and implications mushroomed and set off an unlikely chain of events that drastically altered the outlook and results of the 2011 season.

First, however, there was the matter of a labor dispute between NFL owners and players that kept training camps closed and put the entire 2011 season in jeopardy. Negotiations dragged on into the summer. Many teams' training camp start dates came and went without a resolution. It became obvious: without an 11th-hour settlement, September would arrive without pro football on the weekend calendar. Jokes were made about the nation's passion for football and how a populace demoralized by high unemployment rates, a housing crisis, and the federal debt would not stand for one more blow, like the loss of NFL games.

With the Colts' veteran center Jeff Saturday playing a significant negotiating role on behalf of the players, a late agreement was forged. Workout time was lost, but when it was time to tee it up for the regular season, the league was ready to go.

Colts owner Jim Irsay speaks to the media during the lockout prior to the 2011 NFL season.
SEAN GARDNER/GETTY IMAGES

2011 was marred by a labor dispute between NFL owners and players that kept training camps closed and put the entire season in jeopardy.

For the first time since Manning's arrival in 1998, the Colts had no idea what to do about the starting quarterback position, the most important slot on the team. During his entire Colts career, Manning had rarely left the field for even a snap. As the seasons had been for years, the Colts' 2011 season was about to be defined by Peyton Manning—just in a different way than usual.

Complicating matters somewhat was the fact that Manning's contract was up. Jim Irsay slapped the "franchise tag" on Manning to keep other teams at bay while he and the quartback worked out five-year, $90 million deal. As part of the negotiation, Manning was due a $28 million bonus in March of 2012.

Although his neck prevented him from suiting up, Manning showed up for the opening of training camp and explained that being so highly paid simply added to his commitment to work his hardest and do his best. "I think there is an extra responsibility that comes with it," Manning said. "If they're going to pay you like the highest-paid player, you better play like it." No one would argue that he hadn't already done so.

After the money thing was out of the way, speculation turned to Manning's return date. Just how soon would he slip on his shoulder pads and No. 18 jersey to lead the Colts again? Manning was on the active roster at the end of August. He was doing some throwing and seemed to be merely days away from assuming a full-time practice role. But that never happened.

On September 8, about nine days after that optimistic outlook was advanced, Manning instead had a another neck operation—which was later revealed to be his fourth in 19 months. The spinal fusion procedure repaired a damaged nerve that caused

Colts center Jeff Saturday shares a poignant moment with Patriots owner Robert Kraft during a media session announcing the end of the 2011 NFL lockout. ROB CARR/GETTY IMAGES

weakness in his throwing arm, and the surgery kept Manning sidelined indefinitely.

The new setback ended Manning's record of consecutive starts at 227. The real question was how long it would take to get him back under center. "I miss playing," Manning said. "I really do. If I get cleared to play and I'm good enough, would I play? Absolutely. I'd love to because that's how I'm wired. That's my job and I love my job. If the doctor says you can go, then I'd like to do that."

Injury had finally caught up to one of the most durable players in NFL history. A brief flurry of electricity shot through the city when owner Jim Irsay teasingly tweeted that he was flying to Mississippi to cajole retired Brett Favre into making a comeback. But it wasn't true.

The incumbent backup was Curtis Painter, a 6-foot-4, 230-pound third-year man out of Purdue, most noted for the long, flowing locks that trailed out of his helmet with the horseshoe on it. In 2010, Painter had not thrown a pass. In 2009, he appeared in two games and went 8-for-28 passing.

Late in training camp the Colts talked veteran Kerry Collins out of his recent retirement, announced barely more than a month earlier. In his 16-year career Collins had thrown for more than 40,000 yards and more than 200 touchdowns. Although he had to scramble to cram the playbook's information into his brain, he seemed like a capable fill-in.

Just eight days after he signed with the Colts, Collins was in the backfield for a 17–13 exhibition game win over Cincinnati. Collins was 5-for-10 in about one half of play. It was a rough start. The surprise was that Indianapolis, which is one of the league's poorest preseason teams, won anyway. That was partly due to third-string quarterback Dan Orlovsky's winning touchdown pass, though he was cut before the start of the season.

Peyton Manning grimaces from the sideline during the Colts' disastrous 2011 season. Seeing Manning in street clothes on the sidelines was jarring for NFL fans across the country.
SAM RICHE/MCT VIA GETTY IMAGES

"If they're going to pay you like the highest-paid player, you better play like it." —Peyton Manning

A preseason hope of the franchise was that it could reprise its Super Bowl visit versus New Orleans. For the first time ever, the Super Bowl was scheduled for the Colts' home field in Indianapolis, Lucas Oil Stadium, in February of 2012. The general attitude of club officials, the players, and fans, was that it would be a pretty darned neat thing to play in the Super Bowl at home.

It took less than 60 minutes of play—the season opener—to forget such giddy thoughts. The Colts were traumatized by the Houston Texans. The score, 34–7, didn't even reflect the extent of the thorough beating. It was a stunningly poor showing that seemed to have no good explanation. The Colts were downright awful on all fronts. This was just the beginning of one of the grimmest stretches of football ever played by the franchise, in Baltimore or Indianapolis.

In the third game, against the Pittsburgh Steelers, Collins took a whack

There weren't very many positives for Curtis Painter in 2011, cementing for fans just how impressive Peyton Manning had been over the years. JOE ROBBINS/GETTY IMAGES

Dwight Freeney (93) and David Caldwell (30) bring down Texans running back Arian Foster during the Colts' 19–16 win on December 22, their second and final victory of the 2011 season. Freeney was the team's lone Pro Bowler that year. JOE ROBBINS/GETTY IMAGES

on the head. He was diagnosed with a concussion that ended his season. Painter moved into the starting lineup for the first time in his career, and Orlovsky was rehired.

What perhaps was the strangest year in Colts history unfolded and unraveled. The seventh straight defeat was the most humiliating. The Colts were trampled by the New Orleans Saints 62–7, suffering one of the worst losses in league history. This was an atrocious performance that exposed multiple massive holes in a dike that just wasn't holding back the floodwaters.

It didn't help any that the Colts were ravaged by other critical injuries to star middle linebacker and defensive captain Gary Brackett, tight end Dallas Clark, and cornerback Jerraud Powers. Eventually, defensive coordinator Larry Coyer was fired. Talk began about whether the Colts would qualify for the first overall pick in the 2012 draft. The prize pick figured to be Stanford quarterback Andrew Luck—like Manning, the son of a professional quarterback.

The gallows humor around the league was that the Colts' dire circumstances in Manning's absence proved Manning should be the NFL's 2011 MVP. Coach Jim Caldwell had to work with what he had, and he stuck with Painter despite a stagnant offense. Eventually, Orlovsky got the call to start at quarterback. Orlovsky, 28, had barely played during an NFL career that followed collegiate play for the University of Connecticut, except for some action during the Detroit Lions' infamous 0–16 season in 2008. He was now thrust in command of a team trying to avoid the same winless fate.

Orlovsky made a spectacular start, completing 30 of 37 passes for 353 yards, but the New England Patriots still beat the Colts 31–24. On December 18, the same day the team announced that Manning definitely would not take the field during the 2011 season, the Colts bested the Tennessee Titans 27–13 to eliminate the prospect of finishing winless.

Orlovsky, who had not played quarterback in a winning effort since college seven years earlier, was pleased to be at the controls,

In a tumultuous offseason, Ryan Grigson was hired to replace Chris Polian as the Colts' general manager. Team president Bill Polian was also fired by Jim Irsay. AP PHOTO/MICHAEL CONROY

though he did not have a very special night. "It feels great to finally get one," Orlovsky said. "I'm very humbled to be part of it. It's a lot better than the feeling we've had lately."

To the surprise of many, the Colts banked a second straight win, besting the same Texans team that had slaughtered them in the opener. The Colts went from flirting with an 0–16 record to a mark of 2–13 in just five days, momentarily jeopardizing the No. 1 pick in the draft. The Colts lost at Jacksonville in the season's final game, finishing 2–14 to earn the top pick. Since moving to Indianapolis, the Colts had that choice three previous times and selected Jeff George, Steve Emtman, and Manning. Only one of the three had truly worked out.

The disappointing season set off a chain reaction of change at Colts headquarters. Irsay deemed the year unacceptable. Despite his long and close personal relationship with Bill Polian, who side by side with him had built the Colts in the 2000s, Irsay fired him, as well as Polian's son Chris, the general manager. Irsay had tears in his eyes when he let them go but said it was a business decision for the greater good of the team.

Soon after, Irsay introduced his new general manager. Ryan Grigson, 39, a native Hoosier, who had worked for St. Louis and Philadelphia, was given the top administrator's job and the task of swiftly revamping the Colts.

Irsay and Grigson huddled and at first seemed inclined to retain Jim Caldwell as head coach. Then they reversed field and quickly fired Caldwell and most of his assistants. In the ensuing shakeup, the Colts hired Baltimore Ravens defensive coordinator Chuck Pagano, 51, to preside over the next era of Colts history in Indianapolis. Outside of hiring assistant coaches, the basic authority shifts had been established. That left one huge issue casting a shadow over the Colts' future: What was to become of Peyton Manning?

Owner Jim Irsay said Manning would be the Colts' quarterback, provided he returned to 100 percent health. Things remained murky because no one was sure just how Manning would heal. Armchair medical experts and sports media people said he should never play again. Manning said he would be back.

Despite the huge sum of money Manning was owed, Irsay insisted that the issue was Manning's health. "In terms of if he's healthy and if he's ready to play, I see him back with us," Irsay said. "This is really about, is he [Manning] going to be able to come back and really be the old Peyton Manning and play at a very high level," Irsay said. "What he has meant to the city and to the franchise is incredible."

It was an emotional moment for the Colts franchise and family when Peyton Manning and Jim Irsay stood before the media to announce Manning's departure after 14 years with the organization. JOEY FOLEY/GETTY IMAGES

But as the March 8, 2012, deadline rapidly approached with no resolution on Manning's status, the drumbeat of rumors grew louder that Irsay and Manning would say goodbye, and that the next-generation Colts would draft Andrew Luck— or perhaps Heisman Trophy winner Robert Griffin III—as their future quarterback.

The unthinkable came true on March 7, the day before the deadline. In a rare and dramatic moment, Irsay and Manning conducted a joint press conference. Each choked up over the end of a long and fruitful relationship.

"This is difficult because of the things Peyton has done for our city, our state, and our franchise," Irsay said. "There will be no other Peyton Manning." He also promised that no other Colt would wear Manning's number 18.

Manning thanked Colts fans and the team that had been his home for the entirety of his professional career. As long as the 36-year-old thrower was healthy, he was going to set off free-agent frenzy among teams with quarterback needs. Manning admitted he was not fully healthy yet, indicating he had more work to do and more progress to make.

With heartfelt emotion he addressed the end of his tenure in Indianapolis, where he had played so brilliantly and made his home for nearly a decade-and-a-half. "We all know that nothing lasts forever," Manning said. "Times change, circumstances change, and that's the reality of playing in the NFL. . . . I've truly been blessed."

After his emotional parting with the Colts, Manning was wooed by the Arizona Cardinals, the Tennessee Titans, and the Denver Broncos. The idea of playing under Hall of Fame quarterback John Elway, the Broncos' team president, appealed most to Manning. He signed with Denver, hoping to one day haunt the Colts in the AFC title game and to win another Super Bowl title in the West.

"We all know that nothing lasts forever. Times change, circumstances change, and that's the reality of playing in the NFL."
—Peyton Manning

RESURRECTION...AND A LITTLE BIT OF LUCK

As their reward for unexpectedly becoming the worst team in the National Football League during the 2011 season, the Indianapolis Colts held the No. 1 draft pick in the annual draft of college players the following spring. The prize was Andrew Luck.

Highly touted rookie Andrew Luck was the center of attention from the moment he arrived at rookie minicamp in May 2012. JOE ROBBINS/GETTY IMAGES

The Colts selected the Stanford All-American quarterback, and son of a former NFL quarterback named Oliver Luck, as the top overall pick in 2012. But the Colts brass weren't hoping for the second coming of dad. They were hoping for the second coming of Peyton Manning. Would they be lucky enough to have lightning strike twice?

As the retooling of the franchise began, Irsay gambled that the 6-foot-4, 235-pound Luck was his savior, Peyton Manning 2. The team owner was acting like a car manufacturer who had his product rejected and was rebuilding the engine. He replaced his general manager, coach, quarterback, and more than half of his team. Just about the only thing he retained was the horseshoe on the side of the helmets.

One by one, popular players were released as new GM Ryan Grigson and new coach Chuck Pagano sought to rebuild on the fly. Some well-known Colts departed on their own for other teams, and only a few of the big names stayed. Wide receiver Reggie Wayne, who had known Pagano for years, and defensive stalwarts Dwight Freeney and Robert Mathis hung around.

Free agents and rookies arrived by the boxcar load. Most experts predicted that even a healthy Colts squad, with 36 new faces among the 53 roster sports, could not win more than five games in 2012.

And then the team received another blow when, only a few weeks into the season, Pagano announced that he was suffering from leukemia and needed a leave of absence for treatment. Offensive coordinator Bruce Arians took over as interim coach, doing both jobs, and rather than reeling emotionally, the team rallied.

"It will be a lot of fun to play in this stadium. Hopefully, it's fun for the fans." — Andrew Luck, about Lucas Oil Stadium on the eve of the 2012 season

CHUCK PAGANO

Remarkable Recovery, On and Off the Field

Head coach Chuck Pagano looks on during his first game back after his three-month absence from the team to undergo cancer treatment.
JOE ROBBINS/GETTY IMAGES

Hired in January 2012 to be the new head coach of the Colts, Chuck Pagano was handed the task of revitalizing the franchise after a dismal 2–14 season and a massive organizational shakeup.

The former Baltimore Ravens defensive coordinator set to work putting his stamp on Indianapolis football operations in the offseason, through training camp, and at the start of the 2012 season. But, in September, just three games into his first season as an NFL head coach, Pagano shocked team owner Jim Irsay, his assistant coaches, the fans, and the players by announcing that he had been diagnosed with leukemia and was taking a leave of absence for treatment.

As the 52-year-old coach retreated from the limelight, the Colts rallied under interim coach Bruce Arians, the offensive coordinator. For three months, while Pagano occasionally guided strategy from his hospital bed, the team and city aimed an outpouring of support and prayer in his direction.

Rather than be forgotten in the shadows, Pagano's progress reports were broadcast regularly, his health taken up as a community cause, and in one of the most remarkable sagas in pro football history, the young and inexperienced Colts overachieved under Arians' steady hand and Pagano's long-distance direction.

Not long after being admitted to the Indiana University Health Simon Cancer Center, Pagano was sending emails to update people on his improving condition and upbeat attitude. Colts fans began a CHUCKSTRONG campaign to raise money for leukemia research, players wore T-shirts supporting Pagano's struggle, and some shaved their heads in solidarity, since patients undergoing chemotherapy typically lose their hair. Even some heavily tressed cheerleaders shaved their heads on national television during halftime of a game.

As his strength increased, Pagano appeared at Lucas Oil Stadium to watch games from the owner's box. Pagano's health improved concurrently with the Colts' success. Arians led a squad quarterbacked by rookie Andrew Luck to implausible victory after unlikely win. Mini miracles occurred.

Pagano sent coaching advice via text to rookie T. Y. Hilton, and Hilton promptly returned a punt for a touchdown, a key 75-yard score in a seven-point triumph over Buffalo in late November.

All along Pagano hoped he would be able to resume his place on the sidelines before the end of the regular season. At the end of December, with one game remaining on the schedule, he returned to work full-time at practice. When Pagano arrived at the training complex a gigantic, inflatable Colt figure wore a sign reading, "Welcome Back Chuck."

"We got our commander-in-chief back," said star receiver Reggie Wayne.

Arians called Pagano's December 24 return the "best Christmas gift" the team could get.

Pagano delivered a heartfelt thank-you speech "to the fans, the people of this great city, the great state, and all over the country."

Then Pagano went back to work and his Colts won the next game, finished the seaon 11–5, and qualified for the playoffs, a stunning achievement. Rarely, if ever, has an NFL coach and team exchanged inspiration in such a moving and supportive manner.

It did not take long for Luck to demonstrate uncommon poise as a rookie. When Pagano departed for medical treatment, Indianapolis was 1–2, and Luck already had two 300-yard passing games under his belt. A bye week followed. The team was engulfed by questions, and although the fans kept coming to Lucas Oil Stadium in sell-out numbers each Sunday, it was difficult to predict how the team would fare.

One hint that the Colts might be on the fast track to reinvention was a 30–27 victory over the Green Bay Packers after the bye. That was the day when it first became evident that Luck had special genes and that the partnership between the rookie QB and the veteran receiver Wayne might turn into something special. Against the Packers, a team deemed to be Super Bowl contenders, Luck threw for 362 yards, and Wayne was responsible for 212 of them on 13 catches. Luck's yardage total was a Colts rookie record.

In his NFL regular-season debut, Luck passed for more than 300 yards and one touchdown, but he also threw three interceptions in a 41–21 loss to the Bears in Chicago. JONATHAN DANIEL/GETTY IMAGES

Sure-handed veteran receiver Reggie Wayne hauls in one of his 13 catches in Indianapolis's inspiring 30–27 win over the Green Bay Packers on October 7, 2012. SAM RICHE/MCT VIA GETTY IMAGES

The home crowd was chanting, "Reg-gie! Reg-gie! Reg-gie!" by game's end. Wayne wore orange gloves, the symbol of leukemia awareness. Later, 36 Colts players shaved their heads in solidarity with Pagano.

Wayne's lone touchdown in the game came on a four-yard pass with 35 seconds left. The young Colts were already pulling out dramatic fourth-quarter wins—all this despite entering the contest emotionally stretched because of their coach's illness. Pagano emailed the players from his hospital room urging them not to play for him but for themselves. But his guys shrugged off that sentiment; they were playing for the boss.

"I think it's one of the greatest athletic moments I've ever been a part of," Luck said after the win.

Following the game, Irsay and Grigson made a pilgrimage to the Indiana University Health Simon Cancer Center to present Pagano with the game ball.

Luck celebrates with two of his key ball catchers, T. Y. Hilton (13) and Dwayne Allen, during another clutch Colts victory, a 23–20 win over the Miami Dolphins at Lucas Oil Stadium on November 4, 2012.
GREGORY SHAMUS/GETTY IMAGES

That was really the beginning, the igniter, of one of the most unlikely and swiftest turnarounds in NFL history. From a downtrodden team coping with an epidemic of injuries in 2011, the Colts were transformed into a peppy, fresh-look team led by a man named Luck in 2012.

Indianapolis was still finding its way, however. Arians plugged in new guys at different spots as the Colts were manhandled by the New York Jets, 35–9. But then they pieced together a four-game winning streak, not simply putting up W's but winning the close ones. Indianapolis defeated Cleveland, Tennessee, Miami, and Jacksonville in consecutive weeks, and the margin of victory was six points or less in the first three of those victories.

In the 23–20 win over Miami—secured by a 43-yard field goal by veteran kicker Adam Vinatieri—Luck threw for 433 yards, breaking the year-old NFL record for a rookie passer previously owned by Cam Newton.

Against the Jaguars, defensive back Darius Butler, who hadn't even signed with Indianapolis until late September, intercepted two passes, earning him AFC Defensive Player of the Week honors.

As far as Grigson was concerned, the Colts were still a work in progress, and he was still seeking out new players. Sometimes the new arrivals weren't even recognized by teammates until shortly before game time.

Winning tight ball games, especially at the end, is not a trademark of young teams. But something unusual was happening in Indianapolis. A team that few thought would win often was learning how to make the big plays in the clutch and win regularly.

Pagano also showed up in the locker room briefly to meet with the Colts.

"His presence is felt every day in the facility," Luck said, "but to see him in the flesh, in the locker room, to hear him speak, I think gave all the guys a boost."

Colts fans, as expected, fell in love with Luck immediately, but they were still thumbing through the game programs trying to figure out who the heck the guys were he was throwing to, besides Wayne. Dwayne Allen, a rookie tight end from Clemson, caught 45 passes. Coby Fleener, another tight end and one of Luck's pals from Stanford, had 26 receptions on the year. T. Y. Hilton was a 5-foot-9 end from Florida International who caught 50 passes.

Linebacker Jerrell Freeman, out of the tiny Division III University of Mary Hardin–Baylor, was in on 145 tackles. Freeman also made a pit stop with the Saskatchewan Roughriders before joining the Colts. Whether they knew who he was or not, fans were going crazy cheering for Freeman simply because he wore a horseshoe on his helmet.

The new featured back for a team that hadn't had one in a couple of years was Vick Ballard out of Mississippi State. He led the Colts with 814 yards and 211 carries in 2012.

Luck, who would have been the first guy to tell you that he still had a lot to learn—which is why he spent his free time watching film that didn't star Bruce Willis or Meryl Streep—was a constant. He threw his share of interceptions, but he made up for it by making the big throws, too.

Amidst the successes, there were plenty of glitches, reminders that the Colts were not truly an elite team yet. They were crushed by the New England Patriots, who hung 59 points on them. But even major-league batterings didn't slow Indianapolis for long, and the Colts kept improving. After the thumping by the Patriots, the Colts won three in a row, again by tight margins of 7, 2, and 4 points.

Sometimes there was a bit of serendipity in the victories. It was simply hard to explain how such a young, newly composed roster was able to pull out wins like the one on December 2 against the Detroit Lions. After trailing by 12 points with four minutes to go in the fourth quarter, Indianapolis scored two touchdowns to eke out a 35–33 triumph. A 14-yard pass to receiver Donnie Avery secured Luck's fifth winning drive in the fourth period or overtime of his rookie season.

"Some teams find ways to win, others don't," Arians said. "Ours do. It's never over till the last tick of the clock."

The Colts of 2012 lived by that motto. In their second meeting with the Titans, they fell behind by 13 points in the first half before coming back to win 27–23, with the last six points coming in the fourth quarter on a pair of Vinatieri field goals—the first one a 53 yarder. That was one name Colts fans knew, since Vinatieri is known as Mr. Clutch.

After that triumph, the NFL woke up to see Indianapolis sitting at 9–4, a record that might well get the team into the playoffs.

Playoffs? Just about everybody in Indianapolis believed that the only local pro franchise that might be mentioned in the same breath as that word for a few years would be the NBA's Pacers. There was some concern that this was a bit like Cinderella, and that everything might go *poof* before the postseason arrived.

After falling to 9–5 with a loss to the division-leading Houston Texans, the Colts faced the Kansas City Chiefs. In an all-too-familiar scenario, the game was tied 13–13 entering the fourth quarter. Luck threw a 7-yard touchdown pass to Wayne, and the Colts won it. It was Indianapolis's 10th victory over the year, and it clinched a playoff berth.

"Mission accomplished," Arians said.

Colts fans—always an enthusiastic bunch—came out in full support of Chuck Pagano during his battle with leukemia. JOE ROBBINS/GETTY IMAGES

While offensive coordinator Bruce Arians did a phenomenal job as interim head coach during Chuck Pagano's absence, Arians and the rest of the organization was thrilled to see Pagano return to the sideline for the season finale, a win over the division-champion Houston Texans on December 30, 2012. SAM RICHE/MCT VIA GETTY IMAGES

"It's been an incredible year." —Jim Irsay, on the 2012 season

As he had pledged to do, a rapidly healing Pagano returned to the team in time for the last regular-season game. The Colts trumped the Texans, 28–16. The season took more fairytale overtones when Deji Karim—who had been home parking cars in Oklahoma City a few weeks earlier when summoned to the team—returned a kickoff 101 yards for a touchdown. It was the franchise's first 100-yard return since 1973.

Karim's comment on the astonishing run was, "It parted like the Red Sea."

Indianapolis finished the regular season with an 11–5 record. Luck set a rookie passing record with 4,374 yards gained. Wayne caught 106 passes for 1,355 yards and concluded the year with 968 receptions for his career.

The Colts drew the Baltimore Ravens in the first round, which was ironic on several fronts. The Ravens were Pagano's old team, where he had been defensive coordinator, and Baltimore was the Colts' old home before coming to Indianapolis. It happened to be Baltimore's year, however, and the Ravens defeated the Colts, 24–9, on their way to a Super Bowl championship.

For the Colts, just reaching the playoffs after a double-figure-victory season represented remarkable improvement. Arians, whose record was 9–3, became the first interim coach to win Coach of the Year honors. He was then hired as the new head coach of the Arizona Cardinals.

Arians, who had been such a big part of the miraculous success of the 2012 Colt underdogs, was gone, and the roster would continue to change as the team built for the future with the cornerstones of Ryan Grigson as general manager, Chuck Pagano as coach, and Andrew Luck at quarterback. Together, a fresh version of the Colts was being formed, one that they believed would soon be Super Bowl–bound.

Although it was a short-lived postseason for the Colts, Robert Mathis—the team's regular-season sacks leader with eight—brings down Ravens quarterback Joe Flacco during the AFC Wild Card Playoff Game in Baltimore. ROB CARR/GETTY IMAGES

INDIANAPOLIS COLTS RECORDS, 1998–2012

1998	3–13
1999	13–3
2000	10–6
2001	6–10
2002	10–6
2003	12–4
2004	12–4
2005	14–2
2006	12–4
2007	13–3
2008	12–4
2009	14–2
2010	10–6
2011	2–14
2012	11–5

INDIANAPOLIS COLTS ALL-TIME RECORD BOOK

THROUGH THE 2012 SEASON

INDIVIDUAL HONORS

COLTS IN THE PRO FOOTBALL HALL OF FAME
(minimum two seasons with the Colts)

Name	Position	Years with Colts	Induction Year
Raymond Berry	End	1955–1967	1973
Eric Dickerson	RB	1987–1991	1999
Art Donovan	DT	1950, 1953–1961	1968
Weeb Eubank	Coach	1954–1962	1978
Marshall Faulk	RB	1994–1998	2011
Ted Hendricks	LB	1969–1973	1990
John Mackey	TE	1963–1971	1992
Gino Marchetti	DE	1953–1966	1972
Lenny Moore	RB	1956–1967	1975
Jim Parker	T/G	1957–1967	1973
Joe Perry	RB	1961–1962	1969
Don Shula	Coach	1963–1969	1997
Johnny Unitas	QB	1956–1972	1979

INDIANAPOLIS COLTS RING OF HONOR

Name	Position	Years with Colts	Induction Year
Robert Irsay	Owner	1972–1997	1996
Bill Brooks	WR	1986–1992	1998
Ted Marchibroda	Coach	1975–1979, 1992–1995	2000
Chris Hinton	T/G	1983–1989	2001
Jim Harbaugh	QB	1994–1997	2005
12th Man	Fans		2007
Tony Dungy	Coach	2002–2008	2010
Marvin Harrison	WR	1996–2008	2011
Edgerrin James	RB	1999–2005	2012

FIRST-TEAM ALL-PROS

Name	Position	Years with Colts
Jim Parker	T/G	8 (1958–1965)
Gino Marchetti	DE/T/DT	7 (1957–1962, 1964)
Peyton Manning	QB	5 (2003–2005, 2008, 2009)
Lenny Moore	HB/FL	5 (1958–1961, 1964)
Johnny Unitas	QB	5 (1958, 1959, 1964, 1965, 1967)
Art Donovan	DT/T	4 (1954–1957)
Raymond Berry	E	3 (1958–1960)
Bobby Boyd	DB	3 (1964, 1965, 1968)
John Mackey	TE	3 (1966–1968)
Marvin Harrison	WR	3 (1999, 2002, 2006)
Dwight Freeney	DE	3 (2004, 2005, 2009)
Gene Lipscomb	DT	2 (1958, 1959)
Mike Curtis	LB/FB	2 (1968, 1969)
Eric Dickerson	RB	2 (1987, 1988)
Jeff Saturday	C	2 (2005, 2007)
Bob Sanders	DB	2 (2005, 2007)
Tom Keane	DB/E	1 (1953)
Alan Ameche	FB	1 (1955)
Milt Davis	DB	1 (1957)
Andy Nelson	DB	1 (1959)
Jimmy Orr	FL/E/SE/WR	1 (1965)
Willie Richardson	FL/WR	1 (1967)
Earl Morrall	QB	1 (1968)
David Lee	P	1 (1969)
Tom Matte	RB/QB	1 (1969)
Bob Vogel	T	1 (1969)
Ted Hendricks	LB	1 (1971)
Bubba Smith	DE/DT	1 (1971)

continued

FIRST-TEAM ALL-PROS CONTINUED

Rick Volk	DB	1 (1971)
George Kunz	T	1 (1975)
John Dutton	DT/DE	1 (1976)
Bert Jones	QB	1 (1976)
Rohn Stark	P	1 (1983)
Cary Blanchard	K	1 (1996)
Chris Gardocki	P	1 (1996)
Edgerrin James	RB	1 (1999)
Mike Vanderjagt	K	1 (2003)
Dallas Clark	TE	1 (2009)
Reggie Wayne	WR	1 (2010)

PRO BOWLERS
(players with five or more Pro Bowl selections)

Name	Position	Years with Colts
Gino Marchetti	DE/T/DT	11 (1954–1964)
Peyton Manning	QB	11 (1999, 2000, 2002–2010)
Johnny Unitas	QB	10 (1957–1964, 1966, 1967)
Jim Parker	T/G	8 (1958–1965)
Marvin Harrison	WR	8 (1999–2006)
Lenny Moore	HB/FL	7 (1956, 1958–1962, 1964)
Dwight Freeney	DE	7 (2003–2005, 2008–2011)
Raymond Berry	E	6 (1958–1961, 1963, 1964)
Chris Hinton	T/G	6 (1983, 1985–1989)
Reggie Wayne	WR	6 (2006–2010, 2012)
Art Donovan	DT/T	5 (1953–1957)
John Mackey	TE	5 (1963, 1965–1968)
Bob Vogel	T	5 (1964, 1965, 1967, 1968, 1971)
Jeff Saturday	C	5 (2005–2007, 2009, 2010)

PLAYER RECORDS

SERVICE

Most Seasons

17	Johnny Unitas, 1956–1972
14	Peyton Manning, 1998–2011
13	Gino Marchetti, 1953–1964, 1966
13	Alex Sandusky, 1954–1966
13	Raymond Berry, 1955–1967
13	Dick Szymanski, 1955, 1957–1968
13	Don Shinnick, 1957–1969
13	David Lee, 1966–1978
13	Ray Donaldson, 1980–1992
13	Rohn Stark, 1982–1994
13	Marvin Harrison, 1996–2008
13	Jeff Saturday, 1999–2011

Most Games Played

208	Peyton Manning, 1998–2010
206	Johnny Unitas, 1956–1972
198	Eugene Daniel, 1984–1996

Most Games Started

208	Peyton Manning, 1998–2010
188	Marvin Harrison, 1996–2008
188	Jeff Saturday, 1999–2011

Most Games Started

208	Peyton Manning, 1998–2010
188	Marvin Harrison, 1996–2008
188	Jeff Saturday, 1999–2011

OFFENSE LEADERS

SCORING RECORDS

Most Points Scored

Career

995	Mike Vanderjagt, K, 1999–2005
783	Dean Biasucci, K, 1984–1994
778	Marvin Harrison, WR, 1996–2008

Season

157	Mike Vanderjagt, K, 2003
145	Mike Vanderjagt, K, 1999
135	Cary Blanchard, K, 1996

Game

24	Accomplished 6 times

Touchdowns Scored

Career

128	Marvin Harrison, WR, 1996–2008 (128 rec.)
113	Lenny Moore, HB/FL, 1956–1967 (63 rush., 48 rec., 2 ret.)
78	Reggie Wayne, WR, 2002–2012 (78 rec.)

Season

20	Lenny Moore, HB, 1964 (16 rush., 3 rec., 1 ret.)
18	Edgerrin James, RB, 2000 (13 rush., 5 rec.)
17	Edgerrin James, RB, 1999 (13 rush., 4 rec.)

Game

4	Accomplished 6 times

Most Consecutive Games with a Touchdown

15	Lenny Moore, 10/27/1963–11/29/1964

PASSING RECORDS

Quarterback Wins

Career

141	Peyton Manning, 1998–2010
117	Johnny Unitas, 1956–1972
46	Bert Jones, 1973–1981

Season

14	Peyton Manning, 2005
14	Peyton Manning, 2009
13	Earl Morrall, 1968
13	Peyton Manning, 1999
13	Peyton Manning, 2007

Pass Attempts

Career

7,210	Peyton Manning, 1998–2010
5,110	Johnny Unitas, 1956–1972
2,464	Bert Jones, 1973–1981

Season

679	Peyton Manning, 2010
627	Andrew Luck, 2012
591	Peyton Manning, 2002

Game

59	Jeff George, @ Washington, 11/7/1993

Pass Completions

Career

4,682	Peyton Manning, 1998–2010
2,796	Johnny Unitas, 1956–1972
1,382	Bert Jones, 1973–1981

Season

450 Peyton Manning, 2010

393 Peyton Manning, 2009

392 Peyton Manning, 2002

Game

40 Peyton Manning, @ Houston, 9/12/2010

Completion Percentage

Career (min. 250 attempts)

64.9% Peyton Manning, 1998–2010 (4,682–7,210)

60.7% Jim Harbaugh, 1994–1997 (746–1,230)

58.7% Gary Hogeboom, 1986–1988 (260–443)

Season (min. 100 attempts)

68.8% Peyton Manning, 2009 (393–571)

67.6% Peyton Manning, 2004 (336–497)

67.3% Peyton Manning, 2005 (305–453)

Game (min. 20 attempts)

85.3% Peyton Manning, @ Jacksonville, 12/18/2008 (29–34)

Passing Yards

Career

54,828 Peyton Manning, 1998–2010

39,768 Johnny Unitas, 1956–1972

17,663 Bert Jones, 1973–1981

Season

4,700 Peyton Manning, 2010

4,557 Peyton Manning, 2004

4,500 Peyton Manning, 2009

Game

472 Peyton Manning, @ Kansas City, 10/31/2004

Longest Pass Play from Scrimmage

90 yards Bert Jones to Roger Carr, vs. Jets, 11/16/1975

Most Yards per Game

Career (min. 50 games)

263.6 Peyton Manning, 1998–2010 (54,828–208)

193.0 Johnny Unitas, 1956–1972 (39,768–206)

183.7 Jeff George, 1990–1993 (9,551–52)

Season (min. 10 games)

293.8 Peyton Manning, 2010 (4,700–16)

284.8 Peyton Manning, 2004 (4,557–16)

281.3 Peyton Manning, 2009 (4,500–16)

Most Yards per Attempt

Career (min. 200 attempts)

8.38 Earl Morrall, 1968–1971 (5,666–676)

7.78 Johnny Unitas, 1956–1972 (39,768–5,110)

7.60 Peyton Manning, 1998–2010 (54,828–7,210)

Season (min. 50 attempts)

9.26 Johnny Unitas, 1964 (2,824–305)

9.18 Earl Morrall, 1968 (2,909–317)

9.17 Peyton Manning, 2004 (4,557–497)

Touchdown Passes

Career

399 Peyton Manning, 1998–2010

287 Johnny Unitas, 1956–1972

122 Bert Jones, 1973–1981

Season

49 Peyton Manning, 2004

33 Peyton Manning, 2000

33 Peyton Manning, 2009

33 Peyton Manning, 2010

Game

6 Peyton Manning, @ New Orleans, 9/28/2003; Peyton Manning, @ Detroit, 11/25/2004

Consecutive Games with a Touchdown Pass

47 Johnny Unitas, 12/9/1956–12/4/1960

Most Interceptions Thrown

Career

246 Johnny Unitas, 1956–1972

198 Peyton Manning, 1998–2010

97 Bert Jones, 1973–1981

Season

28 Peyton Manning, 1998

24 Johnny Unitas, 1960

24 Johnny Unitas, 1961

24 Johnny Unitas, 1966

Game

6 Peyton Manning, @ San Diego, 11/11/2007

Fewest Interceptions per Attempt

Career Percentage (min. 200 attempts)

2.11% Jim Harbaugh, 1994–1997 (26–1,230)

2.31% Paul Justin, 1995–1997 (7–303)

2.75% Peyton Manning, 1998–2010 (198–7,210)

Season Percentage (min. 50 attempts)

0.00% Paul Justin, 1996 (0–127)

1.29% Jim Harbaugh, 1997 (4–309)

1.47 Jeff George, 1993 (6–407)

Most Pass Attempts Without an Interception, Game

57 Peyton Manning, @ Texas, 9/12/2010

Quarterback Rating

Career (min. 200 attempts)

94.9 Peyton Manning, 1998–2010

86.6 Jim Harbaugh, 1994–1997

81.6 Gary Hogeboom, 1986–1988

Season (min. 50 attempts)

121.1 Peyton Manning, 2004

104.1 Peyton Manning, 2005

102.5 Bert Jones, 1976

RUSHING RECORDS

Attempts

Career

2,188 Edgerrin James, 1999–2005

1,391 Lydell Mitchell, 1972–1977

1,389 Marshall Faulk, 1994–1998

Season

388 Eric Dickerson, 1988

387 Edgerrin James, 2000

369 Edgerrin James, 1999

Game

40 Lydell Mitchell, @ Jets, 10/20/1974

Yards

Career

9,226 Edgerrin James, 1999–2005

5,487 Lydell Mitchell, 1972–1977

5,320 Marshall Faulk, 1994–1998

Season

1,709 Edgerrin James, 2000

1,659 Eric Dickerson, 1988

1,553 Edgerrin James, 1999

Game

219 Edgerrin James, @ Seattle, 10/15/2000

Longest Run from Scrimmage

80 yards Tom Matte, vs. St. Louis, 10/12/1964; Donald Brown, vs. Tennessee, 12/18/2011

Rushing Yards per Carry

Career (min. 250 carries)

4.84 Lenny Moore, 1956–1967 (5,174–1,069)
4.48 Albert Bentley, 1985–1990 (2,355–526)
4.36 Curtis Dickey, 1980–1985 (3,490–800)

Season (min. 100 carries)

5.19 George Wonsley, 1985 (716–138)
5.13 Tony Lorick, 1964 (513–100)
4.88 Norm Bulaich, 1971 (741–152)

Game (min. 10 carries)

14.2 Lenny Moore, vs. Green Bay, 10/28/1956

Rushing Touchdowns

Career

64 Edgerrin James, 1999–2005
63 Lenny Moore, 1956–1967
45 Tom Matte, 1961–1972

Season

16 Lenny Moore, 1964
14 Eric Dickerson, 1988
13 Edgerrin James, 1999
13 Edgerrin James, 2000
13 Edgerrin James, 2005

Game

4 Eric Dickerson, vs. Denver, 10/31/1988; Joseph Addai, vs. Philadelphia, 11/26/2006

RECEIVING

Receptions

Career

1,102 Marvin Harrison, 1996–2008
968 Reggie Wayne, 2001–2012
631 Raymond Berry, 1955–1967

Season

143 Marvin Harrison, 2002
115 Marvin Harrison, 1999
111 Reggie Wayne, 2010

Game

15 Reggie Wayne, @ Jacksonville, 10/3/2010

Receiving Yards

Career

14,580 Marvin Harrison, 1996–2008
13,063 Reggie Wayne, 2001–2012
9,275 Raymond Berry, 1955–1967

Season

1,722 Marvin Harrison, 2002
1,663 Marvin Harrison, 1999
1,524 Marvin Harrison, 2001

Game

224 Raymond Berry, @ Washington, 11/10/1957 (12 rec.)

Yards per Reception

Career (min. 100 receptions)

19.3 Jimmy Orr, 1961–1970 (5,859–303)
18.8 Roger Carr, 1974–1981 (4,770–254)
17.1 Ray Butler, 1980–1985 (2,890–169)

Season (min. 25 receptions)

25.9 Roger Carr, 1976 (1,112–43)
25.6 Jimmy Orr, 1968 (743–29)
23.5 Glenn Doughty, 1973 (587–25)

Game (min. 5 receptions)

3 Accomplished multiple times

SPECIAL TEAMS

KICKOFF RETURNS

Most Kickoff Returns

Career

176 Terrence Wilkins, 1999–2006
169 Clarence Verdin, 1988–1993
153 Aaron Bailey, 1995–1998

Season

55 Aaron Bailey, 1997
53 Troy Walters, 2002
52 Terrence Wilkins, 2006

Game

9 Brandon James, vs. San Diego, 11/28/2010

Kickoff Return Yardage

Career

4,017 Terrence Wilkins, 1999–2006
3,501 Aaron Bailey, 1995–1998
3,420 Clarence Verdin, 1988–1993

Season

1,272 Terrence Wilkins, 2006
1,206 Aaron Bailey, 1997
1,188 Dominic Rhodes, 2004

Game

236 Dominic Rhodes, vs. San Diego, 12/26/2004

Longest Return

104 Buddy Young, @ Philadelphia, 11/15/1953

Yards per Kickoff Return

Career (min. 25 returns)

32.6 Jim Duncan, 1969–1971 (1,369–42)
27.9 Johnny Sample, 1959–1960 (976–35)
27.5 Buddy Young, 1953–1955 (908–33)

Season (min. 15 returns)

35.4 Jim Duncan, 1970 (707–20)
35.1 Preston Pearson, 1968 (527–15)
30.7 Alvin Haymond, 1965 (614–20)

Game (min. 3 returns)

53.0 Deji Karim, vs. Houston, 12/30/2012 (159–3)

Kickoffs Returned for Touchdown

Career

2 Lenny Lyles, 1958–1961
2 Preston Pearson, 1968–1969
2 Jim Duncan, 1969–1971
2 Aaron Bailey, 1995–1998
2 Dominic Rhodes, 2001–2010

Season

2 Lenny Lyles, 1958
2 Preston Pearson, 1968
1 Accomplished 18 times

Game

1 Accomplished 22 times

PUNT RETURNS

Most Punt Returns

Career

155 Clarence Verdin, 1988–1993
119 Terrence Wilkins, 1999–2006
112 Carl Taseff, 1953–1961

Season

44 Nesby Glasgow, 1979

42 Dewell Brewer, 1994
41 Alvin Haymond, 1965
41 Terrence Wilkins, 1999

Game

9 Nesby Glasgow, @ Kansas City, 9/2/1979

Punt Return Yardage

Career

1,537 Clarence Verdin, 1988–1993
1,065 Terrence Wilkins, 1999–2006
1,012 Howard Stevens, 1975–1977

Season

443 Robbie Martin, 1985
403 Alvin Haymond, 1965
396 Howard Stevens, 1975
396 Clarence Verdin, 1990

Game

148 Carl Taseff, @ Green Bay, 10/14/1956

Longest Run

90 Carl Taseff, @ Green Bay, 10/14/1956
90 T. J. Rushing, @ Oakland, 12/16/2007

Yards per Punt Return

Career (min. 20 returns)

13.5 Ron Gardin, 1970–1971 (405–30)
11.5 T. Y. Hilton, 2012 (300–26)
11.2 Ray Buchanan, 1995–1996 (314–28)

Season (min. 10 returns)

16.8 Ray Buchanan, 1996 (201–12)
13.1 T. J. Rushing, 2007 (249–19)
12.9 Clarence Verdin, 1989 (296–23)

Punts Returned for Touchdown

Career

4 Clarence Verdin, 1988–1993
3 Terrence Wilkins, 1999–2006
2 Carl Taseff, 1953–1961

Season

2 Clarence Verdin, 1992
1 Accomplished 14 times

Game

1 Accomplished 16 times

KICKING

PAT Attempts

Career

346 Mike Vanderjagt, 1998–2005
270 Lou Michaels, 1964–1969
262 Adam Vinatieri, 2006–2012

Season

60 Mike Vanderjagt, 2004
54 Lou Michaels, 1964
52 Toni Linhart, 1975
52 Mike Vanderjagt, 2005

Game

8 Tom Feamster, vs. L.A. Rams, 11/25/1956; Steve Myhra, vs. Green Bay, 11/2/1958

PATs Made

Career

344 Mike Vanderjagt, 1998–2005
263 Lou Michaels, 1964–1969
259 Adam Vinatieri, 2006–2012

Season

59 Mike Vanderjagt, 2004
53 Lou Michaels, 1964
52 Mike Vanderjagt, 2005

Game

8 Tom Feamster, vs. L.A. Rams, 11/25/1956; Steve Myhra, vs. Green Bay, 11/2/1958

PAT Percentage

Career (min. 30 attempts)

100% Cary Blanchard, 1995–1997 (73–73)
100% Matt Stover, 2009 (33–33)
99.4% Mike Vanderjagt, 1998–2005 (344–346)

Most PATs Without a Miss

Season

52 Mike Vanderjagt, 2005
51 Adam Vinatieri, 2010
48 Lou Michaels, 1965

Field Goal Attempts

Career

250 Dean Biasucci, 1984–1994
248 Mike Vanderjagt, 1998–2005
198 Lou Michaels, 1964–1969

Season

41 Cary Blanchard, 1997
40 Cary Blanchard, 1996
39 Steve Myhra, 1961
39 Jim Martin, 1963
39 Lou Michaels, 1966

Game

6 Toni Linehart, vs. Jets, 11/28/1976; Raul Allegre, @ Philadelphia, 10/30/1983; Dean Biasucci, vs. Miami, 9/25/1988

Field Goals Made

Career

217 Mike Vanderjagt, 1998–2005
176 Dean Biasucci, 1984–1994
150 Adam Vinatieri, 2006–2012

Season

37 Mike Vanderjagt, 2003
36 Cary Blanchard, 1996
34 Mike Vanderjagt, 1999

Game

5 Accomplished 7 times

Most Field Goals Of 50+ Yards, Career

18 Dean Biasucci, 1984–1994

Longest Field Goal Made

58 yards Dan Miller, @ San Diego, 12/26/1982

Field Goal Percentage

Career (min. 20 attempts)

87.5% Mike Vanderjagt, 1998–2005 (217–248)
83.8% Adam Vinatieri, 2006–2012 (150–179)
82.9% Cary Blanchard, 1995–1997 (87–105)

Season (min. 10 attempts)

100% Mike Vanderjagt, 2003 (37–37)
92.9% Adam Vinatieri, 2010 (26–28)
92.6% Mike Vanderjagt, 2000 (25–27)

PUNTING

Most Punts

Career

985 Rohn Stark, 1982–1994
838 David Lee, 1966–1978
577 Hunter Smith, 1999–2008

Season

99 Bucky Dilts, 1979
98 Rohn Stark, 1984
92 David Lee, 1978

Game

12 David Lee, vs. Oakland, 12/24/1977; Chris Gardocki, @ Buffalo, 10/6/1996

Total Yardage

Career

43,162 Rohn Stark, 1982–1994
34,019 David Lee, 1966–1978
25,038 Hunter Smith, 1999–2008

Season

4,383 Rohn Stark, 1984
4,124 Rohn Stark, 1983
4,102 Pat McAfee, 2011

Game

551 Chris Gardocki, @ Buffalo, 10/6/1996

Longest Punt

76 yards David Lee, @ Giants, 10/17/1971

Yards per Punt

Career (min. 100 punts)

45.4 Pat McAfee, 2009–2012 (13,170–290)
44.8 Chris Gardocki, 1995–1998 (12,403–277)
43.8 Rohn Stark, 1982–1994 (43,162–985)

Season (min. 40 punts)

47.9 Pat McAfee, 2012 (3,500–73)
46.6 Pat McAfee, 2011 (4,102–88)
45.9 Rohn Stark, 1985 (3,584–78)

Game (min. 4 punts)

58.3 Rohn Stark, vs. Oilers, 9/13/1992 (233–4)

DEFENSE

INTERCEPTIONS

Most Interceptions

Career

57 Bobby Boyd, 1960–1968
37 Don Shinnick, 1957–1969
35 Eugene Daniel, 1984–1996

Season

11 Tom Keane, 1953
10 Milt Davis, 1957
10 Lyle Blackwood, 1977

Game

3 Accomplished 10 times

Interception Return Yardage

Career

994 Bobby Boyd, 1960–1968
518 Rich Volk, 1967–1975
423 Eugene Daniel, 1984–1996

Season

225 Keith Taylor, 1989
221 Ray Buchanan, 1994
219 Milt Davis, 1957

Game

121 yards Milt Davis, @ Chicago, 11/17/1957

Longest Return

97 yards Eugene Daniel, vs. Jets, 10/29/1995

Most Interceptions Returned for Touchdown

Career

5 Jerry Logan, 1963–1972
4 Bobby Boyd, 1960–1968
3 Held by 6 players

Season

3 Ray Buchanan, 1994
2 Accomplished 9 times

Game

1 Accomplished numerous times

SACKS

Most Sacks

Career

107.5 Dwight Freeney, 2002–2012
91.5 Robert Mathis, 2003–2012
50.0 Duane Bickett, 1985–1993

Season

16.0 Dwight Freeney, 2004
13.5 Dwight Freeney, 2009
13.0 Dwight Freeney, 2002

Game

4.5 Johnie Cooks, @ L.A. Raiders, 11/25/1984

FUMBLE RETURNS

Most Fumble Returns for Touchdown

Career

2 Gino Marchetti, 1953–1966
2 Ordell Braase, 1957–1968
2 Derrel Luce, 1975–1978
2 Tony Bennett, 1994–1997
2 Gary Brackett, 2003–2011

TEAM RECORDS

LEAGUE CHAMPIONSHIPS 4 (1958, 1959, 1970 Super Bowl V, 2006 Super Bowl XLI)

Conference Championships 7 (1958, 1959, 1964, 1968, 1970, 2006, 2009)

Division Titles 14 (1968, 1970, 1975–1977, 1987, 1999, 2003–2007, 2009, 2010)

Playoff Berths 25 (1958, 1959, 1964, 1965, 1968, 1970, 1971, 1975–1977, 1987, 1995, 1996, 1999, 2000, 2002–2010, 2012)

WINNING SEASONS 33

Most Wins, Regular Season 14 (2005, 2009)

Most Consecutive Wins 23 (11/2/2008–12/17/2009)

Most Losses, Season 15 (1991)

Most Consecutive Losses 14 (9/13/1981–12/13/1981)

SCORING AND TOTAL OFFENSE

Most Points, Season 522 (2004)

Most Points, Game 58 (vs. Buffalo, 12/12/1976)

Most Points, Half 45 (1st half, vs. Denver, 10/31/1988)

Most Points, Quarter 31 (2nd quarter, vs. Miami, 12/14/1997)

Largest Point Differential, Season 258 (1968, 402–144)

Largest Margin of Victory, Game 56 (56–0, vs. Green Bay, 11/2/1958)

Fewest Points Scored per Game, Season	8.9 (1991, 143 points/16 games)
Fewest Points Scored, Game	0 (accomplished numerous times)
Largest Margin of Defeat	57 (0–57, vs. Chicago, 11/25/1962)
Most Touchdowns, Season	66 (2004)
Most Touchdowns, Game	8 (vs. L.A. Rams, 11/25/1956; vs. Green Bay, 11/2/1958)
Most PATs, Season	64 (2004)
Most PATs, Game	8 (vs. L.A. Rams, 11/25/1956; vs. Green Bay, 11/2/1958)
Most Field Goals Made, Season	37 (2003)
Most Field Goals Made, Game	5 (accomplished 8 times)
Most Yards Total Offense, Season	6,475 (2004)
Most Yards Total Offense, Game	595 (@ Atlanta, 11/12/1967)
Fewest Yards Total Offense, Season	2,483 (1982)
Fewest Yards Total Offense, Game	69 (vs. Detroit, 11/6/1954)
Most First Downs, Season	379 (2004)
Most First Downs, Game	34 (vs. Houston, 9/17/2006)

SCORING AND TOTAL OFFENSE

Most Points, Season	522 (2004)
Most Points, Game	58 (vs. Buffalo, 12/12/1976)
Most Points, Half	45 (1st half, vs. Denver, 10/31/1988)
Most Points, Quarter	31 (2nd quarter, vs. Miami, 12/14/1997)
Largest Point Differential, Season	258 (1968, 402–144)
Largest Margin of Victory, Game	56 (56–0, vs. Green Bay, 11/2/1958)
Fewest Points Scored per Game, Season	8.9 (1991, 143 points/16 games)
Fewest Points Scored, Game	0 (accomplished numerous times)
Largest Margin of Defeat	57 (0–57, vs. Chicago, 11/25/1962)
Most Touchdowns, Season	66 (2004)
Most Touchdowns, Game	8 (vs. L.A. Rams, 11/25/1956; vs. Green Bay, 11/2/1958)
Most PATs, Season	64 (2004)
Most PATs, Game	8 (vs. L.A. Rams, 11/25/1956; vs. Green Bay, 11/2/1958)
Most Field Goals Made, Season	37 (2003)
Most Field Goals Made, Game	5 (accomplished 8 times)
Most Yards Total Offense, Season	6,475 (2004)
Most Yards Total Offense, Game	595 (@ Atlanta, 11/12/1967)
Fewest Yards Total Offense, Season	2,483 (1982)
Fewest Yards Total Offense, Game	69 (vs. Detroit, 11/6/1954)
Most First Downs, Season	379 (2004)
Most First Downs, Game	34 (vs. Houston, 9/17/2006)

PASSING

Most Pass Attempts, Season	679 (2010)
Most Pass Attempts, Game	59 (@ Washington, 11/7/1993)
Most Pass Completions, Season	450 (2010)
Most Pass Completions, Game	40 (@ Houston, 9/12/2010)
Most Net Yards Passing, Season	4,623 (2004)
Most Net Yards Passing, Game	472 (@ Kansas City, 10/31/2004)
Fewest Pass Attempts per Game, Season	21.4 (1973, 300 att./14 games)
Fewest Pass Attempts, Game	7 (@ L.A. Rams, 12/18/1965)
Fewest Pass Completions per Game, Season	9.8 (1973, 137 comp. /14 games)
Fewest Pass Completions, Game	3 (accomplished 4 times)
Fewest Net Yards Passing per Game, Season	104.8 (1953, 1,257 yards/12 games)
Fewest Net Yards Passing, Game	1 (vs. Buffalo, 10/13/1974)
Most Touchdown Passes, Season	51 (2004)
Fewest Touchdown Passes, Season	6 (1982, 9 games)
Most Interceptions Thrown, Season	30 (1978)
Fewest Interceptions Thrown, Season	8 (1975)

RUSHING

Most Rushing Attempts, Season	601 (1983)
Most Rushing Attempts, Game	60 (vs. San Francisco, 11/22/1959)
Most Rushing Yards, Season	2,695 (1983)
Most Rushing Yards, Game	318 (vs. Green Bay, 10/28/1956)
Fewest Rushing Attempts per Game, Season	20.9 (1990, 335 att./16 games)
Fewest Rushing Attempts, Game	10 (accomplished 3 times)
Fewest Rushing Yards per Game, Season	68.9 (1992, 1,102 yards/16 games)
Fewest Rushing Yards, Game	4 (vs. Detroit, 9/22/1991)
Most Rushing Touchdowns, Season	29 (1964)
Most Rushing Touchdowns, Game	5 (accomplished 5 times)
Fewest Rushing Touchdowns, Season	3 (1991)

SPECIAL TEAMS

Most Punts, Season	101 (1979)
Most Punts, Game	12 (vs. Oakland, 12/24/1977; @ Buffalo, 10/6/1996)
Most Yards per Punt, Season	47.9 (2013)
Fewest Punts, Season	42 (1961)
Fewest Punts, Game	0 (accomplished 7 times)
Fewest Yards per Punt, Season	34.5 (1957)
Most Punt Returns, Season	53 (1963)
Most Punt Returns, Game	9 (@ L.A. Rams, 11/22/1964; @ Kansas City, 9/2/1979)
Most Punt Return Yards, Season	485 (1963)
Most Punt Return Yards, Game	164 (vs. Jets, 9/19/1971)
Most Punt Return Touchdowns, Season	2 (1992)
Fewest Punt Returns, Season	12 (1981)
Fewest Punt Return Yards, Season	56 (1981)
Fewest Punt Return Yards, Game	-8 (@ San Diego, 10/23/1988)
Most Kickoff Returns, Season	84 (1981, 2001)
Most Kickoff Returns, Game	9 (accomplished 5 times)
Most Kickoff Return Yards, Season	1,832 (2001)
Most Kickoff Return Yards, Game	274 (vs. Jets, 9/24/1972)
Most Kickoff Return Touchdowns, Season	2 (1958, 1968)
Fewest Kickoff Returns, Season	31 (2011)
Fewest Kickoff Return Yards, Season	578 (2011)
Fewest Kickoff Return Yards, Game	0 (accomplished many times)

DEFENSE

Fewest Points Allowed per Game, Season	10.0 (1971, 140 points/14 games)
Fewest Points Allowed, Game	0 (accomplished many times)
Most Points Allowed, Season	533 (1981)
Most Points Allowed, Game	62 (62–7, @ New Orleans, 10/23/2011)
Fewest Total Yards Allowed per Game, Season	203.7 (1971, 2,852 yards/14 games)
Fewest Total Yards Allowed, Game	49 (@ Buffalo, 10/10/1971)
Fewest Pass Completions Allowed, Season	138 (1982)
Fewest Pass Completions Allowed, Game	4 (vs. Washington, 10/26/1958; vs. Tampa Bay, 10/3/1976)
Fewest Net Passing Yards Allowed, Season	1,726 (1960)
Fewest Net Passing Yards Allowed, Game	6 (@ Houston, 10/23/2005)
Fewest Passing Touchdowns Allowed, Season	6 (2008)
Fewest Rushing Yards Allowed, Season	1,113 (1971)
Fewest Rushing Yards Allowed, Game	4 (@ Buffalo, 10/10/1971)
Fewest Rushing Touchdowns Allowed, Season	5 (1967)
Fewest First Downs Allowed, Season	152 (1982)
Fewest First Downs Allowed, Game	3 (vs. San Francisco, 11/22/1959)
Most Yards on Interception Returns, Season	577 (1959)
Most Yards on Interception Returns, Game	144 (vs. Green Bay, 11/2/1958)
Most Interception Return Touchdowns, Season	4 (1959, 1965, 1968, 1975, 1996)

TURNOVERS AND PENALTIES

Most Fumbles, Season	41 (1986)
Most Fumbles, Game	7 (vs. Miami, 10/23/1983)
Fewest Fumbles, Season	10 (1998)
Most Opponents' Fumbles Recovered, Season	27 (1953)
Most Opponents' Fumbles Recovered, Game	5 (vs. L.A. Rams, 11/23/1958)
Most Penalties, Season	137 (1979)
Most Penalties, Game	16 (@ Denver, 12/11/1983)
Fewest Penalties, Season	51 (1960)
Fewest Penalties, Game	0 (accomplished 5 times)
Most Yards Penalized, Season	1,239 (1979)
Most Yards Penalized, Game	153 (@ Buffalo, 9/18/1983)
Fewest Yards Penalized, Season	433 (1982)

INDEX